SUSTAINABLE MANAGEMENT OF NATURAL RESOURCES

AF184018

European Environmental Law Forum Series, Volume 5

SUSTAINABLE MANAGEMENT OF NATURAL RESOURCES

Legal Instruments and Approaches

Edited by
Helle Tegner Anker
Birgitte Egelund Olsen

intersentia
Cambridge – Antwerp – Portland

Intersentia Ltd
Sheraton House | Castle Park
Cambridge | CB3 0AX | United Kingdom
Tel.: +44 1223 370 170 | Fax: +44 1223 370 169
Email: mail@intersentia.co.uk
www.intersentia.com | www.intersentia.co.uk

Distribution for the UK and Ireland:
NBN International
Airport Business Centre, 10 Thornbury Road
Plymouth, PL6 7PP
United Kingdom
Tel: +44 1752 202 301 | Fax: +44 1752 202 331
Email: orders@nbninternational.com

Distribution for Europe and all other countries:
Intersentia Publishing nv
Groenstraat 31
2640 Mortsel
Belgium
Tel.: +32 3 680 15 50 | Fax: +32 3 658 71 21
Email: mail@intersentia.be

Distribution for the USA and Canada:
Independent Publishers Group
Order Department
814 North Franklin Street
Chicago, IL 60610
USA
Tel.: +1 800 888 4741 (toll free) | Fax: + 1312 337 5985
Email: orders@ipgbook.com

Sustainable Management of Natural Resources
© The editors and contributors severally 2018

The author has asserted the right under the Copyright, Designs and Patents Act 1988, to be identified as author of this work.

No part of this book may be reproduced, stored in a retrieval system, or transmitted, in any form, or by any means, without prior written permission from Intersentia, or as expressly permitted by law or under the terms agreed with the appropriate reprographic rights organisation. Enquiries concerning reproduction which may not be covered by the above should be addressed to Intersentia at the address above.

Cover photograph: George Oze – Alamy Stock Photo

ISBN 978-1-78068-759-9 (paperback)
ISBN 978-1-78068-783-4 (PDF)
D/2018/7849/95
NUR 823

British Library Cataloguing in Publication Data. A catalogue record for this book is available from the British Library.

CONTENTS

PART I
INTRODUCTION

CHAPTER 1

LEGAL APPROACHES TO SUSTAINABLE MANAGEMENT OF NATURAL RESOURCES

Helle Tegner Anker* and Birgitte Egelund Olsen**

Sustainable management of natural resources is a key concern at all levels of society, on a global as well as a local scale. Natural resources are here understood in broad terms encompassing biodiversity, water, air and soil as well as raw materials. Usually, waste is not considered a natural resource; however, in a sustainable management of natural resources, the recycling of waste as secondary raw materials is pivotal and accordingly included in the present understanding of natural resources. The fifth European Environmental Law Forum Conference in Copenhagen in late summer 2017 aimed to highlight key issues regarding legal instruments and approaches and their role in promoting sustainable management of natural resources. This book offers a selection of peer reviewed contributions presented at the conference.[1]

A recurring theme in discussions on sustainability is to strike a balance between environmental, social and economic interests based on the 1987 Brundtland Report's definition of sustainable development as 'development that meets the needs of the present without compromising the ability of future generations to meet their own needs'.[2] It was noted in the Brundtland Report that

---

* The author is professor of law at University of Copenhagen, Denmark (hta@ifro.ku.dk).

** The author is professor of law at Aarhus University, Denmark (beo@law.au.dk).

1 Further information, including conference presentations, can be found at http://law.au.dk/forskning/konferencer/eelf-conference/. Information about the European Environmental Law Forum is available at www.eelf.info. We are grateful to Moritz Reese, Lorenzo Squintani and Bernard Vanheusden for their efforts as regards the EELF activities and also to other environmental law scholars for peer reviews of the contributions to this book. Our special thanks are also addressed to Linda Andersen, who, with a lot of patience, took care of language corrections. We thank Claes Bredahl Petersen for checking footnotes etc.

2 Report of the World Commission on Environment and Development, 'Our Common Future', UN General Assembly, Annex to document A/42/427, 1987, p. 37.

'sustainable development requires that the adverse impacts on the quality of air, water, and other natural elements are minimized so as to sustain the ecosystem's overall integrity.'[3] Thus, it has been argued that the biosphere sets an ultimate bottom-line for sustainable development expressed as strong sustainability or ecological sustainability implying that development must be based on ecological sustainability in order to meet the needs of present and future generations.[4] Calls have been made for ecological sustainability to be the central reference point of environmental law,[5] and that the sustainability of ecosystems should become one of the foundational principles of law everywhere.[6] Further, humans and natural ecosystems are closely interlinked and it must be kept in mind that ecosystems are dynamic and unpredictable. Social-ecological resilience theory has argued that governance systems must be adaptive and based on participatory, collaborative decision-making.[7]

The incorporation of such notions of ecological sustainability and social-ecological resilience into (environmental) policy and law faces many challenges, not least considering a continued quest for (economic) development in the aftermaths of the financial crisis. Furthermore, legal instruments and approaches may in different ways promote sustainable management of natural resources. The contributions in this book shed light on some of those challenges related both to the design of environmental laws, e.g. at EU and national level, and to their implementation and enforcement.

At EU level the ambitions and coherence of EU environmental legislation with respect to sustainability and sustainable management can be discussed. From an internal perspective, the EU sets the frame for sustainable management in the Member States. In **Chapter 2** *Ludwig Krämer* describes the details of the EU framework for managing natural resources and assesses the compliance with the UN Sustainable Development Goals. It is explained that the EU framework shows different features from one sector to another, including also the cooperation between the EU and the national authorities. Among the general characteristics are obligations to draw up management plans with the purpose of achieving specific objectives, obligations to prevent deterioration, obligations to

---

3 Ibid, p. 38.

4 Bosselmann, Klaus (2017) The Principle of Sustainability, Taylor & Francis, 2nd ed.

5 Westerlund, Staffan (2008) Theory for Sustainable Development Towards or Against? in Bugge, H.C. & Voigt, C. (eds), Sustainable Development in International and National Law, Europa Law Publishing, pp. 48-53.

6 Gaines, Sanford (2014) Reimaging Environmental Law for the 21st Century, Environmental Law Reporter, Vol. 44, pp. 10188-10215. Gaines, Sanford (2014) 'The Energy Revolution as Sustainable Development', in L. Squintani and H. Vedder with M. Reese and B. Vanheusden (eds), Sustainable Energy United in Diversity – Challenges and Approaches in Energy Transition in the European Union, European Environmental Law Forum Vol. 1 p. 10.

7 Ebbesson, Jonas (2010) 'The rule of law in governance of complex social-ecological changes', Global Environmental Change 20(3) pp. 414-422.

report to the EU Commission, and the organization of committee meetings at EU level. *Krämer* argues that improvements could be made as regards information to the public, public participation as well as enforcement at EU level. Turning to the Sustainable Development Goals, *Krämer* questions the achievement by the EU both as regards biodiversity, water and air. Calls are made for a policy that will require more and other approaches than envisaged by the EU Commission so far.

In **Chapter 3** *Wybe Douma* focuses on the external effects of EU natural resources use and the extent to which the EU may contribute to building more sustainable and resilient societies also outside the EU. *Douma* examines the EU legal framework addressing the negative consequences of EU production and consumption processes in particular as regards forestry and fisheries. Although both regimes ban illegally harvested products, this relies for forestry products on the laws of the country of origin and for fisheries on the law of the flag state. Another difference is that within the fisheries regime more far-reaching enforcement options are offered as regards states that do not take sufficient measures against illegal, unreported and unregulated (IUU) fishing. Some explanations for these differences are offered, including the exclusive competence of the EU as regards fisheries as well as the existence of international binding norms regarding IUU fishing. *Douma* argues that the coherence of EU policy would benefit from the formulation of an EU strategy on external aspects for sustainable management of natural resources rather than the ad hoc approach applied so far.

EU agricultural policy is one policy area that has significant implications as regards sustainable management of natural resources. *Luchino Ferraris* in **Chapter 4** examines the options for judicial review of the environmental performance of the Common Agricultural Policy (CAP). An overview is provided of the complex process of integrating environmental concerns in the CAP with a particular focus on the so-called 'greening' component of the CAP (2013-reform). It is argued that the CAP 'greening' has ended up being more an instrument to adorn income support than a means to achieve ambitious environmental targets. Based on previous case law regarding the CAP, it is examined whether the inefficiency of the 'greening' component can be subject to judicial review. It is concluded that neither the principle of proportionality, the duty to state reasons, or the principle of environmental integration provides any firm ground for judicial review of the environmental performance of the CAP. *Ferraris* recognizes that consideration must be given to the fact that the CAP reflects politically sensitive and macro-economic choices and that the division of powers between the legislator and the judiciary must be kept in mind.

Another important EU policy area is waste where an emerging issue relates to the handling of pharmaceutical waste. In **Chapter 5** *Katerina Mitkidis, Shona Walter* and *Viktoria Obolevich* discuss the lack of a comprehensive legal framework for the management of pharmaceutical waste. While scientific evidence of detrimental effects of pharmaceutical residue in the environment is growing, many gaps remain, causing regulatory inaction. The authors argue that a way to deal with the inherent complexity and scientific uncertainty of pharmaceutical waste is to take a sustainable, precautionary and life cycle-oriented action with the point of departure in the EU waste hierarchy. It is stressed that the reluctance to trigger the precautionary principle with respect to human pharmaceuticals, and the access to medicines, must be addressed by shifting the discussion from balancing environmental protection and protection of human individuals to balancing the protection of human individuals and the protection of the general public health.

The protection of soil is another issue that has not been addressed comprehensively by the EU, partly due to the failure to adopt the proposed Soil Framework Directive. Despite the EU 2006 Thematic Strategy for Soil Protection and the focus on the issue in the Seventh Environment Action Programme of 2014, the lack of a legal framework is far from being resolved. As explained by *Marta Cenini* in **Chapter 6**, relevant provisions must for the time being be found in other EU directives, in particular the Environmental Liability Directive and the Waste Framework Directive. Another important source is the case law of the EU Court of Justice. *Cenini* argues that it is necessary to clearly establish who is liable/responsible for the clean-up and decontamination of polluted soils and she discusses the liability/responsibility of the landowner in regard to remediation of contaminated soil. This is especially urgent after the *Fipa Group Case* and more recent cases, where the Court of Justice has confirmed that causation of environmental damage is a prerequisite for the duties laid down in the Environmental Liability Directive. Accordingly, mere owners of damaged sites, who are not responsible for the damage, play no part in the system of the directive.

Environmental litigation is a well-known instrument to promote the protection of the environment and sustainable development. In **Chapter 7** *Natalia Kobylarz* systematically examines the case law of the European Court of Human Rights (ECtHR) and the implication of the European Convention on Human Rights (ECHR) general principles for environmental litigation. She argues that due to a large number of environment-related cases, the ECHR organs have gradually expanded the protection of the civil and political human rights to encompass various forms of environmental risk and harm and that the system today efficiently safeguards the natural environment, albeit in a surrogate and somewhat covert manner. *Kobylarz* concludes that although nature has a value in and of itself, it still cannot practically be protected independently of a human being, but will need the agency of a human to defend it through the exercise of his or her own rights.

Samvel Varvaštian in **Chapter 8** explores how the United States courts have interpreted the public trust doctrine and constitutional provisions granting rights to natural resources in an attempt to force the government to take decisive climate change mitigation measures. He outlines that while some state courts have explicitly rejected the idea that the public trust doctrine can protect the atmosphere as a natural resource, others have been more willing to adopt the doctrine. However, it is still unclear whether the doctrine can prove viable at federal level. *Varvastian* argues that the interaction between the atmosphere and water resources may offer a novel angle to the application of the public trust doctrine, which could be successful.

The tension between environmental protection and economic development has come to the fore in The Netherlands. As explained by *Lolke Braaksma* and *Kars de Graaf* in **Chapter 9** a new comprehensive Dutch Environment and Planning Act (EPA) has been adopted with the purpose of working towards a sustainable society while allowing for economic development. This crosscutting Act that incorporates most environmental legislation is based on the concept of (environmental) utilisation space as the 'the legal leeway' for development in a specific area considering the requirements to protect the environment. *Braaksma* and *de Graaf* analyses the origins and implementation of this concept in particular in relation to municipal environmental plans and a programmatic approach. It is revealed that the origins of the EUS concept are related to an ecosystem approach that focuses on the operationalisation of environmental utilization space and works towards sustainable use of ecosystems aimed to maintain ecosystem integrity. The authors suggest, however, that the Dutch legislator may have tried to relate the concept more to economic development than to environmental protection. Also, the EPA leaves it to the local governments to strike the balance through the adoption of municipal environmental plans providing the possibility to adopt tailor-made approaches while adhering to the requirements of EU directives. Another instrument explored by *Braaksma* and *de Graaf* is the programmatic approach which allows the creation of environmental utilisation space and accordingly provides room for economic development. The authors point to the potential risk that detrimental activities will be allowed while the positive results are not yet or only partly manifested. Also the amount of discretion given to local authorities is mentioned as a concern. Thus, the chapter illustrates the difficulties of adopting legislation that on paper may reflect a sustainable management of natural resources, but in practice may turn out to be implemented differently.

In **Chapter 10** *Hendrik Schoukens* analyses another Dutch legislative initiative – the so-called Programmatic Approach to Nitrogen (PAS) – which can be considered a frontrunner to the programmatic approach reflected in the Dutch Environmental and Planning Act. *Schoukens* uses the Dutch PAS system as a benchmark to explore the margins available within the EU nature directives to implement more flexible adaptive management strategies. Adaptive management is presented as an idea that planned experimentation should be used as a means to overcome overly static 'predicative' approaches to environmental impact assessments. The PAS is based on the creation of room for economic development through future reduction and restoration measures in nitrogen sensitive Natura 2000 sites. The legal soundness of the PAS system is, however, questioned considering the case law of the CJEU and it is argued that taking into consideration future restorative actions is at odds with the precautionary principle. *Schoukens* concludes that the reconciliatory and adaptive approach of the PAS leaves a lot to be desired and identifies one of the ultimate flaws as the assumption that the robust recovery of degraded ecosystems can be reconciled with further economic expansion.

The Dutch experience illustrates how the tension between strict (EU) environmental protection requirements and demands for economic development may lead to new – experimental – policy initiatives. In other countries implementation or enforcement of EU environmental law is a well-known concern. In **Chapter 11** *Vojtěch Vomáčka* analyses compliance with the requirements of the EU Habitats Directive based on the case law of the Czech Supreme Administrative Court. The analysis has a particular focus on the options for derogations under Article 6(4) of the Habitats Directive, including the notion of overriding public interests. While it is concluded that the Czech courts interpret individual conditions for derogations in a similar way as the CJEU, it is argued that the goals of EU law are undermined by incorrect transposition and attempts by the Czech government to avoid the protective regime of the Habitats Directive. The EU rules on Natura 2000 have been transposed using the copy and paste method, but the existing nature conservation system has not been amended. Thus, the two systems overlap and the additional requirements from the EU are regarded as an obstacle to industry and infrastructure development. This has resulted in numerous decisions being challenged by environmental NGOs, several of them being successful.

The Czech experience is also analysed in **Chapter 12** where *Ilona Jančářová* explores the role of air quality plans in Czech legislation. An important question is, whether the mere non-compliance with the EU air quality standards is automatically conceived as a failure to establish air quality plans, e.g. without a proper analysis and assessment of the proposed measures. *Jančářová* introduces the basic requirements of the EU Air Quality Directive in view also of the case law of the CJEU. It is argued that the air quality plans are part of the whole set of regulatory instruments to ensure that the level of pollutants does not exceed the limit values of the Directive. Following an analysis of the use of air quality plans in the Czech legal order, it is concluded that air quality plans are programme documents and that the exceedance of limit values in certain zones does not permit the view that the air quality plan is in itself ineffective. The air quality plans must work together with other instruments as a coherent system.

Public participation is often put forward as an important instrument to enhance sustainable development and the integration of a variety of public concerns or interests into decision-making. *Caer Smyth* in **Chapter 13** explores how the underlying rationalist assumptions may shape spaces for public participation in environmental decision-making based on relevant theories and an empirical study of a public inquiry into a major infrastructure project in the UK. It is argued that rationalist philosophy assumes the existence of an objective truth and that logic-based arguments are privileged over experience-based arguments. This may explain the why expert knowledge is prioritized over local knowledge in the public inquiry. *Smyth* suggests that this tendency could conceivably undermine the capacity of participatory governance and have a particularly detrimental impact on the effectiveness of environmental arguments in the decision-making processes.

Participation and consultation may also be an instrument to safeguard specific interests such as those of indigenous peoples. In **Chapter 14**, *Tanja Joona* reflects upon the participatory mechanism of the ILO Convention No. 169 concerning the rights of individual peoples with a particular view to the Sami people in the Artic region and the Finnish legislation. Participation and consultation is viewed as an important means of dialogue to reconcile conflicting interests. Consultation may in particular be a way to achieve a prior informed consent as regards the exploitation of natural resources in indigenous territories. It is, however, argued that the question of representation may not be easily resolved as exemplified in the Finnish legislation where the Sami Parliament represents all the Sami people and not only those who live in the indigenous territories. *Joona* concludes that due to urbanization the definition of indigenous peoples is no longer connected with the traditional livelihoods of the territories. Thus, representativity and legitimacy raise questions of who should be consulted.

In the final **Chapter 15** *Jerônimo Basilio São Mateus* discusses how environmental protection can be fostered through the right to religious freedom. It is argued that the protection of sacred natural sites (SNS) should be enhanced given that religious freedom is a subjective right, which cannot be easily overridden as other land-based rights. Two important principles are advocated, namely first, the participation of religious leaders and communities in the management of protected areas and, second, to reconfigure the environmental discourse to include religious language and values. Furthermore, *Mateus* concludes that litigation may enforce the interactions between nature conservation and religious rights.

Based on the contributions above it can be asserted that despite many efforts there is still a long way to go to achieve sustainable management of natural resources. Several contributions in this book point to the inadequacy of EU environmental legislation when it comes to sustainable management of natural resources both generally (*Krämer*) and within important policy areas such as imports of products (*Douma*), agriculture (*Ferraris*), soil (*Cenini*) and pharmaceutical waste (*Mitkidis, Walter* and *Obolevich*). Even in areas where (EU) legislation establishes that the integrity of ecosystems is the ultimate bottom-line for development the implementation of such ecosystem-based boundaries is difficult and may trigger counterproductive policy responses seeking to avoid undue restrictions as demonstrated by *Schoukens* and *Vomáčka*.

Litigation may be a powerful tool to enforce clear obligations on States – as exemplified by *Kobylarz* and *Varvaštian* – and to some extent also *Vomáčka*. Yet, the law in itself is vulnerable to policy initiatives that may undermine an ecosystem approach.

The formulation and adoption of appropriate legal approaches and instruments remains a key challenge and subject to experiments such as the new Dutch legislation as demonstrated by *Braaksma* and *de Graaf*. Furthermore, well-known instruments to promote socio-ecological resilience such as public participation may also need more attention than just a simple reference in the legislation. Using public participation as an instrument requires thoughts about *who* should participate and *how*. As demonstrated by *Joona* representativity is a major issue as regards indigenous peoples, e.g. in the Arctic. Similarly, *Smyth* questions the way public inquiries shape public participation towards logic-based (expert) arguments over experience-based (lay) arguments with a potentially detrimental impact on the effectiveness of environmental arguments. Similarly, *Mateus* argues that in relation to sacred natural sites participation should be broadened to include religious language and communities as religious rights and nature conservation can be mutually reinforced.

At the end of the day, however, environmental legislation is steered by policy choices and the willingness to give priority to environmental concerns and promote ecological sustainability. Shifting the balance may not be welcome in all societies and it is necessary to carefully consider the most appropriate legal instruments and approaches and their application to avoid counterproductive policies.

PART II

SUSTAINABILITY IN EU AND INTERNATIONAL LAW

CHAPTER 2
SUSTAINABLE MANAGEMENT OF NATURAL RESOURCES BY THE EU

Ludwig KRÄMER*

ABSTRACT

The management of natural resources is shared between the EU and the Member States. While the EU sets a management frame for all Member States, mainly through legislation, the day-to-day management within this frame is ensured by the Member States. This chapter describes the details of the EU management frame and then assesses, if and to what extent the EU is in compliance with the targets for sustainable development of natural resources which were developed by the UN Sustainable Development Goals.

1. INTRODUCTION: CLARIFYING THE TERMINOLOGY

This chapter will examine the management of natural resources by the EU and its contribution to sustainability. In a short first section, the use of the terms 'natural resources', 'management' and 'sustainability' will be clarified. The second section will present the management framework set up by the EU within which the specific management measures by Member States are to be taken. The third section will assess EU achievements concerning natural resources, compared to the Sustainable Development Goals of the United Nations. A short conclusion will end the contribution.

* The author worked for more than 30 years in the Environmental Department of the EU Commission (kramer.ludwig@skynet.be). Currently, he is managing the environmental law consultancy Derecho y Medio Ambiente in Madrid.

The EU environmental policy has to aim at a high level of protection and is committed to ensuring a prudent and rational utilization of natural resources (Article 191(1) TFEU). In this chapter, 'natural resources' will be understood as biodiversity and water, soil, air quality, raw materials and waste. Though marine biological resources – in particular fish – are explicitly mentioned in Article 3 TFEU, they will not be examined outside the discussion on biodiversity. – The term 'management' is very broad and lacks a clear legal shape. In EU law and policy, the term is mainly used in contrast to legislative action, so that it might be appropriate to define it here as the implementation of political objectives within the given legal context. While the implementation – and thus also the management – of EU environmental policy is normally in the hands of the Member States (Article 192(4) TFEU), EU legislation frequently fixes framework conditions which lead to practical management measures which are carried out jointly by EU and by national administrations.

The EU shall work for a sustainable development of Europe and contribute to the sustainable development of Earth (Article 3 TEU); by its external action, it will foster sustainable development of developing countries and help develop the sustainable management of global natural resources (Article 21 TFEU). However, the use of the term 'sustainability' became a fashion at the end of the 1980s, when the United Nations published the Brundtland Report on 'Our common future'. The inflationary use of this term hides the lack of yardsticks to assess, when a policy or a measure is sustainable. It allows almost every measure to be qualified by its authors as sustainable; opinions therefore differ, whether a specific policy or management measure is sustainable or not.

This contribution will not endeavour to give a new content to the notion of sustainability. Instead, it will use the different sustainability goals developed by the United Nations in 2015, and the targets for reaching these goals, as the yardstick to assess if and to what extent EU measures may be qualified as being sustainable – or at least as being on the way to reach sustainability within the time span fixed for the targets of the United Nations' sustainability goals.

2. THE EU FRAMEWORK FOR MANAGING NATURAL RESOURCES

With the exception of measures on soil and on raw materials, the EU sets a legislative framework for the different sectors.[1] Legislation on biodiversity and on air quality does not have the word 'framework' in its title, but functionally the

1 Directive 2000/60/EC, OJ 2000, L 327 p. 1 and Directive 2008/56/EC, OJ 2008, L 194 p. 19 (water); Directive 2008/98/EC, OJ 2008 L 312 p. 3 (waste); Directive 92/43/EEC, OJ 1992 L 206 p. 7 (biodiversity); Directive 2008/50/EC, OJ 2008 L 152 p. 1 (air).

relevant directives fulfil the role of setting the frame for management measures. The different pieces of EU legislation are completed by more specific directives which try to take into due consideration the particularities of the different sectors.

A proposal of 2006 for EU legislation on the protection of the soil was rejected by the Council, mainly because some Member States which already had national legislation on the protection of soils in place – including Germany, United Kingdom and France – successfully blocked the other 22 Member States which favoured an EU directive. With regard to raw materials, no specific EU legislation exists, presumably because many activities concerning raw materials occur outside the EU, and also because the extractive industries frequently succeeded in being exempted from existing EU legislation.

It is common to all EU legislation in the different sectors concerning natural resources that it does not limit itself to fix objectives which are to be reached within a specific period of time. Rather, EU legislation also deals with management issues, to greater or lesser extent. The most obvious examples are outside the subject matter of natural resources, though. They concern chemical products, pesticides and biocides, where EU legislation adopted regulations, not only directives, also in order to be able to go into details of management questions. In these areas, legislation left it to specialized agencies or permanent committees to secure the daily functioning of the respective system, liaise with technical, scientific and socio-economic experts and ensure a balance between free trade, human health and environmental protection interests.

The management of natural resources is far less unified and shows different features from one sector to the other. As regards biodiversity, the Habitats Directive 92/43[2] established a joint procedure between the European Commission (EU Commission) and the Member States for the designation of natural habitats which are of EU-wide importance. Once the lists of habitats of the different biogeographical areas were established, Member States were obliged under EU law, to take the necessary conservation measures in order to ensure a favourable conservation status of the habitats. Derogations and deteriorations of protected habitats were only allowed in the absence of alternative solutions and under strict conditions. For fauna and flora species, an EU-wide list of some 1400 protected species was set up. Again, derogations – hunting, killing, taking from the wild etc. – were only allowed under strictly fixed conditions. The EU Commission is to be informed at regular intervals of such derogations.

Member States have to report every six years on the application of the Habitats Directive. And they meet regularly with the EU Commission in a nature conservation committee to discuss matters of mutual interest, such as the

2 Directive 92/43/EEC, (n. 1, above).

definition of specific terms of the directive, possible amendments or implementation and application questions.

The committee which was set up under Directive 92/43 is not the only committee, where the national authorities meet the EU Commission in committees on biodiversity issues. There are five other committees which were set up by the EU to discuss such issues.[3] Furthermore, the Commission may, at any moment, convene expert group meetings to discuss legislative, policy or management questions; in practice, officials of the national or regional public authorities participate in these meetings, though in theory they only act as experts, and not as representative of their country. Representatives of environmental organizations or other private experts do not participate; discussions are not public.

In the water sector, the Water Framework Directive 2000/60[4] established the frame for EU action. It required Member States to orient their national surface and groundwater administration according to river basins – which required a new administrative structure for a number of Member States. This structure obliged local, provincial, regional and national authorities to cooperate in the establishment of river basin management plans – which the Member States had to draw up and send to the EU Commission. At the same time, pressure was put on the Member States to cooperate with other Member States or with third countries, where a river basin affected two or several countries. The plans need to be updated at regular intervals and sent to the Commission. Furthermore, Directive 2000/60 required the drawing up of surveillance programmes and of programmes related to measures that were to be undertaken. A committee was set up to ensure cooperation and examine the evolution of the status of EU waters and possible adaptations or amendments of the Directive. The readiness of the national authorities to cooperate went so far that an – indicative – implementation plan to apply the Directive in all Member States was agreed.[5]

Committees for cooperation in the application of water directives also exist for drinking water, bathing water, marine waters, nitrates in water, urban waste water collection and treatment, and the prevention of floods.[6] The three directives mentioned last required the drawing up of action plans, application

3 Committees on birds (Directive 2009/147/EC, JO 2010, L 20 p. 7), trade in endangered species (Regulation 338/97, OJ 1997, L 61 p. 1.), import of tropical wood (Regulation 2173/2005, OJ 2005, L 347 p. 1), animals used for scientific purposes (Directive 2010/63/EU) and invasive species (Regulation 1143/2014, OJ 2014, L 317 p. 55). See EU Commission, SWD (2017)594.

4 Directive 2000/60/EC, OJ 2000, L 327 p. 1.

5 Common strategy on the implementation of the Water Framework Directive (2000/60/EC) as agreed by the Water Directors under Swedish Presidency, 2 May 2001.

6 Directives 98/83/EC, OJ 1998, L 330 p. 32 (drinking water); Directive 2006/7/EC, OJ 2006, L 64 p. 37 (bathing water); Directive 2008/56/EC, (n. 1) (marine waters); Directive 91/676/EEC, OJ 191, L 375 p. 1 (nitrates in water); Directive 91/271/EEC, OJ 1991, L 135 p. 40 (urban waste water treatment); Directive 2007/60/EC, OJ 2007 L 288 p. 7 (floods).

plans or management plans.[7] For all these directives, the EU Commission was required to establish an EU report in order to inform on the application of the directives.

Management infrastructure and hence cooperation between the Union's and the national authorities is less intense in the area of clean air. Directive 2008/50[8] installed a cooperation committee and asked Member States to draw up air quality plans where the limit values of the Directive were exceeded; these plans also had to be sent to the EU Commission. However, no link was established between the EU air quality standards and the emissions limit values which were fixed –for industrial installations, cars etc. – in separate pieces of EU legislation; therefore, no discussion at EU level on the interrelationship of air quality standards and emission limit values took place.

The greatest integration between the different pieces of legislation is achieved in the waste sector, where one committee is in charge of the monitoring of more than a dozen waste stream directives and the Regulation on the shipment of waste.[9] Separate committees exist for waste incineration[10] and ship recycling.[11] Most legislative acts on specific waste streams ask Member States to draw up waste prevention and management plans and programmes for the separate collection of waste which are made available to the EU Commission.

In conclusion, it can fairly be stated that the EU environmental legislation sets some infrastructure for the management of biodiversity, water, waste and – with some reservations – air pollution. This frame is marked by the following features:

- a common general legislative framework for the different sectors which is supplemented by accessory legislation;
- the obligation to orient the administrative structures and practices in the Member States according to common criteria: water – river basin administration; biodiversity – Natura 2000 network; air- establishment of zones, agglomerations and sampling points; waste – network of treatment and elimination installations; separate collection of waste.
- the obligation to draw up management plans and/or programmes, in order to realize the general and specific objectives of the EU legislation;
- the obligation to report at regular intervals to the EU Commission on the application of the legislative frame;

7 Directive 91/676/EEC, (n. 6), Article 5, Directive 91/271/EEC, (n. 6), Article 17, Directive 2007/60/EC, (n. 6), Article 7.
8 Directive 2008/50/EC, (n. 1), Article 29.
9 Directive 2008/98/EC, (n. 1), Article 39.
10 Directive 2010/75/EU, OJ L 334 p. 17, Article 75.
11 Regulation 125/2013, OJ 2013, L 330 p. 1, Article 25.

- the obligation to follow specific procedures for derogations from the general provisions and to report on them to the EU Commission;
- the obligation to prevent the deterioration of the environment. This is explicitly laid down in the biodiversity,[12] the water[13] and the air quality areas,[14] though not in the waste framework directive;[15]
- the organization, by the EU Commission, of committee meetings to coordinate the application of the legislation, build consensus on the interpretation of the provisions, agree positions for discussions at international level and prepare revisions, updating or new legislation;
- the obligation for the EU Commission to regularly publish a report on the state of application of the specific directive(s);[16]
- the possibility, for the EU Commission, to call to order a Member State which does not comply with the legal obligations of EU law, and to bring a Member State before the Court of Justice of the EU; this might even lead to financial sanctions (Articles 258 and 260 TFEU).

This management frame is filled out by the national, regional or local administrations of the Member States which have to adopt and implement the daily management measures. The EU Commission is not involved in the daily management of the environmental natural resources, and a change in this regard is not desirable, as it would lead to high centralization which would contradict the repartition of tasks within the EU,[17] require a super-bureaucracy to be set up in Brussels, and would not be likely to produce fair and generally accepted results, as the distance between the decision-maker and the practical local problems simply is too big.

This does not mean that the present management frame could not be improved. The first improvement should take place in the information of the public, as the EU is, according to the EU Treaties, highly committed to the principles of open society.[18] Generally, the Member States, when reporting on the implementation of a directive,[19] inform about the measures which were taken,

12 Directive 92/43/EEC, (n. 1), Article 6; see also Case C-281/16, *Hoekschewaard*.

13 Directive 2000/60/EC, (n. 1), Article 4(1) and 4(7); see also Case C-461/14, *Bund Naturschutz*.

14 Directive 2008/50/EC, (n. 1), Article 1 No. 5 and Article 12.

15 Until now, a general environmental principle of 'no retrocession' which is discussed at international level, has not been recognized at EU level.

16 The obligation to publish a report does not exist in the air quality sector. However, since 2011, the European Environment Agency (EEA) publishes an annual report, see last 'Air quality in Europe -2017 report'. Copenhagen 2017.

17 See Article 192(4) TFEU: the Member States – and not the EU – shall implement EU environmental policy.

18 Articles 1(2), 10(3) and 11(2)TEU, 15(1) and 298 TFEU.

19 Implementation reports on environmental regulations are rather exceptional, though normally such regulations also contain measures which the Member States have to implement.

but almost never on the results. And neither the Member States nor the EU Commission are particularly eager to disseminate environmental information. Also, the Commission's horizontal reports read more as a sort of marketing paper than as a sober analysis of the state of affairs. Examples where more information should be made available concern the biodiversity sector, where in particular the information on derogations made by Member States on the protection of natural habitats[20] and for the protection of species[21] is not made public. Frequently, the names of species are only given in Latin, which leads to limiting discussions to experts. In the water sector, information on national programmes of measures[22] and on monitoring such programmes are not made public, not either the details of the costs of water.[23] The implementation reports by the EU Commission inevitably remain general; as they cover 28 Member States, they cannot and do not give any such details. The river basin management plans are made public, but the background documents for those plans only on request.[24]

The second area, where the management infrastructure of the EU could be improved, concerns the right of the public to participate in the decision-making of public authorities. In the biodiversity sector, no public participation is foreseen,[25] though the recent case law of the Court of Justice seems to favour[26] broad participation rights of environmental organizations. It is true, though, that nature conservation organizations, because of their very great know-how in the area of biodiversity, *de facto* very often participate in decisions on nature conservation measures, though perhaps not in all Member States. In the water sector, the public is entitled to participate in the elaboration of river basin management plans, but not in the elaboration of programmes of measures, derogations, decisions on the cost of water or other decisions. Also in the area of air quality, the public may participate in the elaboration of air quality plans,[27] but nothing is foreseen on decisions concerning sampling points for measuring air pollution or short-term action programmes. In the waste sector, participation in plans and programmes is foreseen. Thus, participation in decisions on plans and programmes is generally provided for,[28] but is rather imperfectly ensured with regard to other decisions.

20 Directive 92/43/EEC, (n. 1), Article 6.
21 Ibid., Article 16.
22 Directive 2000/60/EC, (n. 1), Article 11.
23 Ibid., Article 9.
24 Ibid., Article 16.
25 Directive 92/43/EEC, (n. 1), Article 6(1).
26 Case C-664/15, *Protect Nature*.
27 Directive 2003/35/EC, OJ 2003, L 156 p. 17. This directive only provides for public participation in some plans that are mandatory under EU law.
28 This might be due to the general obligation for Member States to ensure public participation in the environmental impact assessment of plans and programmes, Directive 2001/42/EC, OJ 2001, L 197 p. 30.

A third area is the enforcement of EU law. Indeed, the management of natural resources also includes the obligation to ensure that the management is in compliance with existing legal rules. In this regard, the EU Commission does not insist that Member States completely and timely comply with their reporting obligations. Furthermore, very often the national or regional plans and programmes are not assessed at EU level. In the areas of water and air, the Commission often omits to insist on compliance with the standards that were fixed in EU legislation. And while Member States are obliged to fix penalties for non-compliance with EU directives[29] which shall be effective, proportionate and dissuasive, the Commission does not compare the different penalties or check, whether they are effective, dissuasive and proportionate.

The overall result is that the management of natural resources in the Member States, though it takes place on the basis of rather uniform legislation and in the above-described frame that was set by the EU, leads to rather different results between Member States in the North and the South, in the East and the West of the EU. Different legal cultures – which become apparent for example in the approach to transparency and open society principles or to compliance with the rule of law[30] – contribute to this result. Yet, there is also a responsibility of the EU institutions which do not always ensure that the management frame is filled out in practice.

3. TOWARDS THE UN SUSTAINABLE DEVELOPMENT GOALS

As the term 'sustainability' lacks a concrete legal content, it appears best to refer to the United Nations' Sustainable Development Goals (SDG)[31] which the EU completely adhered to.[32] The SDGs contain 17 objectives and, overall, 169 targets. Of these targets those relating to natural resources – biodiversity, water, air, soil, raw materials and waste – are selected hereafter and EU measures are presented.

29 No such requirement exists, though, in the area of biodiversity.

30 It is this author's conviction that a proverb such as 'fatto la legge, si trova l'inganno' (once the law is made, there will be a way to bypass it) could not exist as a proverb in Scandinavian countries, in the United Kingdom or in some other Member States.

31 UN, 'Sustainable Development Goals, the 2030 Agenda for sustainable development', Resolution adopted on 25 September 2015 by the General Assembly, A/RES/70/1.

32 EU Commission, Communication 'Next steps for a sustainable future. European action for sustainability', COM (2016)739: section 1.2: 'The EU is fully committed to be a frontrunner in implementing the 2030 Agenda on the SDGs, together with its Member States, in line with the principle of subsidiarity'.

The available space only allows rather sketchy presentations of the measures within the EU.[33]

As regards external action, the EU Commission remains rather general. As examples, the declarations on trade and development[34] and on waste and chemicals[35] may be referred to. It is clear that not all measures taken or to be taken can be enumerated. However, to take just two examples, some consideration would have been welcome, whether the environmental clauses in the trade agreements could not be more specific; secondly, it should be questioned whether the export of hazardous and nuclear waste from the EU to developing countries is really sustainable.

Target 6.1: By 2030, safe and affordable drinking water shall be available for all.

Directive 98/83[36] provides for access to drinking water that is safe and affordable. The directive is largely complied with; every year some ten million analyses are carried out; the compliance rate normally is up to 99 per cent.[37] Access to public supply to drinking water is very high, between 98 and 100 per cent of the population, though this figure was only 62 per cent in Romania (2013).[38] Some derogations from the directive's requirements would have to be decided by Member States. Yet it can be fairly expected that by 2030, access to safe drinking water will be possible for all EU citizens.

Target 6.3: By 2030, reducing pollution, halving proportion of untreated water.

Ongoing; pollution was and continues to be reduced via Directives 2000/60[39] and 2008/105.[40] Untreated water is being reduced by the collection and treatment of waste water, on the basis of Directive 91/271.[41]

33 The EU Commission document CSD (2017) 390, which accompanied COM (2017)939 and was supposed to give details of compliance, only referred to the 17 objectives in general, not to the 169 targets.

34 EU Commission, SWD (2016) 390, p. 51: 'In the trade and development policy, the EU has increased the priority given to the sustainable development and conservation of natural resources such as biodiversity and fisheries, notably by the inclusion of dedicated provisions in the trade and development chapters of its trade and investment agreements, in addition to commitments to core environmental agreements'.

35 Ibid., p. 42: 'The EU also supports the sound management of waste and chemicals and the implementation of the related multilateral Environmental Agreements by developing countries'.

36 Directive 98/83/EC, (n. 6).

37 European Court of Auditors, Special Report 12/2017, p. 13.

38 Ibid., p. 18.

39 Directive 2000/60/EC, (n. 1).

40 Directive 2008/105/EC, OJ 2008, L 348 p. 84.

41 Directive 91/271/EEC, (n. 6).

Target 6.5: By 2030, ensure integrated national and transboundary water resources management.

Ongoing, ensured by Directive 2000/60 and river basin management plans which are to be drawn up under that directive and renewed every six years.

Target 6.6: By 2020, protect and restore water-related ecosystems.

No specific measures are foreseen for mountains, forests, wetlands, aquifers and lakes. Protection is attempted through Directive 92/43 (Natura 2000 sites). Large rivers – Danube, Rhine, Elbe, Odra – are subject to management provisions of international conventions and cooperation normally works satisfactorily; other rivers are managed by Member States.

Target 11.6: By 2030, pay special attention to air quality and waste management in urban agglomerations.

Special attention to air quality is paid by the management of Directive 2008/50,[42] but damage through air pollution remains unacceptably high: there are some 400,000 premature deaths due to air pollution in the EU.[43] Waste management is ensured (Directive 2008/98[44]), though waste generation increases and waste prevention and waste recovery results only advance slowly.

Target 12.2: By 2030, achieve sustainable management and effective use of natural resources.

This target is a circular one: whether it is complied with, is just the subject of this contribution.

Target 12.3: By 2030, halve food waste at retail and consumer level, reduce food losses.

Initiatives in this area are mainly taken at national level and by voluntary action. There is no common approach to food losses and to the reduction of food waste. In an action plan on the circular economy of 2015,[45] the EU Commission announced some measures on food and food waste – labelling, measuring, encouraging the avoiding of waste – which have not yet been concretized.

---

42 Directive 2008/50/EC, (n. 1).

43 EEA, Air quality in Europe-2017 report. Copenhagen 2017, p. 55.

44 Directive 2008/98/EC, (n. 1).

45 EU Commission, COM (2015) 614, section 5.2.

Target 12.4: By 2020, sound management of chemicals and all wastes; reduce releases.

Ongoing. The management of chemicals is pursued under Regulation 1907/2006,[46] that of waste under Directive 2008/98[47] and different waste stream directives. The term 'sound management' is unclear and, in practice, compliance is sometimes difficult to assess or to achieve.

Target 12.5: By 2030, substantially reduce waste generation through prevention, reduction, recycling and reuse.

Corresponding objectives are announced under the heading 'circular economy', but realizations so far are limited. 'Substantial reduction' means something different for a country that had no waste prevention or recovery measures taken, and a region such as the EU, where recovery measures are relatively far developed.

Target 12.8: By 2030, ensure that people everywhere have the relevant information and awareness for a sustainable development and lifestyle in harmony with nature.

Within the EU, the necessary information with regard to sustainable development is available; as regards awareness, doubts exist, as poverty, education, traditions and other factors often impede full awareness. Furthermore, to give a concrete example, everybody in the EU has access to information about the negative impact of cars on air pollution, traffic congestion, raw material use, noise, interference in landscape (road construction), etc. However, this does not lead to a significant reduction of the use of cars or other measures to live more in harmony with nature.

Target 14.1: By 2025, significantly reduce marine pollution of all kind.

No specific EU action exists at EU level. Directive 2008/56 on marine water strategy[48] and Directive 2000/59 on port reception facilities for ship waste[49] include activities on marine pollution; Directive 2015/720 on reducing the use of plastic bags[50] might in time also contribute to reducing pollution. However, most of the measures taken by the EU or the Member States are not targeted on marine pollution.

---

46 Regulation 1907/2006, OJ 2006, L 396 p. 1.
47 Directive 2008/98/EC, (n. 1).
48 Directive 2008/56/EC, (n. 1).
49 Directive 2000/59/EC, OJ 2000, L 332 p. 81.
50 Directive 2015/720/EU, OJ 2015, L 115 p. 11.

Target 14.2: By 2020, sustainably manage and protect marine and coastal ecosystems to avoid significant adverse impacts.

Directive 92/43 provides for the management of marine and coastal natural habitats, when these are considered to be of EU importance. Targeted measures to protect ecosystems do not exist at EU level, though EU Member States might be active in this area. A recommendation of 2003 suggested an integrated coastal zone management.[51] It is not clear, whether this recommendation led to significant changes in management.

Target 14.5: By 2020, conserve at least ten per cent of coastal and marine areas.

Directive 92/43 does not provide for a percentage of (land, coastal or marine) natural habitats that are to be protected. The EU Commission's Natura 2000 newsletter indicated in summer 2017 that overall almost 400,000 km^2 were designated as marine habitats of EU importance; considerably more marine habitats were to be designated in particular by Cyprus, Spain, Finland, Greece, Italy, Poland and Portugal.[52]

Target 15.1: By 2020, ensure conservation, restoration and use of territorial and inland freshwater ecosystems and their services.

Directive 92/43 aims at the conservation of natural habitats and wild fauna and flora, not of ecosystems. For the habitats which are of EU importance and listed on the EU lists, the Member States shall take the necessary conservation measures in order to ensure a favourable conservation status. Of course, not all such measures will be taken by 2020.

There are no specific EU measures for forests, wetlands, mountains and drylands.

Target 15.2: By 2020, achieve sustainable management of forests, stop deforestation, restore degraded forests, ensure afforestation and reforestation.

There is no common forest policy in the EU, though EU policies for rural development, employment, climate change, energy and environment influence Member States' forest development, which grew by about 0.4 per cent since

51 Recommendation 2002/413, OJ 2002, L 148 p. 24.
52 EU Commission, Natura 2000 newsletter, July 2017.

1990.[53] Since 2013, the EU has the declared objective to have all forests managed sustainably.

Target 15.3: By 2030, combat desertification, restore degraded land and soil, strive to achieve a land degradation-neutral world.

The EU adhered to the Paris Convention on combating desertification,[54] but has not taken any specific measure to stop or fight desertification within the EU. Measures to restore contaminated sites – old waste dumps, military land, industrial installations etc. – are also left to Member States, though some cooperation exists as to the classification, and identification of such sites, large scale land use for infrastructure measures – urban sprawl, leisure activities etc. – continues.

Target 15.4: By 2030, ensure the conservation of mountain ecosystems.

The EU adhered to the 1991 Salzburg Convention on the protection of the Alps,[55] but has not taken specific measures to implement it. No convention exists or is being prepared for the protection of the Pyrenees or the Carpates. Generally, the protection of mountains is left to Member States.

Target 15.5: Take urgent and significant action to reduce degradation of central habitats, halt the loss of biodiversity and, by 2020, protect and prevent the extinction of threatened species.

Directive 92/43 deals with all habitats of EU importance, without identifying particularly important habitats. The EU did not adhere to the 1971 Ramsar Convention on the protection of wetlands. It does not either have a red list of threatened species, though Directive 92/43 gives some protection status to about 1300 fauna and flora species and Directive 2009/147 tries to protect wild EU birds. An action plan to stop biodiversity loss by 2010[56] did not succeed and was replaced by a plan to stop the loss by 2020.[57] It is likely that this objective will not be reached.

53 EU Commission, a new EU forest strategy: for forests and the forest-based sectors, COM (2013) 659 and SWD (2013) 342.
54 Decision 98/216, OJ 1998, L 83 p. 1.
55 Decision 96/191, OJ 1996 L 61 p. 31.
56 EU Commission, COM (2006) 216.
57 EU Commission, COM (2010) 4 and Council, Doc. 7536 of 16 March 2010.

Target 15.7: Take urgent action to end poaching and trafficking of protected species and address supply and demand of illegal wildlife products.

The EU adopted Regulation 338/97 on the trade in endangered species, which is more stringent than the CITES Convention, to which the EU finally adhered in 2013.[58] The import of tropical wood was also restricted,[59] though developing countries' cooperation could be intensified. An action plan to reduce wildlife trafficking was adopted recently,[60] but controlling and restricting illegal wildlife trade remains difficult.

Target 15.8: By 2020, introduce measures against invasive species.

The EU adopted Regulation 1143/2014,[61] which intends to fight invasive alien species. The EU lists for such species[62] made the inclusion of a species in such a list dependent on economic considerations.

Target 15.9: Mobilize and significantly increase financial measures from all sources to conserve and sustainably use biodiversity and ecosystems.

It was estimated in 2003 – for the 15 Member States at that time; at present, there are 28 Member States – that the annual amount of fully ensured compliance of the Natura 2000 Network with the requirements of Directive 92/43 would require some six billion euro per year. Only a fraction of this sum is made available to Natura 2000 habitats under the different EU structural funds. Member States also continuously under-finance biodiversity and ecosystem projects. An action plan for nature of 2017 tries to obtain more financial resources for nature conservation.[63]

Overall, the assessment of the EU Commission as laid down in the two documents[64] gives the impression that the Commission is of the opinion that the EU is well on the way to reaching the United Nations' SDGs by 2020/2030. The EU is not in need of changing its policy to a significant extent, but may continue with 'business as usual'.

If one looks at the state of the natural resources within the EU, the picture is perhaps less rosy. In the biodiversity sector, the EU did not manage to stop the

58 Regulation 338/97, OJ 1997, L61 p. 1.
59 Regulation 2173/2005 (n. 3); Regulation 895/2010, OJ 2010, L 295 p. 23.
60 EU Commission, COM (2016) 87.
61 Regulation 1143/2014, (n. 3).
62 Commission implementing regulations 2016/1141, OJ 2016, L 189 p. 4 and 2017/1263, OJ 2017, L 182 p. 37.
63 EU Commission, COM (2017) 198.
64 EU Commission, COM (2016) 739 and SWD (2016) 390.

loss of biodiversity and is not likely to do better in future. Whether it is the slow but progressive reduction of the number of birds, of insects or of other species – there is no group of species where the reduction of species has been stopped and the tendency been reversed. The EU did not adopt provisions on biodiversity in general, but limited itself to Directive 92/43 – which deals with specific, 'island-like' habitats – and some accompanying pieces of legislation. It did in particular not succeed in stopping the use of intensive agricultural practice and the use of chemicals – pesticides and fertilizers – in agriculture, and was not really trying to promote large-scale organic farming.

As regards water, the good environmental quality of surface and groundwater was to be achieved fifteen years after the adoption of Directive 2000/60. By 2015, about half of the waters complied with this requirement. And a derogation clause allowed Member States to postpone that date by up to twelve further years; this possibility was used by a number of them, and it is not clear what will happen after 2027. An intention to stop discharges of pollutants into surface waters by 2020[65] was abandoned.

The EU has a very considerable problem with air pollution,[66] but has not taken effective measures to combat pollution at the source, for example by adopting strong measures for car and truck emissions, industrial installations and farming practices. The EU did not, not either under the auspices of climate change, adopt measures to fight desertification and soil erosion. The circular economy approach launched since 2015 did not lead, until now, to a substantive set of rules. It is unlikely that progress in this area will be quick, as the prevention of waste (by reuse, recycling, increased durability, elimination of dangerous substances, suppression of planned obsolescence, etc.) requires an active product policy; however, such an active product policy would go against the doctrine of free enterprise and market economy. In the meantime, the generation of waste per capita increases within the EU.

As regards external policy, the EU has not really managed to fundamentally re-orient its approach by trying to improve the environmental and economic conditions in developing countries. The number of ecological migrants is growing slowly, and if one believes the scientists, their number will be reaching appalling figures in the next thirty years. Fighting environmental impairment at source, one of the principles of EU environmental policy (Article 191 TFEU), also has a territorial application and means that measures should be taken particularly in developing countries. However, such an approach is not really compatible with the doctrine that one euro invested in a third country should bring three euro back to the EU, an example of this being the partnership agreements with developing countries in the fisheries sector. The establishment of the European

65 Directive 2000/60/EC, (n. 2), Article 16.

66 See the number of premature deaths, above, text to n. 43.

Fund for Sustainable Development[67] with a budget of 4,1 billion euro until 2020 hopefully marks a first step in changing the EU external policy.

4. CONCLUDING REMARKS

This contribution is not meant to be pessimistic. Rather it tries to convey the message that the achievement of sustainable development and the compliance with the 17 SDGs of the United Nations requires another EU policy. Business as usual will not be sufficient, and the effective application of the EU environmental legal provisions will require more and other approaches than envisaged by the EU Commission. The Commission's statement in this regard[68] is almost cynical: the Environmental Implementation Review[69] is just another way of informing the public that the Commission will largely stop pursuing infringement cases. In order to see how regressive its proposal is, one should imagine for a second that the Commission substituted its enforcement policy in the competition sector by a 'Competition Implementation Review', which describes cases of breach of EU law instead of enforcing the law. In order to 'facilitate' access to justice, the Commission published a Notice,[70] where it detailed the jurisprudence of the Court of Justice in this matter, carefully avoiding even to take any position itself. And the 'supporting of compliance in Member States' ignores the fact that Article 17 TEU requests the Commission to ensure the application of EU environmental law itself, not just to support Member State action.

The development of natural resources in the EU is not yet in line with the Sustainable Development Goals of the United Nations. The 2030 objective may be reached; however, this would require a major re-orientation of EU natural resources policy.

---

67 Regulation 2017/1601, OJ 2017, L 249 p. 1.

68 EU Commission, COM (2016) 739, p. 9: 'The implementation of the EU's environmental acquis (SDG 6,14,15) remains vital for long-term sustainability and is inseparable from the broad economical and societal challenges. As highlighted in the 7th Environmental Action Programme, maintenance and improvement of our natural resource base is also essential for our economic sectors to deliver their services, e.g. agriculture, fisheries, or energy. The Commission will strengthen the tracking of progress of environmental objectives through Environmental Implementation Review and will launch initiatives to simplify environmental reporting, facilitate access to justice and support environmental compliance in Member States (SDG 17)'.

69 EU Commission, COM (2017) 63.

70 EU Commission, COM (2017) 2616.

CHAPTER 3

SQUARING THE CIRCULAR ECONOMY: TOWARDS MORE COHERENCE IN THE EU SUSTAINABLE MANAGEMENT OF NATURAL RESOURCES

Wybe Th. Douma*

ABSTRACT

The sustainable management of natural resources by the EU is in our own interest and also contributes to global sustainable development. What we import can have serious consequences in exporting countries. Such external effects of EU natural resources use have been discussed at length by the EU institutions, but a clear and coherent policy framework has not emerged. Instead, an ad hoc approach has been followed. Over time, the EU has thus developed separate policy regimes with distinct features for numerous individual natural resources. Two such regimes, regarding forestry and fisheries, are examined in this contribution. The manner in which they aim at ensuring that only legally harvested natural resources are put on the EU market or imported has turned out to be quite different. While the specific characteristics of the natural resources in question do not seem to play a decisive role here, it does seem that other factors do. A prominent factor seems to be the fear of violating rules of international trade law. Another factor could be that the EU has an exclusive competence to adopt fisheries measures, but not when it comes to forestry products. In order to enhance the effectiveness of the individual regimes, it is concluded that it is worth

* The author is lecturer International and European Environmental Law at Hague University, the Netherlands, independent legal researcher (w.t.douma@gmail.com) and editor of several legal journals and the European Environmental Law website www.eel.nl and its news service.

striving for enhanced coherence of the EU's policy regarding sustainable management of natural resource.

1. INTRODUCTION

The European Union (EU) is highly dependent on the import of resources from third (non-EU) countries. This brings economic advantages for those countries, but some of the EU imports have environmental and social disadvantages for the producing countries that stand in the way of their sustainable development. They can have negative economic consequences where natural resources (like timber, minerals and fish) are illegally harvested and payment of taxes is avoided. These negative consequences for third countries of EU production and consumption processes can also affect the Union itself, notably through rising greenhouse gas emissions due to illegal logging or burning of forests to clear land for oil palm plantations. They can also contribute to destabilisation and increased migration to Europe. Only by paying attention to the external consequences of EU use of natural resources, for instance in terms of environmental effects, rights of indigenous persons and their livelihoods and food security, can the EU ensure that it does not add to the problems of developing countries and instead contribute to building more sustainable and resilient societies.

Since the entry into force of the Treaty of Lisbon on 1 December 2009, the duty to contribute to the sustainable development of the planet and especially of developing countries has explicitly been laid down in EU primary law.[1] The duty to integrate environmental concerns into other policy areas of the EU in order to contribute to sustainable development was already introduced years earlier in the form of the integration principle.[2] But as experiences with the latter provision have shown, it can be a while before the law on paper also becomes the law in practice.[3]

Over time, the EU institutions discussed ways and means to ensure that natural resources used in the EU would be managed sustainable at length. At times, attention was also paid to the external aspects. Various instruments aimed at stimulating the legality and at times also the sustainability of natural resources

1 Notably in Article 3(5) and 21(2)(d) TEU.

2 Nowadays Article 11 TFEU: "Environmental protection requirements must be integrated into the definition and implementation of the Union's policies and activities, in particular with a view to promoting sustainable development." The integration principle was already introduced in the treaties in 1987 through the Single European Act, albeit without a reference to sustainable development.

3 On the slow process of integrating environmental concerns in the EU's trade policy, see Douma, W.Th. (2017) 'The Promotion of Sustainable Development through EU Trade Instruments', European Business Law Review, Vol. 28, No. 2, pp. 193-212.

that are put on the EU market were introduced. These instruments regulate the production, consumption and waste management in the EU itself in the first place, but at times also touch on the sustainable management of natural resources outside the EU. Focusing on the external aspects of EU legislation, the manner in which the individual instruments are designed and operate varies considerably. This comes as somewhat of a surprise, considering that the instruments all have the same goal. Partially, the differences might be due to dissimilarities where the individual resources are concerned. The lack of a more detailed theoretical underpinning of ways and means to deal with external aspects of EU production and consumption patterns also could play a role. Other reasons could be the difference in EU competences, and the fear of violating international trade law. The latter topic is not dealt with at length in this paper, in order to keep within the limits of this publication.

In this contribution, first of all the attempts at formulating a general framework on such external aspects will first be discussed (section 2). After that, two policy areas in which the EU has introduced a distinct regime aimed at ensuring the legality and – in one of the two cases – sustainability of natural resources are turned to, namely forestry (section 3) and fisheries (section 4). In the final section 5, concluding remarks are presented.

2. ATTEMPTS AT CREATING A GENERAL FRAMEWORK FOR EXTERNAL ASPECTS OF GLOBAL VALUE CHAINS

In 1998, a study on Integrated Product Policy (IPP) was published that only focuses on the EU itself.[4] The European Commission (Commission) issued a Green Paper on this issue in 2001.[5] The European Parliament (EP) stressed the importance of indicators for monitoring achievement of IPP. It insisted that the Commission would analyse the implications of global supply chains for IPP and IPP's role in developing countries, and would start putting the IPP into practice. In 2003, a study on the external environmental effects related to the life cycle of products and services confirmed that external effects can and need to be taken into account.[6] In the same year, the Commission announced that IPP would be a

4 Ernst & Young, Integrated Product Policy. A study analysing national and international developments with regard to Integrated Product Policy in the environment field and providing elements for an EC policy in this area, Brussels, March 1998. See also http://ec.europa.eu/environment/ipp/2001developments.htm and DG XI, *Workshop on Integrated Product Policy, Final Report*, Brussels, 8 December 1998.

5 COM (2001) 68.

6 Bio Intelligence Service and O2 France, External environmental effects related to the life cycle of products and service, Brussels, February 2003.

key part of the implementing measures for the forthcoming Thematic Strategy on the Sustainable Use of Resources.[7] It also promised that suitable indicators would be developed.[8] The European Parliament regretted that the communication provided only limited guidance on how to move society in the direction of sustainable systems of product development and design.[9] Taking up some of the critique, the 2005 Thematic Strategy on the sustainable use of natural resources[10] explained that the EU is highly dependent on resources coming from outside Europe, and that the environmental impact of resource use by the EU is felt globally. It described 'sustainable use' as a key ingredient of long-term prosperity both within the EU and globally. This encompasses both the production and the consumption phase, hence the whole value chain, including the effects outside the EU. The Strategy was supposed to apply for 25 years and lead to reducing the environmental impact of 'resource use'. No quantitative targets were proposed, because of a lack of knowledge and indicators (needed to measure progress in achieving targets) at that moment in time – in spite of the 2003 promises to develop such indicators. Targets would however be developed within five to ten years.[11] Member States were asked to take the lead, except in areas where the EU has exclusive competence. A 2011 progress report[12] underlined that although the Resource Strategy had highlighted the importance of the international dimension, the increasing import of resources and their related environmental impacts outside Europe still was not sufficiently addressed in EU policies. Quantitative targets also still had not been formulated due to the complexity of setting targets on resource use or related environmental impacts and the absence of examples of this on national level.[13] The Ecological Footprint is mentioned as one example of a widespread environmental impact indicator and a good communicative tool, but its analytical power was described as widely disputed because of its methodological weaknesses.[14]

The 2005 Strategy was replaced by no less than three new policy documents. The EU 2020 Strategy[15] and the accompanying Flagship initiative entitled 'A resource-efficient Europe'[16] set the EU on the path to transformation.

7 COM (2003) 302, p. 6.
8 Ibid., p. 17.
9 Resolution P5_TA (2004)0349, OJ 2004, C 104 E, p. 726. A framework directive for IPP aimed at establishing coherence and consistency in the area of product-related environmental protection was called for, because so far, IPP instruments had only had an isolated impact.
10 COM (2005) 670.
11 Ibid., p. 6.
12 SEC (2011) 1068.
13 Ibid., p. 9.
14 Ibid., p. 21.
15 COM (2010) 2020.
16 COM (2011) 21.

Furthermore, the 'Roadmap for a Resource-Efficient Europe'[17] sets out how Europe's economy is to become sustainable by 2050. While the quest for robust, easily understandable and widely accepted indicators continued, it was proposed to start measuring progress with the help of a provisional lead indicator.[18] The latter indicator did not take external aspects into account, however, so it needed to be complemented by other indicators.[19]

At the end of 2011, the Eco-innovation Action Plan (Eco-AP) was adopted.[20] It aims to achieve a more efficient and responsible use of natural resources. In the period 2012-2014, eco-innovation objectives were to be integrated in the revision of existing policies. The 7th European Action Programme 'Living well, within the limits of our planet' entered into force in January 2014.[21] It identifies resource-efficiency as one of its policy objectives. Commissioner Malmström from DG Trade issued the 2015 Trade for All strategy.[22] It stressed that the Commission takes concerns about environmental aspects of trade agreements seriously, and sets out that a responsible management of global value chains is crucial to ensure trade policy meets EU values. Conflict minerals, illegal logging, sustainability criteria for biofuels[23] and non-financial reporting regarding supply chain issues[24] are among the examples mentioned. It was announced that the Commission will further develop these policies in the coming years through a mix of soft and innovative tools and legislative changes.[25] More specifically, the Commission intends to increase transparency in supply chains and improve consumer information by creating additional incentives for supply-chain due diligence reporting by large EU companies, notably by publishing annually a list of reports submitted by 'responsible supply chain reporting' companies. Furthermore, new sectoral or geographic opportunities for additional responsible supply chain

17 COM (2011) 571.

18 Ibid., p. 20. The indicator covers resource productivity, measured by the ratio of GDP to Domestic Material Consumption (expressed in Euro/tonne). A higher ratio would indicate better performance, with growth consuming relatively fewer resources. It is admitted that this only captures the material resources aspects and does not deal with other resources or the potential shift of burden across countries.

19 Ibid., p. 21.

20 COM (2011) 899.

21 Article 5 of Decision No. 1386/2013/EU of the European Parliament and of the Council of 20 November 2013 on a General Union Environment Action Programme to 2020 'Living well, within the limits of our planet', OJ L 354, 28.12.2013, p. 171.

22 COM (2015) 497.

23 Laid down in Commission regulation 2014/1307/EU, OJ 2014, L 351 and the Renewable Energy Directive 2009/28/EC, OJ 2009, L 140.

24 Directive 2014/95/EU, OJ 2014, L 330 and Directive 2013/34/EU, OJ 2013, L 182. On the implementation in the Netherlands and a number of other EU countries, see S. van der Velde, *De implementatie van Richtlijn 2014/95/EU in Nederland. Niet-financiële rapportage door grote ondernemingen*, The Hague, 2017.

25 Trade for all, p. 24.

partnerships will be identified and assessed.[26] It was also explained that human rights breaches that may be found in global supply chains such as the worst forms of child labour and land grabbing "deserve particular attention".[27]

In its communication 'Closing the loop – An EU action plan for the Circular Economy' that appeared a few months after the Trade for All strategy, the Commission set out that attention must be paid to the environmental and social impacts of the production of primary raw materials, both in the EU and in non-EU countries. The action plan is to implement the EU's 2020 strategy flagship initiative. The Commission explained its plans to promote the sustainable sourcing of raw material globally, for example through policy dialogues, partnerships and its trade[28] and development policy. It is underlined that industry has a key role to play by making specific commitments to sustainable sourcing and cooperating across value chains.[29] The global dimension of the circular economy and supply chains is described as prominent in areas such as sustainable sourcing, and an increasingly globalized market for secondary raw materials. To tackle these external aspect, the Commission announced that it will cooperate closely with international organizations and other interested partners as part of the global efforts to reach the 2030 Sustainable Development Goals.[30]

3. EU TIMBER TRADE POLICY

3.1. INTRODUCTION

While the EU had immense difficulties to persuade Poland to stop logging in Europe's last primeval forest,[31] it is following a dual approach to ensure that timber from outside the Union that is put on its market stems from legally logged sources. On the one hand, since 2003 the EU aims at concluding bilateral agreements that ensure forestry management and law enforcement in major producing countries meet minimum standards. Consignments from those countries in principle can be put on the EU market with the permits issued in the country of origin. On the other hand, importers of timber from countries with which no such partnership agreement was concluded are obliged to provide evidence of the legality of individual shipments of timber through a due diligence system. The latter rules applied since 1 March 2013, but enforcement in the EU

26 Ibid., p. 25.
27 Ibid.
28 The Communication refers here to the 'Trade for all' strategy discussed above.
29 COM (2015) 614, p. 5.
30 Ibid., p. 20.
31 See Case C-441/71 R, *Commission* v *Poland,* (interim relief), Case C-441/17. See also Douma, W.Th. 'A new and practical way of stopping EU law violations', EU Observer, 14 September 2017.

Member States is taking off only slowly. Some examples of the first national case law from Sweden, the Netherlands and Germany will be mentioned in this respect. The Commission instigated an infraction procedure against one Member State for not enforcing the applicable rules.

3.2. SCALE OF THE PROBLEM

Estimates about the percentage of forestry products stemming from illegal logging operations are that they amount to up to one third of total operations and are worth between 10 and 100 billion USD per year. The damage is even higher if the related crimes are also taken into account. Forestry crime including corporate crimes and illegal logging is estimated to account for up to $152 billion every year, i.e. more than all official development aid combined.[32] On top of that, tropical forests contain a high share of the world's terrestrial biodiversity, provide carbon storage and help to regulate the climate as well as water cycles.

The EU supports the global targets of halting and reversing global forest cover loss by 2030 at the latest and of reducing gross tropical deforestation by at least 50 per cent compared to 2008 levels by 2020. However, research has shown that the EU is responsible for the deforestation of about 9 million hectares of land per year, through the import of products associated with deforestation.[33]

3.3. EU INITIAL RESPONSE: FLEGT

In 2003, the EU adopted the Forest Law Enforcement, Governance and Trade (FLEGT) Action Plan.[34] It sets out a range of measures available to the EU and its Member States to tackle illegal logging. In 2005, the FLEGT Regulation was adopted.[35] It formed the basis for a series of prolonged negotiations with major timber producing countries of so-called Voluntary Partnerships Agreements (VPAs). These bilateral agreements contain detailed rules on the regulation of logging, the enforcement of legislation, the licensing of timber by the exporting VPA country and the monitoring and verification of the functioning in practice of the system. The loggers and other traders need to meet all applicable laws and regulations of the VPA country that regulate origin and production process, subsequent processing, transport, and trade activities, and the licensing authorities are to verify that the timber has been legally produced in accordance with the applicable legislation. If it can be ensured in this manner that the law on

32 Erik Solheim, Head of UN Environment, quoted at http://www.unep.org/newscentre/loopholes-regulations-allow-illegal-logging-thrive-worldwide.

33 COWI, Feasibility Study on options to step up EU Action against Deforestation – Part II.

34 COM (2003) 251.

35 Council Regulation (EC) No. 2173/2005 on the establishment of a FLEGT licensing scheme for imports of timber into the European Community, OJ 2005, L 347, p. 1.

paper is applied and enforced in practice throughout its territory, the exporting country can issue FLEGT licences for shipments of timber destined for the EU. In their turn, the EU countries in principle will accept the FLEGT licensed timber as proof of legality.[36] Although a functioning VPA relationship thus opens the EU doors for timber from exporting countries, the VPA with Indonesia to date is the only one that started operating at the end of 2016.

3.4. ADDITIONAL MEASURES: EUTR

When it became clear that not all major producing countries would be able and/or willing to conclude VPAs, and existing instruments showed not to be very effective in tackling illegal logging and trade (in other words, it was easy to keep putting illegally harvested timber on the EU market, which did not make the conclusion of VPAs an urgent matter), pressure grew to adopt stronger measures. This resulted in the adoption of the EU Timber Regulation (EUTR) on 20 October 2010.[37] As of 3 March 2013, the EUTR prohibits the placing on the EU internal market of illegally harvested timber and timber products. Whether the timber is legal depends on whether it was harvested in accordance with the applicable legislation in the country of harvest, even if it is not an EU country. Elements of the legislation to be taken into account are the rights to harvest timber within legally gazetted boundaries, due payments and duties, environmental and forest legislation, legal rights of third parties concerning land use and land tenure, and trade and customs formalities. Nevertheless, timber that meets the legality requirement is not necessarily also sustainable timber; it merely is legal in the sense that it meets the legal requirements of the producing country, even if these are not in conformity with international standards on sustainable forestry.

It is up to the companies that place timber on the EU market to verify that the timber from non-VPA countries is legal. They must implement what the EUTR describes as a due diligence system. The system requires that the company collects verifiable data on the origin of the timber, from the harvest to the moment it is placed on the European market, so that it can be established that it was legally harvested for the entire 'chain of custody'.

Depending on the circumstances in the country, or even in the specific region of the country where the timber originates, a risk inventory, analysis and assessment must also be made. Where necessary, risk mitigation measures must

36 Also see Ozinga, S. (2011) EU forestry partnerships: Rethinking timber trade agreements, Biores, Vol. 5, No. 2, and Cerutti, P.O., Putzel, L., Pacheco, P. and Baxter, J. (2015) 'Tackling illegal logging in the tropics: From good intentions to smart policies', Biores, Vol. 9, No. 4.

37 Regulation (EU) 995/2010 of the European Parliament and of the Council of 20 October 2010 laying down the obligations of operators who place timber and timber products on the market, OJ 2010, L 295, p. 23.

be taken – except where the risk identified in the course of the risk assessment procedures is negligible. There is not a single accepted system for risk assessment. Rather, the level of risk can only be assessed on a case-by-case basis, as it depends on a number of factors. As a general rule, the operator has to address the questions regarding the prevalence of illegal harvesting of specific tree species, the prevalence of illegal harvesting practices in the place of harvest, and the complexity of the supply chains. Furthermore, specific information related to the timber or timber product itself needs to be used, notably a description, the country of harvest (and, where applicable, the sub-national region and concession), the supplier and trader, and documentation showing compliance with applicable legislation. Although the EUTR covers all companies that put timber on the EU market for the first time, whether they are Transnational Companies (TNCs) or Small and Medium Sized Enterprises (SMEs), the scope of the EUTR is limited in other ways. Only certain types of timber and timber products are covered, while too many products made out of timber (including books, coffins, seats, clothes hangers, tools and musical instruments) are exempted from the regulation.

The EU's timber regime is an example of how the Union is creating regulatory mechanisms that foster CSR initiatives by making these legally binding. This is in line with the Lisbon Treaty's provisions that demand that EU external trade policy takes fundamental rights and environmental protection issues on board. The dual system of due diligence on the one hand and VPAs on the other certainly can improve timber governance in producing countries, and thus contribute to the sustainable development of third countries, in line with the EU's self-imposed treaty obligations described above.

3.5. THE VPA SYSTEM IN PRACTICE

As indicated above, the 2005 FLEGT Regulation aimed at concluding so-called Voluntary Partnership Agreements (VPAs) with countries that export considerable amounts of timber to the EU. In spite of their name, the VPAs place a legally binding obligation on partners to implement a licensing scheme for timber within the schedule stipulated in each VPA, and ensure that sufficient enforcement activities take place.

The VPA with Indonesia entered into force on 1 May 2014. Over 80 pages long, it sets out detailed requirements that are to be met before FLEGT licenses can be issued by Indonesian authorities, a definition of legally-produced timber (i.e. timber harvested and produced in accordance with the legislation as set out in Annex II to the VPA), rules on control of the supply chain, verifications procedures, and rules on independent monitoring. The entry into force did not mean that Indonesia could start issuing FLEGT licenses. The FLEGT licensing scheme started operating on 15 November 2016 after an evaluation of the compliance of the Indonesian Timber Legality Assurance System (TLAS) with the criteria set out in the VPA.[38] From that moment on, EU importers from Indonesia no longer needed to apply the EUTR due diligence system, because the EUTR exempts timber originating from partner countries listed in Annex I FLEGT Regulation.[39] This timber shall be considered to have been legally harvested. Indonesia profited from its new status by issuing 11817 licenses for shipments to the EU worth a total value of US$ 409 million in the period 15 November 2016 – start of April 2017.[40]

The VPA contains an obligation to periodically have an independent third party evaluate whether the TLAS is functioning as described.[41] The evaluation is to include visits to forest harvesting areas, offices, forest checking stations and export points, as well as sampling and spot check methods to evaluate the work of the forest regulatory agencies in Indonesia. Evaluations are to take place at least once every year and are to be released to the public. In this manner, it is to be ensured that the exporting country continues to meet the requirements of the VPA and keeps the right to issue FLEGT licences.

Five other countries have already signed a VPA with the EU and are currently developing the systems needed to control, verify and license legal timber. These countries are Cameroon, the Central African Republic, Ghana, Liberia, and the Republic of the Congo. Negotiations with nine more countries are ongoing.

3.6. THE EUTR IN PRACTICE

The EUTR was adopted on 20 October 2010 and offered the Member States and companies a lengthy period to prepare the application of the new rules in practice, namely until 3 March 2013. Nevertheless, many of the EU Member States were late in abiding by the rules of the EUTR regime, and by 2015 the Commission opened infringement procedures against four states that still did not

---

38 Decision 1/2016 of the Joint Implementation Committee set up by the Voluntary Partnership Agreement between the European Union, of the one part, and the Republic of Indonesia, of the other part of 15 September 2016 concerning the start date of the Forest Law Enforcement Governance and Trade (FLEGT) licensing scheme [2016/1797], OJ 22.10.2016, L 274, p. 62.

39 Indonesia was placed on the Annexes to the FLEGT Regulation, indicating that certain timber and timber products from the country would be able to be placed on the EU internal market on the basis of Indonesian licenses. See Commission delegated regulation (EU) 2016/1387 of 9 June 2016 amending Annexes I and III to Council Regulation (EC) 2173/2005 following a Voluntary Partnership Agreement with Indonesia for a FLEGT licensing scheme for imports of timber into the European Union, OJ 18.8.2016, L 223, p. 1.

40 ClientEarth, EUTR News – March to May 2017, Newsletter, 19 June 2017.

41 Article 15 sub (a) and Annex VI.

meet all requirements.[42] In April 2017, Slovakia was asked to provide evidence for rules on penalties in case of breach of the EUTR.[43] In Belgium, important quantities of timber are placed on the EU market. The country was accused of not managing to carry out enough EUTR verifications at the end of 2017. Since the entry into force of the EUTR in 2013, apparently a mere handful of inspections had been carried out – by less than 1 FTE.[44]

A first official evaluation of the EUTR was published by the Commission on 18 February 2016 and covers the period March 2013 – March 2015.[45] The report showed that implementation and enforcement of the EUTR was slow and uneven during these first two years and remained incomplete. Checks carried out on operators remained limited during the evaluation period, and in many Member States the allocated staff to carried out such checks was not proportionate to the number of operators in that country. This did not stimulate companies to actively develop and use a due diligence system. The uneven implementation and the patchy enforcement did not yet facilitate the establishing of a level playing field, which would protect operators from unfair competition of products made of illegally logged timber.

Sweden appears to be the first country where a company was found to have violated the EUTR. On 5 October 2016, the administrative court of Jönköping confirmed that a timber importer called Almträ Nordic did not comply with the EUTR due diligence requirements of the EUTR when it imported teak from Myanmar.[46] What makes this case particularly interesting is the fact that the importer possessed a so-called 'Green folder' demonstrating that its purchase complied with Myanmar's forest laws. Such folders are compiled by the Myanmar Forest Products Merchants' Federation. They include permits issued by the state-owned company Myanmar Timber Enterprise (MTE), the sole official seller of forestry products from this country, and other official documents. Despite those papers, the Swedish Forest Agency (*Skogsstyrelsen*) was not convinced that the timber was legally harvested in the sense of the EUTR. While forest areas where the timber had been logged were identified, documentation clearly tracing the timber supply chain from MTE back to the forest of harvest was lacking in the 'Green Folder'. The Swedish agency was quite right not to trust the situation and demand for additional evidence. Several reports have shown that Myanmar exports huge quantities of illegally harvested timber, presumably with the help of

42 Namely Hungary, Greece, Spain and Romania. See European Commission, Report on the EU Timber Regulation, COM (2016) 74 final, p. 4 and the accompanying Commission staff working document SWD (2016) 34 final.

43 European Commission, April infringement package, 27 April 2017.

44 Meynen, N. 'Houtmaffia krijgt vrij spel', De Standaard, 24 mei 2017.

45 European Commission, Report on the EU Timber Regulation, COM (2016) 74 final, p. 4 and the accompanying Commission staff working document SWD (2016) 34 final.

46 Förvaltningsrätten Jönköping (Administrative court Jönköping) 5 October 2016, Case No. 2095-16, *Almträ Nordic AB* v *Skogsstyrelsen*.

employees of MTE.[47] The distrust is also in line with the Commission's Guidance Document for the EUTR, which explains, *inter alia*, that shortcomings in governance can undermine the reliability of documents proving compliance with applicable legislation. It is therefore necessary to take into account the degree of corruption prevalent in a specific country, precisely the kind of circumstances relevant in Myanmar. No appeal was brought against the Swedish court ruling. The company in question announced that it would stop importing wood directly from Myanmar. Although the EUTR only foresees in the possibility to act against individuals consignments of timber products from a certain country (unlike the fisheries regime discussed below), in practice it seems as if Sweden and Denmark have banned the import of timber from Myanmar.[48]

The Netherlands followed suit. The Dutch competent authority (*NVWA*) claimed that a timber importer did not comply with the EUTR rules when introducing a shipment of Azobé timber from Cameroon on the Dutch market. A measure was introduced whereby the operator would forfeit € 1,800 for each cubic meter of wood and / or timber products from Cameroon placed on the European market up to a maximum of € 90,000. The Authority reasoned that because of the high level of corruption in Cameroon, there is a high chance that the wood was not legally harvested, and the company should have exercised more caution. The importer appealed against the penalty decision, but the appeal was rejected in a ruling of 24 May 2017.[49] According to the District Court in Noord-Holland, the importer collected insufficient verifiable information. It did not identify the origin of the shipment of timber, and the risk inventory did not meet the requirements of the EUTR. Moreover, none of the risk-limiting measures required by the situation in Cameroon was taken. The Court therefore agrees with the NVWA that the due diligence requirements of the EUTR have not been fully complied with. Because of this infringement, the competent authority was allowed to sanction the company.

In a more recent ruling of 4 July 2017, the Amsterdam District Court found that the competent authorities failed to enforce the EUTR without a proper reason in a number of cases where companies had imported timber from Brazil, without abiding by the EUTR due diligence requirements.[50] Greenpeace Netherlands had requested the Dutch competent authority to inspect a number of companies that were importing timber from the Brazilian Amazon region, and to

47 See for instance Environmental Investigation Agency, Overdue diligence. Teak exports from Myanmar in breach of European Union rules, October 2016.

48 See for more details Douma, W.Th. 'Towards a 'due diligence' jurisprudence the EU Timber Regulation's requirements in courts', Doing Business Right Blog, 27 July 2017.

49 *B.V. X* v *de staatssecretaris van Economische Zaken*, Rechtbank Noord-Holland 24-5-2017, AWB – 16 5358, ECLI:NL:RBNHO:2017:4474.

50 *Stichting Greenpeace Nederland* v *de staatssecretaris van Economische Zaken*, Rechtbank Amsterdam 4-7-2017, AMS 15/5067, ECLI:NL:RBAMS:2017:4926.

prosecute those noncompliant with the EUTR. Upon this request, inspections were carried out showing that several Dutch companies were indeed not complying with the EU due diligence system. The request to prosecute these companies was rejected, however. Instead, merely written warnings were issued to them. The authorities refused to sanction the companies notably because the rules were still rather new. They found it reasonable to give them the chance to bring their business operations in line with the new legal regime. A guidance document on the enforcement policy under nature protection legislation also prescribed warnings to first offenders.[51]

Greenpeace successfully appealed this decision. The Amsterdam Court notably found the Dutch enforcement policy to be unreasonable where it classified violations of articles 4(2) and (3) and 5 EUTR as minor issues, resulting in warnings only for first time offenders. Furthermore, it recalled that the EUTR was adopted on 20 October 2010 and entered into force on 3 March 2013, allowing market participants a considerable amount of time to prepare for meeting the Regulation's requirements. Finally, the Court set out that when companies violate the law, the law ought to be enforced. Authorities can decide not to do so only in special circumstances. In view of the lack of such circumstances, the decision not to prosecute companies violating the EUTR was deemed insufficiently motivated and was therefore quashed. The authorities were ordered to take a new decision within six weeks, in which they are to demonstrate all the facts on the basis of which they decide to enforce the law or not to and, if so, in which manner they plan to take enforcement action. By the time this contribution was submitted in March 2018, still no news on this case had emerged.

These first cases show that several judges are willing and able to apply the EUTR in a manner that does justice to the need for sustainable management of natural resources inside and outside the EU. The due diligence system thus offers the authorities and the judiciary a means to fight illegal logging.

4. EU AND ILLEGAL, UNREPORTED AND UNREGULATED FISHING

4.1. SCALE OF THE PROBLEM

It is estimated that up to 26 million tonnes of seafood – representing 19 per cent of global yields and 10 billion euros per year – are caught via Illegal, Unreported

51 NVWA, Specific Intervention Policy Nature Protection Legislation (Specifiek interventiebeleid natuurwetgeving), IB02-SPEC08 natuur, version 2.1 of 16 July 2015.

and Unregulated (IUU) fishing[52] each year.[53] IUU fishing worldwide depletes fish stocks, destroys marine habitats, undermines food security, nutrition and livelihoods, distorts competition, puts fishers that abide by the rules at a disadvantage and weakens coastal communities, particularly in developing countries. This poses serious challenges to human rights and security; maritime security; economic activity and trade, both at sea and on land. IUU fishing also poses a serious environmental threat to fish stocks and can lead to the collapse of fisheries.[54] The United Nations recognised the importance of the fight against IUU fishing in the UN Sustainable Development Goals as one of the issues to tackle under goal no. 14.4 concerning the conservation and sustainable use the oceans, seas and marine resources for sustainable development. As WWF pointed out, our oceans are nearly in collapse with over 80 per cent of global fish stocks overexploited, but with our ballooning population we cannot afford to lose the systems that provide us with food.[55]

The EU is the largest importer of fish products in the world in terms of value. EU trade – comprising extra-EU imports and exports, and intra-EU exchanges – amounted to EUR 45,9 billion and 13,8 million tonnes in 2014. In that year, the EU imported fish and seafood for a value of some EUR 21 billion.[56] The quantity of illegal products imported into the EU each year was (conservatively) estimated

52 'Irregular' indicates a violation of relevant national laws or international obligations (Article 2 sub 2 IUU Regulation); 'unreported' means not reported, or misreported, to the relevant national authority or regional fisheries management organisation, in contravention of applicable laws and regulations (Article 2 sub 3); 'unregulated' covers fishing in the area of application of a relevant regional fisheries management organisation by fishing vessels without nationality, by fishing vessels flying the flag of a State not party to that organisation or by any other fishing entity, in a manner that is not consistent with or contravenes the conservation and management measures of that organisation; or conducted in areas or for fish stocks in relation to which there are no applicable conservation or management measures by fishing vessels in a manner that is not consistent with State responsibilities for the conservation of living marine resources under international law (Article 2 sub 4).

53 See *inter alia* MRAG and University of British Colombia, The global extent of illegal fishing, Fisheries Ecosystems Restoration Research, Fisheries Centre, 2008, UNODC, 'Transnational Organized Crime in the Fishing Industry: Focus on Trafficking in Persons, Smuggling of Migrants, Illicit Drugs Trafficking', in Focus on: Trafficking in Persons, Smuggling of Migrants, Illicit Drugs Trafficking (Vienna), 2011 and Agnew, D. J., J. Pearce, G. Pramod, T. Peatman, R. Watson, J.R. Beddington and T.J. Pitcher (2009) Estimating the worldwide extent of illegal fishing. PLoS ONE, Vol. 4, No. 2, pp. 1-8.

54 Commission Communication on the application of Council Regulation (EC) 1005/2008 establishing a Community system to prevent, deter and eliminate illegal, unreported and unregulated fishing, COM (2015) 480 final, 1 October 2015.

55 http://wwf.panda.org/wwf_news/?244850 %2FEU-Lifts-Yellow-Card-Warning-on-Philippine-Fisheries.

56 European Market Observatory for Fisheries and Aquaculture Products (EUMOFA), The EU fish market, 2015 edition, European Union, Brussels, 2015. To compare, it is estimated that 20-32 per cent of wild-caught seafood import to the United States, worth between US$ 1.3-2.1 billion, is illegal. See Pramoda, G. K. Nakamurab, T.J. Pitchera and L. Delagran (2014) 'Estimates of illegal and unreported fish in seafood imports to the USA', Marine Policy, Vol. 48, pp. 102-113.

at 500 000 tonnes worth 1.1 billion Euro.[57] The interest of the EU to combat IUU fisheries in all likelihood is also motivated by the fact that its Member States have fishing fleets in every ocean of the world.

4.2. EU RESPONSE

In order to tackle these problems, in 2002 the EU IUU Action Plan was adopted.[58] It was directly inspired by the FAO International Plan of Action adopted in 2001 to prevent, deter and eliminate IUU fishing.[59] The Action Plan was followed by the EU IUU Strategy of 2007,[60] which was accompanied by a proposal for the IUU Regulation.[61] The European Council of Fisheries Ministers formally adopted the IUU Regulation[62] in September 2008, together with the Regulation concerning authorisation for fishing activities.[63] The IUU regulation entered into force on 1 January 2010. As foreseen in this regulation, the Commission adopted an Implementing Regulation[64] laying down technical details in the areas of inspections of third country fishing vessels in Member States ports, catch certification schemes,[65] sightings and mutual assistance. Furthermore, in November 2009, the Regulation establishing a Community Control System for ensuring compliance with the rules of the Common Fisheries

---

57 Commission Communication on a new strategy for the Community to prevent, deter and eliminate Illegal, Unreported and Unregulated fishing, COM (2007) 601 final of 17 October 2007, p. 2.

58 Commission Communication, Community action plan for the eradication of illegal, unreported and unregulated fishing, COM (2002) 280 final.

59 FAO, International plan of action to prevent, deter, and eliminate illegal, unreported and unregulated fishing, adopted at the 24th session of COFI, Rome, Italy, 2 March 2001, http://www.fao.org/DOCREP/003/y1224e/y1224e00.htm.

60 Commission Communication on a new strategy for the Community to prevent, deter and eliminate Illegal, Unreported and Unregulated fishing, COM (2007) 601 final.

61 COM (2007) 602 final.

62 Council Regulation (EC) 1005/2008 of 29 September 2008 establishing a Community system to prevent, deter and eliminate illegal, unreported and unregulated fishing, OJ L 286, 29.10.2008, pp. 1-32.

63 Council Regulation (EC) 1006/2008 of 29 September 2008 concerning authorisations for fishing activities of Community fishing vessels outside Community waters and the access of third country vessels to Community waters, OJ L 286, 29.10.2008, pp. 33-44.

64 Commission Regulation (EC) 1010/2009 of 22 October 2009 laying down detailed rules for the implementation of Council Regulation (EC) 1005/2008 establishing a Community system to prevent, deter and eliminate illegal, unreported and unregulated fishing, OJ L 280, 27.10.2009, pp. 5-41.

65 The catch certificate scheme encompasses certificates with information such as vessel name, fishing licence number, flag state, description, date of catch, and estimated weight for all landings, transhipments, and imports of fish products into the EU. It also requires competent authorities of the flag state of the catching vessel to certify that the catches concerned have been made in accordance with the applicable laws, regulations, and international conservation and management measures.

Policy was adopted.[66] A Handbook on the IUU Regulation aims to provide technical advice to administrations and operators and to answer the most frequent questions.[67]

The IUU Regulation prohibits the importation into the EU of fisheries products obtained from IUU fishing.[68] Fishing products are defined as all products falling under certain tariff headings, with the exception of those listed in Annex I.[69] The flag states are to certify that the fisheries products are indeed legal. The system encompasses flag State notifications, catch certificates and the process for the identification of non-cooperating third countries (green, yellow and red cards system).

The EU regime builds on international fisheries law, where it is envisaged that states have a 'due diligence' obligation to exercise best possible efforts and to do their utmost to prevent IUU fishing. This includes the obligation to adopt the necessary administrative and enforcement measures to ensure that fishing vessels flying their flag, their nationals, or fishing vessels engaged in their waters are not involved in activities that infringe the applicable conservation and management measures of marine biological resources, and in case of infringement to cooperate with other states in order to investigate and, if necessary, impose sanctions which are sufficient to deter violations and deprive offenders of the benefits from their illegal activities and to consult.

The IUU Regulations enables the Commission to assess the fisheries governance performance of non-EU countries and where necessary enter into a dialogue with them. If this dialogue does not bring about improvements in the fight against IUU fisheries, the Commission can issue a so-called pre-identification notification. These notifications are accompanied by proposed tailored measures to address the identified shortcomings by a specified deadline. This procedure creates a framework for collaboration to achieve improved fisheries governance. If the country fails to sufficiently improve its fisheries governance, a yellow card can be issued.[70] In cases where the country still remains unable to resolve its IUU fishing problems, the Commission can draw the red card, i.e. identify it as a non-cooperating country in the fight against IUU fishing,[71] and can propose the Council to place the country on the list of non-

---

66 Council Regulation (EC) 1224/2009 of 20 November 2009 establishing a Community control system for ensuring compliance with the rules of the common fisheries policy, OJ L 343, 22.12.2009, pp. 1-50.

67 European Commission, DG Maritime Affairs and Fisheries, Handbook on the practical application of Council Regulation (EC) 1005/2008 of 29 September 2008 establishing a Community system to prevent, deter and eliminate illegal, unreported and unregulated fishing (the IUU Regulation), Brussels, Belgium, 2009.

68 Article 12(1) IUU Regulation.

69 Article 2 sub 8 IUU Regulation.

70 Article 32 IUU Regulation.

71 Article 31 IUU Regulation, the identification procedure.

cooperating third countries.[72] Identification and subsequent blacklisting lead to trade measures, including the prohibition of imports of fishery products from these countries into the EU, and the prohibition of EU vessels from operating in their waters.[73]

4.3. ENFORCEMENT AND THE INSTRUMENTS IN PRACTICE

An interesting feature of the EU fisheries regime is that EU Member States are obliged to inspect a minimum of five per cent of all vessels flying a non-EU flag that bring fish or fisheries products to an EU port per year.[74] In case of vessels known or suspected of IUU fishing, inspection is mandatory.[75] Customs authorities supervise the import, export and transit of goods including fishery products. They also ensure that the control measures relating to the IUU Regulation – notably regarding the presence of valid catch certificates – are performed prior to releasing the fisheries products for free circulation. The Commission is in charge of the green, yellow and red cards system, while it is up to the Council to decide on blacklisting countries that persist in IUU fishing.

If we compare the central role of the Commission in the fisheries regime with the role that the 28 competent authorities in the EU Member States need to play where illegal logging is concerned, the long time before Member States get their act together where timber is concerned is remarkable.

According to the Commission's own assessment that was presented on 1 October 2015, five years after the entry into force of the IUU Regulation a number of tangible results can be seen.[76] The benefits of fighting IUU fishing include increased revenues to the local or State budget of non-EU countries, revenues which would otherwise be lost to the benefit of IUU operators.[77] In 2012 and 2013, some 1500 inspections of fishing vessels were carried out in EU ports. Since 2010, over 200 import consignments were refused, for instance

72 Article 33 IUU Regulation, the listing procedure.

73 Article 38 IUU Regulation. Also see Article 18(1)(g) IUU Regulation.

74 Article 9(1) IUU Regulation.

75 Article 9(2) IUU Regulation.

76 Communication on the application of Council Regulation (EC) 1005/2008 establishing a Community system to prevent, deter and eliminate illegal, unreported and unregulated fishing, COM (2015) 480 final. Next to this 10 page document more details can be found in the Study on the state of play regarding application and implementation of the IUU Regulation, DG MARE, April 2014.

77 Ibid., p. 10.

because of false, non-valid, erroneous or incomplete catch certificates.[78] Some 4.2 million EUR in fines were imposed by various coastal States.[79]

Over 200 cases of presumed IUU fishing by vessels from 27 countries were investigated by the Commission, based on information collected by the Commission itself or received from Member States, third countries and stakeholders. As a direct consequence of these investigations eight flag States[80] and four coastal States[81] have imposed sanctions amounting to more than 8 million EUR of fines and fees against more than 50 vessels. As these cases have led to sanctions imposed by flag and/or coastal state, there had been, until then, no need to include vessels on the EU list under Article 27(1) IUU Regulation. At the same time the Commission encouraged the flag States concerned to initiate administrative and legislative reforms to reinforce their control of the activities of their fishing fleets.

By 18 July 2017, yellow cards were issued to 24 non-EU countries. In ten of these cases (*inter alia* Curaçao and the Philippines), the yellow card was revoked after the countries in question made sufficient progress (green card or de-listing). Thailand is among the countries for which the yellow card still holds. In six cases, a red card was issued by the Commission, and the Council subsequently blacklisted these countries meaning that they could no longer export their fisheries products to the EU. Subsequently, half of these countries (Belize, Republic of Guinee and Sri Lanka) were delisted again. The remaining three, Cambodia, Comoros and St Vincent and Grenadines, were still blacklisted as of 18 July 2017.[82]

Thailand is the world's third-largest seafood exporter. Its fishing industry relies heavily on migrant workers. The country received a yellow card from the Commission in April 2015 due to its inadequate legal framework for fighting unlawful fishing and poor monitoring, control and traceability systems. According to the Commission, Thailand lacked the necessary legal and administrative environment to ensure efficient and effective performance of their duties as flag, coastal and market state.[83] Like all pre-identified countries,

---

78 Ibid., p. 4. Other reasons to refuse consignments can be a breach of national or RFMO conservation and management measures, including quotas; illegal transhipment at sea; catch by a fishing vessel that is not included on the list of vessels authorised to operate in the relevant RFMO area or a lack of cooperation or inadequate action taken by the flag State responsible for certifying the catch.

79 Ibid., p. 4.

80 Belize, Brazil, Comoros, Lithuania, Panama, Republic of Guinea, Republic of Korea and Spain.

81 Liberia, Republic of Guinea, Sierra Leone and Guinea Bissau.

82 See for a detailed overview see https://epthinktank.eu/2017/11/27/illegal-unreported-and-unregulated-iuu-fishing/.

83 Commission Decision of 21 April 2015 on notifying a third country of the possibility of being identified as a non-cooperating third country in fighting illegal, unreported and unregulated fishing, OJ C 142, 29.4.2015, pp. 7-17.

Thailand was proposed an action plan to address shortcomings. The Commission has been evaluating progress, but in 2016 indicated that the dialogue with the country was proving difficult and there remained serious concerns about the steps taken by Thailand to fight IUU fishing activities.[84] By July 2017, reportedly still not enough progress was made to withdraw the yellow card.[85]

It is clear from this brief overview that the IUU fishing regime is being enforced much more effective than the EUTR.

5. CONCLUDING REMARKS

The EU aims at promoting sustainable development inside and outside the EU. Where natural resources are concerned, it actively promotes the sustainable management of forestry and fisheries products. For each of these resources, legal regimes were adopted that aim at ensuring that the products that are offered on the EU markets have been legally harvested, or that they meet sustainability criteria. The instruments introduced in these regimes differ from each other in the manner in which the aim is to be reached. Where forestry and fisheries products are concerned, a ban on putting illegally harvested products on the EU market for the first time and a ban on importing IUU fisheries products respectively were introduced. In the case of forestry, legality depends on the laws of the country of origin, in that of fisheries, on the law of the flag state. Where fisheries products are concerned, the EU regulation offers extra options that are more far-reaching than the timber regime: states that do not take sufficient measures against IUU fishing can receive a yellow card warning, and if they persist a red card can be issued banning fisheries products from that country to enter the EU.

Traders in forestry products are responsible for ensuring the products in question are legal; they need to utilise a due diligence system to substantiate this. The fact that the fisheries regime encompasses more far reaching enforcement rules could have to do with the fact that fisheries forms a part of the Union's exclusive competences and the fact that the rules in question were adopted in the form of a Council regulation, without the EP as co-legislator. The factor that in all likelihood played an important role in the shaping of the manner in which trade limitations regarding countries were held possible under the fisheries rules, but not where the timber trade was concerned, has to do with the existence of international binding norms regarding IUU fishing. The existence of such norms makes it less likely that states faced with import restriction could bring a

84 European Commission – Press release, Fighting illegal fishing: Warnings for Kiribati, Sierra Leone and Trinidad & Tobago, while Sri Lanka is delisted, Brussels, 21 April 2016.

85 Wipatayotin, A. 'EU tipped to keep Thai 'yellow card' IUU warning', Bangkok Post, 18 July 2017.

successful WTO claim against the EU. In the area of the trade in timber products, almost no such binding standards exist in international law, making it harder to introduce sanctions against states that merely allow their territory to be robbed of its natural resources without violating international law.

The advantages of the EU involvement with external aspects of natural resources use and sustainable management of natural resources are plentiful. It increases public revenues in the countries of origin, decreases unfair competition for legal activities, allows local SMEs to compete, prevents corruption and money flowing to criminals and terrorists, protects the environment from overexploitation, protects the livelihoods of the local population etc. There are also clear advantages for the EU itself. For instance, shared environmental resources are protected better, climate change is countered, and environmentally induced migration or migration due to the inability of failed states to offer a future to its populations is prevented.

The coherence of EU policy would benefit from the formulation of an EU strategy on external aspects of sustainable management of natural resources. Some suggestions to do so were made, notably in the 2005 Strategy. In practice, at the EU level no coherent indicators were developed that could inform policy makers to set goals or standards. Instead, and as a result an *ad hoc* approach ensued for different natural resources. Having examined the regimes developed for fisheries and forestry it became apparent that these regimes could benefit from the experiences with the application and enforcement of the rules of the respective regimes. At the same time, it could help if a practical set of indicators was developed after all that would offer guidance on the manner in which EU use of natural resources affect third countries.

CHAPTER 4

JUDICIAL REVIEW OF THE ENVIRONMENTAL PERFORMANCES OF THE EU AGRICULTURAL POLICY

Luchino FERRARIS*

ABSTRACT

In the 2013 EU Common Agricultural Policy (CAP) reform, the attention paid to the environmental impact of the EU CAP and the fight against climate change became a key concern for the EU legislator. However, an assessment of the outcomes of the measures put in place to this aim reveals that the results achieved are unsatisfactory, particularly with reference to the substantial resources shown to have been consumed. While waiting to see – particularly in the light of the Commission Communication of November 2017 – if in the future CAP the main mistakes are corrected, this chapter will examine whether and to what extent the failure by the EU legislator to address the environmental impact of the EU agricultural policy may be challenged before the European Court of Justice.

1. INTRODUCTION

As far as the EU agricultural policy is concerned, the recurrent leitmotiv is that the wide discretion accorded to the EU legislator is justified by the political sensitivity of the subject matter, which implies the consideration of several

* The author is PhD Candidate at the Sant'Anna School of Advanced Studies (luchino.ferraris.mail@gmail.com). This contribution, in some parts, will draw extensively from his previous work Ferraris, L. (2018, forthcoming) 'The Role of the Principle of Environmental Integration in Maximising the 'Greening' of the Common Agricultural Policy', European Law Review.

intertwined factors and delicate political choices. Therefore, while keeping in mind the division of powers between the legislator and the judiciary, this contribution aims – on the one hand – at taking stock of the situation concerning the extent of the judicial review of secondary legislation in the light of existing case-law; and – on the other hand – at exploring the matter of whether and to what extent some general principles of EU law or provisions having general application may suggest coming to a different interpretative solution. This, as will be seen, is particularly relevant with regard to an assessment of the legality questions related to the principles of proportionality and the principle of environmental integration, as well as the requirement to state reasons.

It is worth remembering that on 29 November 2017 the new Communication on the future of food and farming was published, which also endeavours to bring some changes to the way the CAP should tackle the environmental challenge.[1] Amongst other things, this policy document purports to undertake a so-called 'delivery model' vis-à-vis several aspects of the CAP, including its environmental performance. Time will tell whether and to what extent the resolutions of this Communication will give rise to real commitments. However, even in the best-case scenario, thoroughness and completeness of judicial review will always be key components used to assess the legality of rules put in place to give substance to political objectives, particularly that of the sustainable management of natural resource.

Against this background, this chapter will first give an overview of the long-standing and complex process of integration of environmental concerns in the CAP, and then assess the extent of the judicial review of the CJEU *vis-à-vis* the environmental dimension of the CAP under the existing case-law. Subsequently, due attention will be paid to the matter of the principle of proportionality, the duty to give reasons and the principle of environmental integration, so as to see to what extent a more careful consideration of them may give rise to a more rigorous approach while reviewing secondary agricultural legislation. In fact, while the approach of the CJEU seems to be settled, an argument will be made – as a sort of 'thought experiment' – to suggest that an extensive interpretation of the above-mentioned principles may pave the way for an enhanced consideration of the environmental performance of the CAP at judicial level.

---

1 Communication from the Commission to the European Parliament, the Council, the European Economic and Social Committee and the Committee of the Regions – The Future of Food and Farming, COM (2017) 713 final.

2. THE CAP AND THE ENVIRONMENT: A LONG STORY

It is nowadays uncontested that there is a two-way relationship between agriculture and the environment, and that this is so in particular with respect to climate change. On the one hand, agriculture is an important driver for greenhouse gas (GHG);[2] on the other, climate change impairs the survival of the agricultural sector as a whole. This is especially significant in the light of the projected world population growth, which is estimated to reach 9.6 billion by 2050,[3] and in respect of the harmful agricultural effects on the environment not being limited to climate change.[4]

It is well-known that agriculture can play a significant role in minimising environmental damage,[5] and it is for this reason that EU policy-makers have been trying to integrate sustainable development into the design of EU agriculture during the course of the last three decades.

It was in 1985 that the Commission first issued a Green Paper on the future of the CAP.[6] In so doing, it drew attention to the unsustainable agricultural production patterns of the CAP, which characterized EU agriculture in the 70s and the early 80s. This resulted in a gradual shift from price support to coupled payments, and then later to decoupled payments. Since 1992 further steps have been taken in the successive MacSharry, Fischler and Fischer-Boel reforms.[7] A follow-up of this discussion can be found in the 2006 Commission Communication on the integration of environmental concerns into the CAP,[8]

2 According to the IPCC, Agriculture, Forestry and Other Land Use (AFOLU) contributes to about 24 % of the overall GHG emissions worldwide. See IPCC (2014) Climate Change 2014, Mitigation of Climate Change: Fifth Assessment Report; at the same time, agriculture alone is supposed to contribute about 10.3 % in the EU: EEA (2015), Agriculture and Climate Change. On the relationship between agriculture and climate change at global level, see more extensively FAO (2016) The State of Food and Agriculture: Climate Change, Agriculture and Food Security.

3 UN Department of Economic and Social Affairs – Population Division, Population Estimates and Projections Sections (2012) World Population Prospects: The 2012 Revision

4 Önder, M., E. Ceyhan and A. Kahraman (2011) 'Effects of Agricultural Practices on Environment', ICPBEE, Vol. 24, p. 28.

5 Andúgar, A. (2010) 'The Positive Contribution of Agriculture and Forestry to Combating Climate Change – La Contribution Positive De L'Agriculture Et De La Sylviculture À La Lutte Contre Le Changement Climatique – Der Positive Beitrag Von Land- Und Forstwirtschaft Zur Bekämpfung des Klimawandels', EuroChoices, Vol. 9, p. 30.

6 Communication from the Commission to the Council and the Parliament – Perspectives for the Common Agricultural Policies, COM (85) 333.

7 For the history of the integration of environmental considerations in the CAP, see Matthews, A. (2013) 'Greening Agricultural Payments in the EU's Common Agricultural Policy', Bio-Based and Applied Economics, Vol. 2, p. 1.

8 Communication from the Commission to the Council and the European Parliament – Development of agri-environmental indicators for monitoring the integration of environmental concerns into the common agricultural policy, COM (2006) 508.

and it resulted in the 2008 CAP Health Check introducing specific agricultural activities involving additional agri-environment benefits under the support of Pillar I. Nowadays, from a legal point of view, a strong influence is exerted by the principle of environmental integration (Article 11 TFEU), which compels the EU legislator to introduce environmental considerations in every Union policy, including therefore in EU agriculture (this principle will be analysed in-depth *infra*, paragraph 4.3.).

The 2013 reform is the latest outcome of these efforts, and its interventions were shaped in compliance with the traditional structure of the CAP. In terms of structure, the CAP's intervention is divided into two Pillars: Pillar I – which includes the Direct Payments Regulation ('DPR')[9] – supports farmers' income in the form of direct payments and market measures and is entirely financed by the European Agricultural Guarantee Fund ('EAGF'); and Pillar II – which is constituted by the Rural Development Regulation ('RDR')[10] – is the support provided for the development of rural areas in the form of Rural Development Programmes ('RDPs') and is co-financed by the European Agricultural Fund for Rural Development ('EAFRD') together with the Member States. The greening of the CAP – even more so further to the formal introduction of the battle against climate change as one of the leading values of the 2013 reform – concerns both Pillar I and Pillar II.[11] As for the latter, rural development measures – many of which are conceived for environmental purposes – are laid down in the RDR. As for the former, apart from the standards enshrined in the so-called cross

9 European Parliament and Council Regulation (EU) 1307/2013 establishing rules for direct payments to farmers under support schemes within the framework of the common agricultural policy (Direct Payments Regulation) [2013] OJ L347. The DPR establishes common rules on payments granted directly to farmers (direct payments) and additional payments triggered in specific circumstances (e.g. basic payment scheme, payments for farmers in areas with natural constraints, young farmers, etc.).

10 European Parliament and Council Regulation (EU) 1305/2013 on support for rural development by the European Agricultural Fund for Rural Development (Rural Development Regulation) [2013] OJ L347. The RDR lays down general rules, objectives and measures to be adopted in order to implement rural development policy programs financed by the European Agricultural Fund for Rural Development (EAFRD).

11 Other than the DPR and the RDR, the 2013 CAP also contains:
- European Parliament and Council Regulation (EU) 1306/2013 on the financing, management and monitoring of the common agricultural policy (Horizontal Issues Regulation) [2013] OJ L347;
- European Parliament and Council Regulation (EU) 1308/2013 establishing a common organization of the markets in agricultural products (Market Organisation Regulation) [2013] OJ L347;
- European Parliament and Council Regulation (EU) 1310/2013 laying down certain transitional provisions as regards the application of the four basic regulations in the year 2014 [2013] OJ L347.

compliance,[12] the most remarkable environmental tool of the 2013 reform is constituted by the so-called 'greening measures'. Because of the fact that this policy choice is new to the CAP and in the light of the considerable investment made to set these measures up, this chapter will particularly focus on such the 'greening measures'. In this connection, 30 % of the annual ceiling that the Member States receive under Pillar I (*i.e.* the 'Basic Payment Scheme' provided for by the DPR) is required to be used for the implementation of three 'greening measures'. The said measures include crop diversification,[13] the maintenance of permanent grassland[14] and the establishment of ecological focus areas,[15] together with a series of 'equivalent practices'[16] that are currently recognised as being equal to the three basic measures and ensuring the same level of environmental benefit.[17] The 'greening measures' only pertain to Pillar I. Pillar II provides for additional funding only if, and on the condition that, more targeted agri-environmental measures listed in the RDR are undertaken and managed at farm-level so as to go beyond the baseline as set by Pillar I.[18] There are many ways through which such Pillar II measures – which touch upon, *inter alia*, water management, air, soil, food safety and organic farming – attempt to integrate environmental requirements into the CAP.[19]

However, a close examination of how the 'greening' of the CAP has been carried out did not result in a change in farming practice sufficient to ensure a valuable improvement of environmental performances of the CAP. This is true both in terms of general political choices made and in terms of the outcomes of the single 'greening' instruments.

---

12 According to the official CAP glossary, 'In order to receive direct payments and some other forms of support, farmers are required to respect certain rules. This requirement is known as cross-compliance. These rules concern food safety, animal health, plant health, the climate, the environment, the protection of water resources, animal welfare and the condition in which farmland is maintained'. Cf. https://ec.europa.eu/agriculture/sites/agriculture/files/glossary/pdf/index_en.pdf (acceded on 4 December 2017).

13 Regulation (EU) 1307/2013 OJ L347, Article 44.

14 Regulation (EU) 1307/2013 OJ L347, Article 45.

15 Regulation (EU) 1307/2013 OJ L347, Article 46.

16 Regulation (EU) 1307/2013 OJ L347, Article 43(3). The list of 'equivalent practices' is contained in Annex IX.

17 For the detailed analysis of the 'greening measures', see European Commission – DG for Internal Policies (2012) 'Environmental Public Goods in the New CAP: Impact of Greening Proposals and Possible Alternatives'.

18 According to the CAP Glossary, agri-environmental measures are 'practices, undertaken voluntarily by farmers, over a set period. Support may be provided through Rural Development programmes. The practices bring environmental benefits and /or help to mitigate and adapt to climate change'; Nazzaro, C. and G. Marotta (2016) 'The Common Agricultural Policy 2014-2020: Scenarios for The European Agricultural and Rural Systems', Agric Econ, Vol. 4, p. 16.

19 Petrescu-Mag, R.M. and P. Burny (2015) The Principle of Environmental Integration Under Scrutiny. An Analytical Legal Framework on How EU Policies are Becoming Green, Accent, p. 74.

With respect to political choices, the main criticisms raised concern the decision to concentrate most of the available resources in Pillar I instead of Pillar II. While on this point I make reference to the extensive analysis already conducted in scientific literature;[20] for the purpose of this contribution the second aspect deserves more attention. In other words, what really matters here is the problem of the concrete results achieved – particularly in connection with the significant resources pulled out of the Union budget.

In fact, according to several studies, the delivery of environmental benefits resulting from the use of the greening measures has proved to be – at most – insignificant, in spite of the costs to set them up.[21] Remarkably, this conclusion was affirmed by the EU Court of Auditors in December 2017, emphasising the low level of requirements, which largely reflect the normal farming practice, and also estimating that greening has led to a change in farming practice on only around 5 % of all EU farmland.[22]

In conclusion, notwithstanding the considerable efforts displayed in the 2013 reform, little environmental benefit is likely to be expected from the measures adopted. Indeed, the Impact Assessment issued prior to the reform focused on – among other matters – the environmental impact of all the options potentially available for the EU legislator. However, this was only done very generically, without spelling out the expected improvements, in numerical terms, for each component of the natural environment (water, air, soil and so forth). An in-depth consideration would require first and foremost an evaluation of the actual impact

20 Stock of the situation is taken in Ferraris, L. (2018, forthcoming) 'The Role of the Principle of Environmental Integration in Maximising the 'Greening' of the Common Agricultural Policy', European Law Review. The most prominent studies conducted on this point include Cardwell, M.N. (2015) 'The Direct Payments Regime: Delivering 'a Fair Standard of Living for the Agricultural Community' in J.A. McMahon and M.N. Cardwell (eds.), Research Handbook on EU Agricultural Law, Edward Elgar, p. 41; Matthews, A. (2013) 'Greening Agricultural Payments in the EU's Common Agricultural Policy', Bio-Based and Applied Economics, Vol. 2, p. 1; Cardwell, M. (2013) 'European Union Agricultural Policy and Practice: The New Challenge of Climate Change', Environmental Law Review, Vol. 13, p. 271; Dhondt, N. (2003) Integration of Environmental Protection in Other EC Policies, ELP, p. 259; Baldock, D. *et al.* (1992) 'The Integration of Environmental Protection Requirements into the Definition and Implementation of Other EC Policies, Institute for European Environmental Policy papers, p. 29.

21 Before the entry into force of the CAP see the predictions made by Hart K. and Baldock D. (2011) 'Greening the Cap: Delivering Environmental Outcomes Through Pillar One', Institute for European Environmental Policy papers, available at: https://ieep.eu/uploads/articles/attachments/1639ede9-590d-46f4-9695-b4c07c64badb/Greening_Pillar_1_IEEP_Thinkpiece_-_Final.pdf?v=63664509757 (acceded on 4 December 2017); after the entry into force of the CAP, see the report issued by European Environmental Bureau (2016) 'The Hidden Truth: Environmental Impact of New EU Rural Development Programmes', available at: http://www.birdlife.org/sites/default/files/attachments/the_hidden_truth_factsheets_-_eu.pdf (acceded on 4 December 2017); Hart, K., A. Buckwell and D. Baldock (2016) 'Learning the Lessons of the Greening of the CAP', Institute for European Environmental Policy papers.

22 European Court of Auditors (2017) 'Greening: a more complex income support scheme, not yet environmentally effective', Special Report, No. 21.

of EU measures when applied at farm-level. Disappointingly, the Commission avoided doing this, as was also pointed out by the Court of Auditors from the outset.[23] In other words, there is no numerical target set *vis-à-vis* each component of the natural environment. It is therefore correct to say that the 'targets' set out in the EU policy documents and legislation in the area of agriculture are not fleshed out in detail, but they remain more like political slogans. In 2016, the Commission 'reviewed' the 'greening' performances of the CAP, but the conclusion was that 'the actual impact on environmental outcomes depends – for certain aspects – on the choices made by Member States and farmers', with no reference to facts and figures relating to the expected outcomes.[24]

In conclusion, CAP 'greening' widely ends up being more an instrument to adorn income support than a means to achieve ambitious environmental targets. Moreover, considering that 30 % of the annual ceiling that the Member States receive under Pillar I shall be used for it, it can be said that a significant amount is earmarked for compliance with the 'greening measures', thus implying a lot of public money being invested for this purpose. Against this background, the question is whether there is any room to review judicially the environmental performance of the CAP. In other words, is it completely lawful under EU law to 'green inefficiently'?

3. CASE-LAW ON THE JUDICIAL REVIEW OF THE COMMON AGRICULTURAL POLICY

Traditionally, the CJEU has always recognised an ample discretion accorded to the EU legislator in the shaping of the EU agricultural policy, which is the oldest and probably the most complex European policy, at the heart of which lie huge political and economic interests, social repercussions and ideological divisions.[25] Moreover, the CJEU is generally – and understandably – more available to annul administrative rather than legislative acts, precisely by virtue of the higher political contentiousness of the latter.[26]

---

23 'Scientific evidence exists which justify [sic] the effectiveness and necessity of measures such as crop diversification and ecological focus areas (for biodiversity, the quality of water, for soil etc.). However, the regulation does not specify the concrete objectives, which should be achieved by the farming community'. Cf. European Court of Auditors (2011) 'Is Agri-Environment Support Well Designed and Managed?', Special Report, No. 7.

24 Commission Staff Working Document – Review of greening after one year, SWD (2016) 218 final, p. 19.

25 Cf. the review of Türk, A. (2009), Judicial Review in EU Law, Edward Elgar, p. 137.

26 Tridimas, T. (1999) 'Proportionality in European Community Law: Searching for the Appropriate Standard of Scrutiny' in E. Ellis (ed.), The Principle of Proportionality, Hart, p. 68.

Accordingly, the Court is constant in holding that in agricultural matters judicial review must be limited to the verification that the measure challenged is not vitiated by any manifest error or misuse of powers, and that the authority concerned has not manifestly exceeded the limits of its discretion.[27]

As for the review of proportionality, the lawfulness of a measure adopted in that sphere can be affected only if the measure is manifestly inappropriate in terms of the objective that the competent institution is seeking to pursue.[28] Such a stance is confirmed even in the most recent decisions, in which the discretion of the EU legislator is deemed to derive, after the entry into force of the Treaty of Lisbon, from Articles 40 and 43 TFEU.[29]

Unsurprisingly, results are the same when the CAP is challenged on environmental grounds. In the case of *Bettati* – concerning legislation on ozone protection – the Court did not consider itself entitled to review the exercise of the wide discretion accorded to EU institutions, which also includes the choice of the measures to adopt in order to implement the environmental policy.[30] The CJEU also clarified that such a review is generally limited to where there is a clear inadequacy having regard to the aim pursued or an obvious error of appraisal.[31]

The application of specific environmental principles in agricultural matters leads to analogous conclusions. This is particularly true – for instance – with regards to its assessment of the precautionary principle. When this principle is invoked by EU institutions to justify legislative acts, the CJEU acknowledges that the EU legislator has a wide discretion when it adopts risk management measures, including political choices on its part and complex assessments, while the validity of a measure adopted in that area can be affected only if the measure is manifestly inappropriate.[32]

It could therefore be concluded that the likelihood of the EU agricultural legislation being reviewed, for reason of a lack of sufficient integration of environmental concerns, is rather limited.[33] The CJEU will likely only review legislation that does not provide for environmental integration at all,[34] but not

---

27 The milestone in this respect is Case C-189/01, *Jippes and others*, para. 80; Case C-331/88, *Fedesa and Others*, paras. 8 and 14.

28 Case C-310/04, *Spain v. Council*, para. 98.

29 Case C-422/16, *Verband Sozialer Wettbewerb eV v TofuTown.com GmbH* (TofuTown), not yet published (Court reports – general), para. 46.

30 Case C-341/95, *Bettati v Safety Hi-Tech Srl*, para. 32.

31 Ibid., paras. 32 and 35.

32 Joined Cases C-78/16 and C-79/16, *Pesce and others/Serinelli and others, not yet published*, para. 49; Case C-477/14, *Pillbox 38, not yet published*, para. 49; Case C-77/09, *Gowan Comércio Internacional e Serviços*, para. 82.

33 This is also the conclusion of Jans, J. H. and Vedder H. H. B. (2012) European Environmental Law: After Lisbon, 4th edition, Europa Law Publishing, p. 26.

34 This is the case of European Parliament and Council Directive 2004/25/EC on takeover bids (Takeover Directive) [2004] OJ L142. See the analysis developed by Beate, S. (2009) Towards a

that which claims to take the environment into account even though the actual environmental benefit is very limited in practice.

As mentioned above, this chapter will suggest that in the light of some general principles, the consideration of some of the environmental deficiencies of the CAP may, or ought, to justify a different interpretation.

4. TOWARDS A DIFFERENT APPROACH?

4.1. THE PRINCIPLE OF PROPORTIONALITY

The principle of proportionality, in its traditional meaning, operates to 'prevent obligations being imposed by legislative measure or administrative act save to the extent to which such obligations are necessary in the public interest to attain the purpose of the measure/decision in question'.[35] Although the Court first introduced the principle, express recognition was subsequently given in Article 5(4) TEU. The latter provides that 'under the principle of proportionality, the content and the form of Union action shall not exceed what is necessary to achieve the objectives of the Treaties'.

The reason why this principle may be of interest here is indeed intuitive. The unsatisfactory outcome of 'greening' is accompanied by a very substantial investment of economic resources, particularly into Pillar I. It follows that such a gap between the actual results achieved and the resources seen to be invested – not only relating to the 30% greening component, but also to the additional administrative burden – leads to the conclusion that the EU legislator may be blamed for not having adopted measures which were less burdensome, particularly for EU taxpayers, who may be – indeed quite indirectly, but somehow at least ideally – affected every time EU expenditure is not effected efficiently. In other words, it may be said that the 'greening measures' included in the Direct Payments Regulation were not proportionate.

The general test of proportionality normally contains two elements, *i.e.* appropriateness of the means employed to achieve the Union's objectives and the necessity of these means to attain them.[36] It is a matter of fact, as pointed out above, that in carrying out this test the CJEU shows a systematic deference to the EU legislator and that such a deference is particularly tangible in agricultural matters. The proof of this approach is given by the Court's requirement that

---

Sustainable European Company Law: A Normative Analysis of the Objectives of EU Law, Wolters Kluwer, p. 592.

35 Gordon, Richard, Moffat and Rowena (2014) EU Law in Judicial Review, Oxford University Press, 2nd edition, p. 340.

36 Case 66/82, *Fromancais v FORMA*, para. 8.

review in this area would be appropriate only if there were a 'manifest error of misuse of powers'.[37]

Against this background, it then appears clear that the rationale suggested above is unlikely to be accepted by the Court in the near future. Being mistaken on the cost-effectiveness of certain measures – even when the mistake may appear evident – is still not sufficient to give rise to a 'manifest error' as the question of whether an error is manifest or not can be solved only if such an error is recognizable *ex-ante*. In the case of the CAP, this would have been impossible, for the very simple reason that no numerical parameter may serve as a benchmark.

As a result, the principle of proportionality as currently interpreted by the Court does not allow a thorough review of the environmental dimension of the CAP. That said, it may be argued that a limited space for a more penetrating control may be present when the Court adds a third element to the proportionality test, *i.e.* the need that measures do not have a disproportionate effect on a claimant's interest.[38]

4.2. DUTY TO STATE REASONS

In the European system there is a wide-ranging duty to give reasons, which is nothing but a corollary of the principle of effective judicial protection.[39] It is, indeed, ineffective for a public administrative body to adopt legislation without sufficiently justifying the rationale underlying it, which also significantly hampers the right to defence. Other functions of the principle are recognised by the EU Courts to provide the possibility for such Courts to exert their supervisory function and for the Member States and citizens to ascertain the circumstances in which EU institutions came to a certain decision;[40] the necessity of self regulation for the institution adopting the act; and the need for the EU Parliament to effectively exert its political scrutiny.[41] As a result, Article 296 TFEU provides that 'legal acts shall state the reasons on which they are based'. The reference to 'legal acts' makes clear that the duty applies both to legislative and to administrative measures.

The theoretical potential of the duty – for the EU policymakers – to state reasons in the ambit of a review of the environmental dimension of the CAP is

37 Case C-84/94, *United Kingdom v Council*, para. 58.

38 Case C-331/88, *R v MAFF, ex p FEDESA*, para. 13.

39 Heukels, T. and J. Tib (2002) 'Towards Homogeneity in the Field of Legal Remedies: Convergence and Divergence' in P. Beaumont, C. Lyons and N. Walker (eds.) Convergence and Divergence in European Public Law, Hart Publishing, p. 114.

40 Case 24/62, *Germany v Commission*, para. 69.

41 For an in-depth analysis of the rationale of the principle, see Shapiro, M. (1992) 'The Giving Reasons Requirement', University Chicago Legal Forum, 179, p. 182.

rather straightforward. Environmental benefits of the measures envisaged by the Rural Development Regulations and (above all) the Direct Payments Regulation are spelled out only in generic terms in the respective preambles. There is no scientific study supporting the choice of those measures as beneficial for the environment (in the sense explained *supra*, paragraph 2). Nor is it clarified as to what extent such measures are expected to have a positive environmental impact. The latter, in particular, is clearly dependent upon good environmental management at farm level, which is neither fostered nor provided for at all by the CAP. As a result, a rigorous interpretation of the duty to state reasons may suggest that the 'greening measures' may be reviewed judicially because the reasons for their inception in the CAP are not sufficiently explained, with the only limit stemming from the need to respect the political discretion of the law-maker.

What is clear anyway is that the review of legislation under this principle depends on the specific circumstances of the case, particularly the content of the measure, the nature of the reasons given and the interest of the parties in obtaining such reasons.[42]

In the case of legislative measures of general application, such as the regulations of the CAP, it is considered as fully acceptable to simply mention in the preamble the circumstances leading to the decision in question and its general objective,[43] without a careful report of all stages of the law-making process.[44]

All in all, it is possible to assert that the threshold of the review which can be carried out by this principle is rather limited and offers few opportunities to re-examine the exercise of powers of the EU institutions. Unsurprisingly, such a limited scope of judicial protection derives precisely from the necessary power of appraisal of EU institutions, which is indispensable in order to be able for them to fulfil their tasks.[45]

In conclusion, the more environmentally-friendly interpretation of the principle proposed above does not have any foundation or recognition in the case-law of the CJEU, which seems – again – to sanction EU institutions only when the lack of reasons given is absolute or at least particularly blatant.

---

42 Case C-113/00, *Spain v Commission*, paras. 47 ff.
43 Case C-5/67, *Beus*, para. 95.
44 Case T-114/92, *Bemim v Commission*, para. 41.
45 Case C-269/90, *Technische Universität München v Hauptzollamt München-Mitte*, paras. 13 ff.

4.3. THE PRINCIPLE OF ENVIRONMENTAL INTEGRATION

According to Article 11 TFEU, 'environmental protection requirements must be integrated into the definition and implementation of the Union's policies and activities, in particular with a view to promoting sustainable development'. Introduced by the Single European Act, the Lisbon's version of the principle of environmental integration ('PEI') is worded more strongly.[46] However, it has been argued that the current wording represents a step back compared to the old pre-Lisbon Article 6 EC Treaty, particularly as the principle lost its status as the 'general principle of EU law'.[47] In fact, the principle is now contained in Title II of the Part of TFEU dedicated to the principles (Part I), *i.e.* amongst the 'provisions having general application'. Thus, the PEI does not have the same legal value as the principle of proportionality. This downgrade can be confirmed by examining the wording of the PEI in the Charter of Fundamental Rights of the European Union, where Article 37 provides for the same in a similar yet weaker wording.[48]

In the writer's opinion, this is truer in theory than in practice, as the normative impact of the principle at judicial level has been less marked than the political pressure exerted by the same principle at law-making level.[49] Moreover, the clear link made with 'sustainable development' implies that the principle does not mean there is an obligation to prioritize by default environmental protection, but to strike a *balance* between economic, social and environmental considerations depending on the specific circumstances. Needless to say, such a balance may also lead to the prioritisation of other objectives, provided that environmental protection is *taken into account*.[50] That said, the PEI has indeed contributed to driving the inception of some of the most important

---

46 Article 130r of the Single European Act provided that 'environmental protection requirements shall be a component of the Community's other policies'.

47 Amongst other things, this appears to be particularly true in the light of the proliferation of integration clauses. Cf. Jans, J.H. (2010) 'Stop the Integration Principle?', Fordham Int'l L. J., Vol. 33, p. 1544.

48 Charter of Fundamental Rights of the European Union [2000] OJ C 364, Article 37: 'A high level of environmental protection and the improvement of the quality of the environment must be integrated into the policies of the Union and ensured in accordance with the principle of sustainable development'. Cf. Jans, J. H. and Vedder H. H. B. (2012) European Environmental Law: After Lisbon', 4th edition, Europa Law Publishing, p. 29 where the authors stress the sole reference of the Charter to 'EU policies' and not 'EU activities', claiming that an interpretation of Article 11 TFEU in line with the Charter would result in further downgrading of the principle.

49 Such a conclusion is – perhaps – supported by a reading between the lines of Usui, Y. (2005) 'The Principle of Environmental Integration in the European Union: From a Discursive Constructivism', Bulletin of Niigata University International and Information Studies: Department of Information Culture, Vol. 8, p. 110.

50 Case C-371/98, *First Corporate Shipping, Opinion of AG Léger*, para. 54. The Advocate General affirmed: 'The concept 'sustainable development' does not mean that the interests of the environment must necessarily and systematically prevail over the interests defended in the

breakthroughs in terms of greening of the agricultural sector, but it is basically not applied judicially to review the environmental dimension of EU agricultural legislation on its basis.

On the one hand, it could be argued that after all Article 11 TFEU only lays down an obligation of means of an 'interstitial' nature. Only an unexpected reform at Treaty level could change the state of play, through the insertion of defined standards to be adhered to, or to be achieved, in respect of secondary legislation. It is therefore true that, being more the 'fossilisation' of a political slogan than a fully-fledged legal rule, the integration principle will always have more potential to influence the EU legislator than to trigger judicial review.

On the other hand, though, if it is true that the environmental objective must not be prioritised as such, it is also true that it must not be *a priori* sidelined *vis-à-vis* other objectives. According to EU institutions a wide discretion in the development of EU policies is only meaningful if the said institutions are left free to choose *how* to strike a balance between the components of sustainable development. If no balance is struck at all, the obligation arising from sustainable development – however broad – cannot be said to have been respected. Amongst other things, striking a balance would imply, in the author's view, substantive awareness of the positive and negative effects of the proposed measures. In the current CAP, there is no mechanism or method that allows for the *evaluation* of the actual environmental impact of a measure by comparison with other social and economic considerations.

However, this only lies within the ambit of political observations. In fact, it is true that *politically speaking* the EU would significantly gain in legitimacy and credibility from a more thorough judicial control of the correspondence between objectives declares, resources displayed to pursue them and results obtained. This should be the outcome of a meaningful interpretation of the concept of 'high level of protection and improvement of the quality of the environment' enshrined in Article 3(3) TUE. That having been said, *legally speaking* the wording of the PEI does not allow one to come to such a conclusion.

5. CONCLUSION

The analysis conducted above has shown that a progressive integration of environmental considerations has taken place in EU agriculture in the last few decades and particularly as a result of the last reform of 2013.

---

context of the other policies pursued by the Community... On the contrary, it emphasizes the necessary balance between various interests which sometimes clash, but which must be reconciled'. On this point, cf. also de Sadeleer, N. (2015) 'Sustainable Development in EU Law: Still a Long Way to Go', Jindal Global L. Rev., Vol. 6, p. 51.

However, the examination of CJEU case-law shows that a full judicial review of the environmental performance of the EU agricultural policy does not appear to be a concrete option in the current state of play. This is true in spite of the significant progress made in CJEU case-law, where there is some evidence of the concept that 'high level of protection and improvement of the quality of the environment' has sometimes fostered teleological interpretations by the Court of Justice.[51] As a result, it would appear that the process of judicial review in respect of environmental measures set out in the CAP will continue to be limited even in the near future, as well as remaining characterized by the ample discretion accorded to the EU institutions.

In conclusion, it must be recognised that there is a clear reason for this being the current position in terms of the law. Consideration must be given to the fact that in the event that there were to be a penetrating review of politically sensitive and macro-economic choices made by the EU, the CJEU would then 'be faced with endless challenges by applicants seeking to argue an alternative balancing of potentially conflicting factors'.[52] If this view is to be accepted, then it must also be pointed out that there are other considerations and real needs to be met that should properly be taken into account, and that there is a balance of these requirements to be struck by the EU policymakers. Further, any such balance should also properly be subject to the legality check of the EU Courts. These other considerations pertain – firstly – to the exigency that EU measures are elaborated in accordance with solid scientific evidence supporting the suitability of such measures to reach their targets, which also include the capability of such measures to trigger radical changes in the farming practice; and – secondly – to the protection of taxpayers' concerns that EU money is spent in an efficient and proportionate way. In the examination of the existing case-law, the latter issues do not seem to be taken into consideration as much as they deserve.

51 Misonne, D. (2015) 'The Importance of Setting a Target: The EU Ambition of a High Level of Protection', Transnational Environmental Law, Vol. 4, No. 1, p. 26 and case-law cited therein.

52 Gordon, Richard, Moffat and Rowena (2014) EU Law in Judicial Review, Oxford University Press, 2nd edition, p. 346.

PART III

SUSTAINABLE MANAGEMENT OF WASTE

CHAPTER 5

TOWARDS RESPONSIBLE MANAGEMENT OF PHARMACEUTICAL WASTE IN THE EU

Katerina MITKIDIS,* Shona WALTER** and Viktoria OBOLEVICH***

ABSTRACT

Medicines improve and save lives; however, when disposed to the environment, active pharmaceutical ingredients (APIs) designed to treat humans may have unintended negative effects on other species and ecosystems. APIs are released to the environment as waste during production, consumption and disposal of medicines. While scientific evidence of detrimental effects of pharmaceutical residue in the environment is growing, many gaps remain, causing regulatory inaction. This chapter introduces the issue of pharmaceutical waste and reviews the applicable legal framework. Unsurprisingly, it is found that the legal framework is far from comprehensive. On this background, we identify obstacles to sustainable pharmaceutical waste management and possible ways to overcome those and reflect on the issue of pharmaceutical waste management in light of the waste hierarchy. We argue that a shift in public discourse is necessary to allow for the adoption of precautionary, sustainable and life cycle-based legal measures. This shift should move the focus from balancing the environmental protection with public health to balancing individuals' health concerns with public health protection (through the protection of the environment).

* Associate professor of law, PhD, Aarhus University, Denmark (katpe@law.au.dk). This chapter was written within 'Pharmaceuticals in the Environment: Legal Solutions Informed by Behavioral Science' project (PiE project) funded by the Aarhus Universitets Forskningsfond.

** Research assistant at the PiE project, Aarhus University, Denmark (shona.walter@law.au.dk).

*** PhD, Research assistant at the PiE project, Aarhus University, Denmark (vao8008@gmail.com).

1. INTRODUCTION

Medicines improve and save lives; however, when disposed to the environment as waste, active pharmaceutical ingredients (APIs) designed to treat humans may have unintended negative effects on other species and ecosystems.[1] Moreover, through their impact in the environment, they may also pose a threat to human health.[2] Designed to act on living cells, to resist the acid environment of the stomach and to be administered according to a specific schedule, human pharmaceuticals impact the environment in a complex way. Of particular concern are endocrine-disrupting pharmaceuticals, cancer treatment drugs, antibiotics, anti-inflammatory drugs and sedatives.[3] The pharmaceuticals in the environment (PiE) problem is recognized as a growing issue by academics, regulators, the general public and the pharmaceutical industry. Recently, the United Nations (UN) Strategic Approach to International Chemicals Management adopted 'Environmentally Persistent Pharmaceutical Pollutants' as an emerging policy issue.[4] This chapter addresses the PiE from the waste management perspective.

In 2015, the UN set forth seventeen goals to achieve sustainable management of natural resources.[5] Minimizing waste disposed to the environment is one target running throughout the whole document. Pharmaceutical waste has a special position within waste in general, being long perceived as a necessary by-product of access to medicines. In other words, following the advancement in the treatment possibilities and access to them, the amount of pharmaceutical waste got larger and more varied. With growing scientific evidence of the negative impact of pharmaceutical waste in the environment and consequently on public health this leading to an increased need of more and new medicines, the current vicious circle has been brought to the public's attention. Voices calling to better balance patient access with the protection of human health and sustainable management of natural resources have been raising.

On this background and after introducing the issue of pharmaceutical waste in the context of PiE (section 2) and the applicable legal framework (section 3),

1 This chapter focuses on medicinal products for human use. Veterinary medicinal products are not considered due to the differences in the applicable legal frameworks. The terms 'medicines', 'pharmaceuticals' and 'medicinal products' are used interchangeably.

2 Williams, E.S. and B.W. Brooks (2012) 'Human Health Risk Assessment for Pharmaceuticals in the Environment: Existing Practice, Uncertainty, and Future Directions' in B.W. Brooks and D.B. Huggett (eds.) Human Pharmaceuticals in the Environment, Springer.

3 Infra notes 12-15.

4 Strategic Approach to International Chemicals Management, Nomination for new emerging policy issue: environmentally persistent pharmaceutical pollutants, SAICM/ICCM.4/7, 27 July 2015.

5 United Nations, General Assembly, Transforming our world: the 2030 Agenda for Sustainable Development, A/RES/70/1, 21 October 2015 (2030 Agenda for Sustainable Development).

the aim of the present chapter is twofold. Firstly, to identify obstacles to sustainable pharmaceutical waste management and possible ways to overcome those (section 4). Secondly, to reflect on the issue of pharmaceutical waste management in light of the waste hierarchy (section 5). In the conclusion, we argue that a shift in public discourse is necessary to allow for the adoption of precautionary, sustainable and life cycle-based legal measures.

2. WHAT DO WE KNOW?

Pharmaceutical waste enters the environment through three routes: production processes, patient use and disposal of unused medicines. During production, pharmaceuticals enter the environment through unintentional leaks or as residue from manufacturing sites' effluents. While pharmaceutical waste from production processes is considered negligible within the EU,[6] the concentration of APIs in effluent from industrial processes is much higher than in urban wastewaters, thus having the potential to significantly alter the balance in the local environment.[7] The therapeutic use of pharmaceuticals arguably accounts for the majority of the PiE. Approximately 30-90 per cent of APIs consumed by patients are excreted unchanged,[8] and current waste water treatment plants are unable to eliminate all APIs from the water.[9] The problem is further exacerbated by pharmaceutical over-prescription and overuse. Finally, considerable amounts of pharmaceuticals enter the environment during the disposal of unused and expired medicines. Unused and expired pharmaceuticals should be collected through take-back schemes.[10] However, on average 50 per cent of unused pharmaceuticals are disposed of improperly.[11]

---

6 The European Federation of Pharmaceutical Industries and Associations estimates this to be 2 % of all PiE, see BIO Intelligence Service, Study on the environmental risks of medicinal products, prepared for Executive Agency for Health and Consumers, Final Report, 2013 (BIOIS Report), pp. 45-46. This number is doubted as it is largely based on estimations. Moreover, the number is low since most APIs for pharmaceuticals manufactured and used in the EU are produced outside of the EU. However, the outsourced pollution by pharmaceutical waste is likely to impact EU's population, see e.g. D.G.J. Larsson (2014) 'Pollution from drug manufacturing: review and perspectives', Philosophical transactions of the Royal Society of London, Series B, Biological sciences, 369(1656), p. 4.

7 Larsson, *supra* note 6, p. 4.

8 BIOIS Report, p. 48.

9 Bound, J.P. and N. Voulvoulis (2005) 'Household Disposal of Pharmaceuticals as a Pathway for Aquatic Contamination in the United Kingdom', Environmental Health Perspectives, 113(12), Table 2.

10 Directive 2001/83/EC on the Community code relating to medicinal products for human use (Directive 2001/83/EC), Article 127b.

11 European Environment Agency, Pharmaceuticals in the Environment, Results of an EEA Workshop, Technical Report No. 1/2010, p. 26.

The presence of PiE has caused a range of major negative changes in the environment, such as the population decline of certain species,[12] changes in animals' behaviour,[13] feminization of fish[14] and the rise of anti-microbial resistance.[15] The same level of negative effects on human health has not yet been positively proven.[16] The World Health Organization (WHO) concluded in 2011 that the levels of pharmaceuticals in drinking water are very unlikely to cause 'appreciable adverse health impacts to humans.'[17] However, the WHO also acknowledged the lack of knowledge about the effects of long-term chronic exposure to low levels of pharmaceuticals and the possible combined effects of their mixtures upon organisms in water and soil.[18] While each API might be present in concentrations too low to have a negative impact on the environment and human health, their combination is likely to be more harmful.[19]

The growing scientific evidence of the negative impact of pharmaceuticals and their metabolites in the environment both on the integrity of natural resources and human health as well as the persistent gaps in the scientific knowledge are arguably reasons to adopt cautious regulation. However, thus far, the EU has taken a weak approach to regulating the effects of pharmaceutical waste on the environment and the legal framework remains scattered.

3. LEGAL FRAMEWORK[20]

There is no comprehensive legal framework in the EU for the management of pharmaceutical waste, which mirrors the regulation of the PiE problem in general. The PiE problem lies on the border of environmental and pharmaceutical law. Due to the different competences and competing economic and protective

12 Green, R.E. *et al.* (2004) 'Diclofenac poisoning as a cause of vulture population declines across the Indian subcontinent', Journal of Applied Ecology, 41(5).

13 Bean, T.G. *et al.* (2014) 'Behavioural and physiological responses of birds to environmentally relevant concentrations of an antidepressant', Philosophical transactions of the Royal Society of London, Series B, Biological sciences, Vol. 369, No. 1656.

14 Larsson, D.G.J. *et al.* (1999) 'Ethinyloestradiol — an undesired fish contraceptive?', Aquatic Toxicology, Vol. 45, No. 2.

15 Larsson, *supra* note 6, p. 5.

16 But see, e.g., Pomati, F. *et al.* (2006) 'Effects of a Complex Mixture of Therapeutic Drugs at Environmental Levels on Human Embryonic Cells', Environmental Science & Technology, Vol. 40, No. 7.

17 WHO, Pharmaceuticals in Drinking-water, 2011, WHO/HSE/WSH/11.05, p. 28.

18 Ibid., p. 29. See also, Brooks and Huggett, *supra* note 2, p. 7.

19 Thrupp, T.J. (2018) 'The consequences of exposure to mixtures of chemicals: Something from 'nothing' and 'a lot from a little' when fish are exposed to steroid hormones', Science of The Total Environment, Vols. 619-620.

20 We focus on the legal framework applicable specifically on pharmaceutical waste. For the EU legal framework applicable on the PiE in general, see, BIOIS report.

interests of the EU in the two sectors, they are regulated in fundamentally different ways; while environmental legislation focuses on environmental protection, pharmaceutical legislation is primarily focused on the creation of good market conditions for pharmaceutical companies. Thus, although the primary purpose of the pharmaceutical sector is to deliver medicines for the treatment of citizens, the majority of legislative acts in this area was adopted based on the internal market legal basis,[21] rather than the public health legal basis,[22] not to speak about the environmental one.[23]

The most general regulation is contained in Directive 2001/83/EC, specifically Article 8(3)(g) requiring an environmental risk assessment (ERA) within the marketing authorization procedures. However, unlike in the case of veterinary medicinal products, a negative ERA of medicinal products for human use cannot lead to the refusal of a marketing authorization application.[24] Moreover, it concerns only the finished product, while the manufacturing process is expressly excluded.[25]

Furthermore, the water legislation newly requires monitoring of six APIs in the environment and compels the European Commission to act.[26] Monitoring is necessary to understand better the PiE extent, but water quality is only a small part of the overall problem, focusing on remedying the problem rather than its prevention.

When looking at the three main routes for entrance of pharmaceutical waste into the environment, we see a picture of scattered regulation. As already stated, the presence of pharmaceuticals in effluents and/or possible leaks from production processes are not considered in the ERA carried out during the market authorisation procedure. Instead, this is considered during the environmental impact assessment (EIA) carried out prior to the construction of a pharmaceutical manufacturing plant, as required by the EIA Directive.[27] Interestingly, the EIA Directive requires an EIA for the production of APIs, whereas Member States have the discretion to require or not require an EIA for an installation which will produce the final medicinal product.[28] The possible

21 The Treaty on the Functioning of the European Union (TFEU), Article 114 (ex. Article 95).
22 TFEU, Article 168 (ex. Article 152).
23 TFEU, Article 192 (ex. Article 175).
24 Directive 2001/83/EC, Article 26(1)(a) in connection to Article 1(28a).
25 European Medicines Agency, Guideline on the Environmental Risk Assessment of Medicinal Products for Human Use, EMEA/CHMP/SWP/4447/00 corr 2(2006), p. 3.
26 Directive 2000/60/EC establishing a framework for Community action in the field of water policy (Water Framework Directive) and Directive 2008/105/EC on environmental quality standards in the field of water policy (as amended by Directive 2013/38/EU) (Directive 2008/105/EC), Articles 8b and 8c.
27 Directive 2014/52/EU on the assessment of the effects of certain public and private projects on the environment.
28 EIA Directive, Article 4(1) and Annex I (6)(e) compare to Article 4(2) and Annex II (6)(b).

reasoning here is that the production of final pharmaceutical products have a lower environmental impact. However, this is questionable when you consider the cumulative impact of various plants with other approved or existing projects on the local environment, which must since 2014 be considered by Member States when exercising their discretion under Article 4(2) of the EIA Directive.[29] Furthermore, industrial discharges from production processes into water and soil are regulated by the Industrial Emissions Directive (IED).[30] According to the IED, listed industrial processes cannot be executed without a permit stipulating emission limit values for specified substances. The emission limit values are based on Best Available Techniques (BAT) summarized in the so-called BAT Reference Documents (BREFs). Several BREFs apply to the pharmaceutical industry;[31] however, none sets limits for APIs. Arguably, the IED leaves out limits on APIs because the environmental impact of pharmaceuticals is already reviewed within the marketing authorization procedure.[32] Furthermore, APIs, except for anti-cancer treatment, are not considered hazardous waste.[33] Therefore, no special treatment of them is necessary. However, under the Urban Waste Water Treatment Directive, industrial waste water must be pre-treated before it enters the urban waste water treatment system, so it does not adversely affect the environment.[34]

Regarding the second route of pharmaceuticals' entrance to the environment – human excretion, is not considered waste under the Waste Framework Directive.[35] Instead, it is covered by the Urban Waste Water Treatment Directive, which requires collection systems for urban waste water to use the 'best technical knowledge not entailing excessive costs.'[36] Current waste water treatment plants are not able to remove 100 per cent of APIs from waste water.[37] New waste water treatment technologies are thus being developed, however, their installation and running costs are perceived as high,[38] therefore likely not passing the cost-

29 Directive 2014/52/EU, Annex III (3)(g).

30 Directive 2010/75/EU on industrial emissions (integrated pollution prevention and control).

31 E.g. BREF–Large Volume Organic Chemicals (2017).

32 Läkemedelsverket, Platform to enable the initiation of a revision of EU legislation on Good Manufacturing Practice, GMP, in order for legislation also to comprehend environmental considerations, Report from the Medical Products Agency, 16 June 2011, p. 27.

33 Commission Decision 2000/532/EC, waste codes 18 01 08, 18 02 07 and 20 01 31; for anti-cancer treatment, see waste codes 18 01 09, 18 02 08 and 20 01 32.

34 Annex I, section C Directive 91/271/EEC concerning urban waste water treatment (Urban Waste Water Treatment Directive). The details of the pre-treatment are prescribed by individual Member States, see Urban Waste Water Treatment Directive, Article 11(2).

35 Directive 2008/98/EC on waste (Waste Framework Directive), Article 2(1)(f).

36 Urban Waste Water Treatment Directive, Annex I (A).

37 D. Nicole (2014) 'Pharmaceuticals in Wastewater Treatment Plant Effluent Waters', Scholarly Horizons: University of Minnesota, Morris Undergraduate Journal, Vol. 1, No. 2, p. 4.

38 Doerr-MacEwen, N.A. and M.E. Haight (2006) 'Expert Stakeholders' Views on the Management of Human Pharmaceuticals in the Environment', Environmental Management, Vol. 38, No. 5, p. 859.

effectiveness requirements set out in Annex I to the Urban Waste Water Treatment Directive and Article 8c of Directive 2008/105/EC.[39] In addition, the focus of the Directive is again on end-of-life treatment and not on prevention of waste production.

Finally, disposal of unused and expired pharmaceuticals is harmonized only leniently in the EU. Member States shall introduce collection schemes,[40] but there are no guidelines on how such schemes should be designed and financed, and there is no control or evaluation of the schemes. Moreover, the schemes' operators are not required to be registered or to receive a permit to handle pharmaceutical waste.[41] The collection system must be referred to on the outer packaging of a medicinal product, but only 'where appropriate,'[42] i.e. where 'the possibility of environmental risks cannot be excluded.'[43]

The problem of pharmaceutical waste is thus not adequately tackled in the applicable legal framework, considering the known detrimental effects on the environment and human health. The questions to ask is why there has not been more done and what could the way forward be.

4. WAY FORWARD

The reasons for the scattered legal framework can be seen both as problems but also as fuel for action. The reasons include the balancing of major interests, the complexity of the pharmaceutical industry and the lack of scientific certainty.

4.1. FROM COMPETING MAJOR INTERESTS TO SUSTAINABILITY

When regulating the PiE, major interests must be balanced. These are primarily ensuring the common market in pharmaceuticals, the protection of public health and the protection of the environment. The European Commission's Renewed Vision for the Pharmaceutical Sector from 2008 mentioned all three interests.[44] The Commission's primary focus was on the local and global competitiveness of the sector and on ensuring the widest possible access of patients to the newest,

39 An ongoing discussion in some Member States suggests that based on the polluter pays principle the high costs of the water treatment solutions should be shared by the industry. See e.g. Gawel et.al., Arzneimittelabgabe, UBA-Texte 115/2017 (available at the homepage of the Federal Environment Agency: Umweltbundesamt).

40 Directive 2001/83/EC, Article 127b.

41 Waste Framework Directive, Preamble 17.

42 Directive 2001/83/EC, Article 54(j).

43 European Medicines Agency, *supra* note 25, p. 9.

44 European Commission, Safe, Innovative and Accessible Medicines: a Renewed Vision for the Pharmaceutical Sector, COM 666 final, 2008, p. 4.

cheapest and safest treatment (Objectives 1-11). Environmental protection came in as the last objective under the first heading (Objective 12). Since then the environmental protection has gained more attention, also due to the adoption of the 2030 Agenda for Sustainable Development by the UN.

The 2030 Agenda for Sustainable Development comprises 17 goals and 169 associated targets. No goal is more important than another one, they are 'integrated and indivisible.'[45] Relevant to the problem of pharmaceutical waste, goal 3 speaks to ensuring public health, access to medicines and support to pharmaceutical R&D, and goals 6, 14, 15 and partially goal 12 focus on environmental protection. The EU declared support to the 2030 Agenda for Sustainable Development and stated that together with its Member States, it will 'implement the 2030 Agenda across all internal and external policies in a comprehensive and strategic approach.'[46] To that end, the EU will '… take action to address global health threats, such as epidemics and antimicrobial resistance … and address chemical pollution'[47] and '… promote resource efficiency and sustainable consumption and production, including the sustainable management of chemicals and waste … .'[48]

The endorsed international policy provides the EU with a background to tackle the pharmaceutical waste problem. It places all the major policy interests on the same level. The EU thus has the mandate to overcome the possible prioritization of the common market and public health objectives over the environmental ones stemming from the integration principles in Article 11 and 168(1) of the TFEU.[49] However, it might be naïve to expect that a perfect balance can be reached.

4.2. FROM SCIENTIFIC UNCERTAINTY TO PRECAUTION

Section 2 above introduced some scientific evidence of the detrimental effect of pharmaceutical waste in the environment; but it also pointed out scientific uncertainty regarding its harmfulness on human health. Scientific uncertainty may invoke the application of the precautionary principle.[50] The EU guidelines

45 2030 Agenda for Sustainable Development, primarily paras. 6 and 18.

46 Joint Statement by the Council and the Representatives of the Governments of the Member States Meeting Within the Council, the European Parliament and the European Commission, The New European Consensus on Development, 'Our World, Our Dignity, Our Future', 7 June 2017, para. 7.

47 Ibid., para. 27.

48 Ibid., para. 43.

49 Nowag, J. (2017) Environmental Integration in Competition and Free-Movement Laws, OUP, pp. 4-8.

50 Rio Declaration on Environment and Development (1992), Principle 15.

on the precautionary principle[51] and EU case law[52] settled that in order to apply the precautionary principle, a scientific risk assessment should be performed. Meaning precautionary actions cannot be introduced relying purely on a hypothetical risk.[53] Yet the precautionary principle requires us to 'take protective measures without having to wait until the reality and seriousness of those risks become fully apparent.'[54] This draws a thin line for regulators between acting and non-acting. For example, in respect to including the results of ERA into the risk-benefit analysis for introducing a new medicinal product on the market, the European Medicine Agency seems to consider available scientific evidence inadequate to trigger the precautionary principle application.[55] However, acquiring scientific evidence of the causal relationship between the presence of pharmaceuticals in the environment and their negative effect on ecosystems and human health is possible only in rare cases, due to the 'cocktail effect' and a long-time span between an exposure and its effects.[56]

It is important to mention the different application of the precautionary principle in the two spheres: environmental protection and protection of public health. Even though the precautionary principle was initially introduced as a part of environmental law, it has received a general applicability.[57] In fact, so far the principle has been more frequently applied within health law than environmental law, possibly due to larger available scientific evidence.[58] It may also reflect the preference given to public health in the legal framework.[59] Also, while the EU case law established that the protection of human health takes precedence over economic considerations,[60] the same has not been established regarding

51 Communication from the Commission on the Precautionary Principle, COM (2000) 1 final, 2 February 2000, section 5.1.2.

52 T-70/99, *Alpharma v Council* (T-70/99, Alpharma), para. 162.

53 C-36/01, *Monsanto Agricoltura*, para. 106; C-192/01, *Commission v Denmark*, para. 49; C-42/02, *Commission v Netherlands*, para. 52; E-3/00 *EFTA Surveillance Authority v Norway* (2000–2001) EFTA Ct. Rep. 73, para. 29.

54 T-13/99, *Pfizer Animal Health SA v Council*, para. 139.

55 Brooks and Huggett, *supra* note 2, p. 28.

56 Keil, F. (ed), Pharmaceuticals for Human Use: Options of Action for Reducing the Contamination of Water Bodies A Practical Guide, 2008, Institute for Social-Ecological Research (ISOE) GmbH.

57 Joined T-74/00, T-76/00, T-83/00 to T-85/00, T-132/00, T-137/00 and T-141/00, *Artegodan*, para. 184.

58 Sadeleer, N. (2006) 'The Precautionary Principle in the EC Health and Environmental Law', European Law Journal, Vol. 12, No. 2, p. 172.

59 TFEU, Article 11 ('Environmental protection requirements must be **integrated** into the definition and implementation of the Union policies and activities …') compared with Article 168(1) (A high level of human health protection shall be **ensured** …) (emphases added).

60 T-13/99, *Pfizer*; T-70/99, *Alpharma*.

environmental protection.[61] All this reflects also the fact that humans tend to be more anthropocentric than ecocentric. Thus, in order to facilitate the application of the precautionary principle, we might change the framing of the PiE from only an environmental to both an environmental and a public health problem. The focus of scientists is already shifting from the negative effects of PiE on wildlife to the negative effects on humans.[62]

Such a reframing has been instrumental in the application of the precautionary principle in the area of veterinary medicinal products and their effect on the environment.[63] While the same APIs are often used in both human and veterinary medicines, veterinary products are regulated more strictly, arguably due to the risk of veterinary products entering humans' food chain and, thus, representing a potential threat to public health.[64]

While it is understood that the authorities with democratic legitimacy have the competence to evaluate the risks of PiE, there is little support for them not to take a precautionary approach in respect to human pharmaceuticals, as they do in the case of veterinary products, since the risks to the environment mean according to the growing scientific evidence also risks to human health.

4.3. FROM COMPLEXITY TO LIFE CYCLE ACTION

Pharmaceuticals' life cycle is highly complex: pharmaceutical companies produce medicines, regulatory authorities issue market approvals, healthcare professionals prescribe medicines, pharmacies dispense them, health insurance companies (partially) pay for them, and citizens use them.[65] This (still simplified) picture shows the difficulty in distributing responsibility for pharmaceutical waste fairly.[66]

Built on the environmental protection legal basis, the Waste Framework Directive implements the polluter pays principle. However, establishing who the

---

61 Jobling and Owen speak about the cost-effectiveness requirement as the 'Achilles Heel' of the precautionary principle, see Jobling, S. and R. Owen (2013) 'Ethinyl oestradiol in the aquatic environment' in European Environment Agency, Late lessons from early warnings: science, precaution, innovation, EEA Report No. 1/2013, p. 296.

62 Hotchkiss, A.K. *et al.* (2008) 'Fifteen years after "Wingspread"—environmental endocrine disrupters and human and wildlife health: where we are today and where we need to go', Toxicological Science, 105(2); and Jobling and Owen, *supra* note 61.

63 T-13/99, *Pfizer*; T-70/99, *Alpharma*.

64 Regulation (EC) 470/2009 laying down Community procedures for the establishment of residue limits of pharmacological active substances in foodstuffs of animal origin, Article 7(d).

65 Healthcare centres and hospitals are excluded from the analysis here as they raise a range of specific questions in respect to pharmaceutical waste.

66 Amster, E.D. (2016) 'Mitigating pharmaceutical waste exposures: policy and program considerations', Israel Journal of Health Policy Research, Vol. 5, No. 1, p. 3.

polluter is proves tricky.[67] Article 14 refers to the 'original waste producer or … the current or previous waste holders.' The 'polluter' thus differs depending on the route of pharmaceuticals' entrance to the environment. Regarding industrial pharmaceutical waste, pointing a finger seems simple. Human excretion of pharmaceutical residues is covered by the Urban Waste Water Treatment Directive, as discussed above. Article 9 of the Water Framework Directive stipulates that the different users (industrial and urban) of water systems must contribute to the cost of maintaining these services.[68] As both pharmaceutical manufacturers and patients discharge their waste water into urban treatment systems, they are both considered polluters.[69] The fairness of this assumption is questionable in respect to patients since they do not choose what a product is composed of and when speaking of prescription-only products if to use it at all (it is the doctor's choice). Finally, in respect to the disposal of unused or expired pharmaceuticals, the situation is not easier. The patient might not have decided alone to buy it (if prescribed), might not be to blame for not using it all and might not know how to properly dispose of it.

Some EU Member States implement the extended producer responsibility concept through industry-financed take-back schemes.[70] Here producers are seen as the primary polluter.[71] However, the pharmaceutical industry may oppose this, arguing that they do not decide which treatment is used by patients and that they cannot influence the choice as the advertising of pharmaceuticals is strictly limited.[72] Nevertheless, it is widely reported that promotional efforts of pharmaceutical companies towards healthcare professionals often amount to bribery.[73] Yet, some argue that financing collection schemes by industry will not successfully combat over-prescription as it remains more profitable for

67 Opinion of Avocate General Kokott in Commune de Mesquer v Total France SA and Total International Ltd., C-188/07, 24 June 2008.

68 Water Framework Directive, Article 9. European Court of Auditors (2015) 'EU-funding of urban waste water treatment plants in the Danube river basin: further efforts needed in helping Member States to achieve EU waste water policy objectives', Special Report No. 2, European Union, p. 40.

69 See also note 39 above.

70 Waste Framework Directive, Article 8. For an overview of industry-financed take-back schemes in the EU, see http://calpsc.org/products/pharmaceuticals/international-epr-programs-for-pharmaceuticals/ (acceded on 10 February 2018).

71 Barnett-Itzhaki, Z. *et al.* (2016) 'Household medical waste disposal policy in Israel', Israel Journal of Health Policy Research, Vol. 5, No. 1, p. 3.

72 Directive 2001/83/EC, Title VIII.

73 E.g. India Medical Times, Novartis fined $49 million for bribing doctors to prescribe its drugs, 28 April 2017, available at: http://www.indiamedicaltimes.com/2017/04/28/novartis-fined-49-million-for-bribing-doctors-to-prescribe-its-drugs/ (acceded on 15 February 2018).

pharmaceutical companies to sell large amounts of pharmaceuticals and pay the collection schemes than to reduce the sold amounts and thus collection costs.[74]

The complexity of both the pharmaceutical industry and application of the polluter pays principles in the waste sector calls for minimizing waste creation throughout the whole pharmaceuticals' life cycle. While we cannot presume that the production of pharmaceuticals will decrease in future (due to, *inter alia*, growing and aging population), we should aim to reduce the amounts of medicines entering the environment, targeting every stage of and all actors in the pharmaceuticals' life cycle.

5. WAY FORWARD? GOING BACK TO THE WASTE HIERARCHY

In light of the previous, it is evident that the management of pharmaceutical waste is a complex matter. The way to deal with this complexity and related scientific uncertainty is to take sustainable, precautionary and life cycle-oriented action. In our view, this action should take the starting point in the waste hierarchy as prescribed in Article 4 of the Waste Framework Directive.

5.1. PREVENTION

According to the waste hierarchy, the primary focus should be on the prevention of pharmaceutical waste creation, without compromising access to medicines. Fighting overconsumption is one possible focus. Legal measures to this end may entail regulating the size of medicines packaging,[75] combatting illegal promotional activities and bribery in the pharmaceutical sector,[76] and educating patients about pharmaceuticals' rational use and proper disposal. The barrier to overcome is the pushback by pharmaceutical companies and long waiting time to see the results of patients' education.

While the measures outlined above are possibly the most cost-effective at our hands today, designing APIs that are less harmful to the environment would solve the problem at its source. This movement is known as 'green pharmacy.'[77] While this idea is gaining support across various stakeholders, there is an issue of costs

---

74 Alev, I. *et al.* (2015) 'Extended Producer Responsibility for Pharmaceuticals', Georgia Tech Scheller College of Business Research Paper No. 2015-19, p. 15, available at: https://ssrn.com/abstract=2693169 (acceded on 14 February 2018).

75 This is already implemented in some jurisdictions, e.g. Denmark (Danish Medicines Act, § 57).

76 Alev *et al.*, *supra* note 74, p. 14.

77 Daughton, C.D. and I.S. Ruhoy (2011) 'Green pharmacy and pharmEcovigilance: prescribing and the planet', Expert Review of Clinical Pharmacology, Vol. 4, No. 2; K. Kümmerer and M. Hempel (eds.) (2010) Green and Sustainable Pharmacy, Springer.

and a lack of incentives from the EU's regulator. In order to make this idea more appealing to the pharmaceutical industry, both more stringent laws on the environmental impact of medicinal products (e.g. the inclusion of the ERA results into the risk-benefit analysis within the marketing authorization procedures) and positive incentives (e.g. quicker market entry for 'green' pharmaceuticals) would have to be adopted.

5.2. (PREPARING FOR) RE-USE

Considering the characteristics of pharmaceuticals – perishable products, whose consumption is not (entirely) patient-driven – they have not been considered suitable for re-use or recycling.[78] Some, however, argue that unused pharmaceuticals returned to pharmacies are a waste of both economic and natural resources and in many instances could be re-used for treatment of other patients.[79] Before allowing this on a general basis, multiple safety, legal, ethical and economic issues need to be solved. The quality of unused and returned medicines must be guaranteed, and a responsible subject must be identifiable. The costs of redispensing unused pharmaceuticals should not outweigh the financial benefits. Finally, the patients given these products must be fully informed about the 'second hand' character and willing to take these medicines.[80] Without these issues fully solved, the practice has nevertheless developed spontaneously. In Greece, strangled by the long-lasting economic crisis, society has self-organized to make access to medicines possible to those without economic means through so-called 'social pharmacies.' However, the legality of social pharmacies' operation has recently been questioned.[81]

5.3. RECOVERY

We skip the recycling step of the waste hierarchy as no recycling of human pharmaceuticals (except for their packaging) is possible. The possibility of recovery is also very limited. The recommended disposal solution for

78 Alev *et al.*, *supra* note 74, p. 3.

79 Mackridge, A.J. and J.F. Marriott (2007) 'Returned medicines: waste or a wasted opportunity?', Journal of Public Health, 29(3); For the rationale of pharmaceuticals' re-use, see, J.M. Pomerantz (2004) 'Recycling Expensive Medication: Why Not?', Medscape General Medicine, Vol. 6, No. 2.

80 Bekker, C.L. *et al.* (2017) 'Redispensing of medicines unused by patients: a qualitative study among stakeholders', International Journal of Clinical Pharmacy, Vol. 39, No. 1.

81 Letter by the Panhellenic Pharmaceutical Association, 'Establishment and Operation of Social Pharmacies', 19 October 2017, available at: http://www.pfs.gr/ΕνημέρωσηΣυνδικαλιστικάΝέα/ΑνακοινώσειςΠΦΣ/tabid/101/newsid416/3019/Default.aspx (in Greek) (acceded on 14 February 2018).

pharmaceutical waste is incineration in high temperatures,[82] optimally with energy recovery. Incineration may be a good solution for municipal waste including improperly disposed medicines. In that way, the problem of pharmaceuticals' mixtures would also be solved. However, incineration of pharmaceutical waste releases toxic pollutants to the air and thus other technologies of waste treatment – e.g. through chemical or steam-based processes – appear, but they do not involve energy recovery.[83]

5.4. DISPOSAL

Disposal of pharmaceuticals happens at the household level as well as at the professional level by healthcare centres, such as hospitals, though these are excluded from our analysis here.[84] As already noted, the EU vaguely requires its Member States to implement take-back collection systems. Each Member State can decide how the collection system should be operated and financed. There is thus a variety of collection systems across the EU, making it hard to monitor whether the obligation imposed on the Member States is complied with and whether the collection systems are 'appropriate' and effective. Unification of the collection systems, and the mutual learning among them, is perceived as an important measure for fighting the PiE problem.[85]

Additionally, more environmentally responsible disposal could possibly be reached by re-classification of (selected) APIs from non-hazardous to hazardous waste, as 'it is not possible to make a sound distinction between those medicaments exceeding the concentration limits [that render the waste hazardous] and those not exceeding them.'[86]

Finally, new developments of more financially and technologically accessible waste water treatment are necessary. However, the polluter pays principle should be carefully considered here.

---

82 Richman, C. and S. Castensson (2008) 'Impact of waste pharmaceuticals: an environmental hazard or "greenwash"?', The Pharmaceutical Journal, Vol. 280, p. 335.

83 Ibid. See also Health Care Without Harm Europe, Non-Incineration Medical Waste Treatment Technologies in Europe, Resource Book, June 2004, available at: http://www.env-health.org/IMG/pdf/altech_Europe_updated_version_10_12_2004.pdf (acceded on 14 February 2018).

84 *Supra* note 65.

85 Clayton, H., DG Environment, European Commission Proceedings of EU workshop of 11 September 2014 on the development of a strategic approach to pollution of water by pharmaceutical substances, available at: https://circabc.europa.eu/faces/jsp/extension/wai/navigation/container.jsp (acceded on 15 February 2018).

86 Entry of the Czech Republic suggesting to move all pharmaceutical waste under hazardous waste, Ökopol GmbH, Review of the European List of Waste, Final Report, November 2008, part 4. This is already implemented in Finland, see Ökopol GmbH, Review of the European List of Waste, Executive Summary, November 2008, p. I – 23.

6. CONCLUSION

The problem of pharmaceutical waste has attracted the attention of scientists, regulators, the media and the general public. However, persistent lack of reliable monitoring and scientific data has hindered moves to regulatory responses. That is especially true for the lack of data about impacts of PiE on human health. The proven negative effects on the environment have not been enough to trigger the application of the precautionary principle in respect to human pharmaceuticals, as it happened in respect to veterinary pharmaceuticals.[87] Only now, the European Commission is preparing a Strategic Approach to PiE.[88] However, the available documents show that the measures to be taken are rather cosmetic as the regulator is not prepared to restrict citizens' access to medicines.[89] Indeed, in the past the EU has been willing to apply the precautionary principle more readily in the area of public health than environmental protection.[90] Thus, if we intend to effectively protect the natural environment and natural resources, we might need to shift the discussion from balancing the environmental protection and the protection of human individuals' health to the discussion on balancing the protection of human individuals' health and the protection of general public health (through the protection of the environment).

Future legal measures should be based on the principles of sustainability and precaution and take into account the whole life cycle of pharmaceuticals, imposing some obligations on each involved actor, rather than targeting only one. By such action, we may hope for a more sustainable use of our natural resources rather than closing our eyes in front of the growing problem of pharmaceutical waste.

87 T-13/99, *Pfizer*; T-70/99, *Alpharma*.

88 DG Environment, Communication on a strategic approach to pharmaceuticals in the environment, Ares (2017)2210630.

89 No phase-out strategies are possible as in respect to other emergent pollutants. For the level of support provided to different solution, see Clayton, *supra* note 85.

90 de Sadeleer, *supra* note 58, p. 172.

CHAPTER 6

ENVIRONMENTAL LIABILITY AND WASTE: WHICH RESPONSIBILITIES FOR LANDOWNERS?

Marta Cenini*

ABSTRACT

A recent report elaborated by the European Environmental Agency has drawn public attention to the alarming conditions of soils in the European territory. A significant number of lands require urgent remediation measures to halt the loss of biodiversity and health risks as well as to secure soil sustainable use for the future. The European Union has already issued a Thematic Strategy for Soil Protection in 2006 and then tackled the issue in the Seventh Environment Action Programme of 2014, but the question is far from being resolved. From a juridical point of view, it is necessary to clearly establish who is liable/responsible for the clean-up and decontamination of polluted soils and the chapter discusses the liability/responsibility of the owner of a contaminated soil in regard to its remediation. The boundaries of this liability/responsibility are not well defined since soil is not subject to a comprehensive and coherent set of rules at EU level; the relevant provisions must thus be found in the EU directives in force and in particular in the Directive on Environmental Damage (Directive 2004/35/EC) and the Waste Framework Directive (Directive 2008/98/EC).

* The author is aggregate professor of private law at University of Milan, Italy (marta.cenini@unimi.it).

1. INTRODUCTION

A recent report by the European Environmental Agency estimates that in 2011 local soil contamination amounted to 2.5 million potentially contaminated sites in the 39 EEA countries, of which about 45 per cent have been identified to date and to 342,000 contaminated sites, of which about 1/3 have been identified.[1] Only about 51,000 of these identified sites have already been remedied and the others are still awaiting the necessary clean-up and preventive measures, increasing health risks and causing irreparable loss of biodiversity. The EU had already considered this issue in 2006 when it adopted a Thematic Strategy for Soil Protection[2] with the objective to protect soils across the EU; in 2014 the EU returned on the topic and elaborated the Seventh Environment Action Programme,[3] which recognized that soil degradation is a serious challenge and laid down a series of objectives to be reached by 2020.[4] The United Nation also considered the restoration of degraded land and soil as well as the halt of the loss of biodiversity as an urgent goal in the 2030 Agenda for sustainable development issued in 2015.[5]

From a juridical point of view, if we want to secure remediation of contaminated sites and soil sustainable use, we need to clearly establish who is liable/responsible for the clean-up and decontamination of polluted soils. Generally speaking, the person or undertaking who caused the environmental loss, including soil contamination and the damages caused by waste abandonment, should be considered liable in the first place, but case law and literature have identified other possible responsible parties.

The chapter discusses the liability/responsibility of the owner of a contaminated soil in regard to its remediation and in particular focuses on the position of the 'innocent' and/or 'not-responsible' landowner, that is to say, the owner of a contaminated land who is not the causer of the soil pollution nor of improper waste disposal but nevertheless is claimed to be financially responsible

---

1 Source: Progress in the management of contaminated sites in Europe (2014; last modified 4 Sep 2015). For further information see http://www.eea.europa.eu/data-and-maps/indicators/progress-in-management-of-contaminated-sites-3/assessment.

2 Thematic Strategy for Soil Protection (COM (2006) 231) issued on 22 September 2006.

3 Seventh Environment Action Programme entered into force on 17 January 2014.

4 The Seventh Environment Action Programme provides that by 2020 land is managed sustainably in the Union, soil is adequately protected and the remediation of contaminated sites is well underway; it also commits the EU and its Member States to increase efforts to reduce soil erosion and increase soil organic matter, and to remediate contaminated sites. See http://ec.europa.eu/environment/soil/index_en.htm.

5 See Transforming our world: the 2030 Agenda for sustainable development, available at http://sustainabledevelopment.un.org. See in particular goal 15.

for certain costs or is asked to carry out specific remedial measures.[6] The boundaries of this liability/responsibility are not well defined since soil is not subject to a comprehensive and coherent set of rules at EU level and only a few Member States have specific legislation on soil protection.[7] The relevant provisions must thus be found in EU directives in force and in particular in the Environmental Liability Directive (Directive 2004/35/EC, hereinafter ELD) and the Waste Framework Directive (Directive 2008/98/EC, hereinafter WFD).

This chapter is divided into four parts. Part 2 offers a general overview about the principles and liability mechanisms established by the ELD, focusing on the rules and related literature that discuss the position of the landowner with regard to the duties imposed to them by the ELD; part 3 analyses the WFD comparing it with the ELD and examines what underlies its different rationales, with a particular interest in the position of the waste owner and holder; part 4 discusses the controversial application of the WFD to cases of accidental pollution and the possible clash between the two directives; and part 5 draws some conclusions regarding the individuation of the responsible party in order to secure the remediation of contaminated soils and their sustainable use.

2. LANDOWNER'S LIABILITY IN THE ELD

Regarding the remediation of contaminated soils, scholars and case law of the Court of Justice of European Union (hereinafter, Court of Justice or Court) have recently pointed out that there may be an overlap or even a clash between the ELD and the WFD.[8] This assumption could be surprising at first sight, since the two directives have very different scopes of application and rationales.

6 On the relationship between property and environment, see in particular Winter, G. (ed.) (2016) Environmental and Property Protection in Europe, The Avosetta Series (12), Proceedings of the Avosetta Group of European Environmental Lawyers, Europa Law Publishing, Groningen; Pozzo, B. (ed.) (2007) Property and Environment. Old and new remedies to protect natural resources in the European Context, Stampfli Publishers Ltd., Berne; Waite, A. and G. Jones QC and V. Fogleman (ed.) (2016) Waite and Jewell: Environmental Law in Property Transactions, Fourth Edition, Bloomsbury.

7 For further details see Pozzo, B. and B. Vanheusden and L. Bergkamp *et al.* (2015) 'The Remediation of Contaminated Sites and the Problem of Assessing the Liability of the Innocent Landowner: A Comparative Law Perspective', in ERPL, pp. 1071 ff.; Fogleman, V. (2015) 'Landowners' liability for remediating contaminated land in the EU: EU or national law?', Part II: National law', in 2 Env. Liability: Law, Policy and Practice, pp. 42 ff.

8 Valerie Fogleman was the first scholar who pointed out a possible clash between the ELD and the WFD in case of soil contamination. See in particular Fogleman, V. (2015) 'Landowners' liability for remediating contaminated land in the EU: EU or national law? Part I: EU law, 1 Env. Liability: Law, Policy and Practice', pp. 6 ff.; *Ibid.* (2015) 'Landowners' liability for remediating contaminated land in the EU: EU or national law? Part II: National law', in 2 Env. Liability: Law, Policy and Practice, pp. 42 ff.

As is well known, the ELD deals with the prevention and remediation of environmental damage and focuses on the activity that causes the environmental damage, which is defined as the damage to protected species and natural habitats, water damage and land damage. The latter in particular is 'any land contamination that creates a significant risk of human health being adversely affected as a result of the direct or indirect introduction, in, on or under land, of substances, preparations, organisms or micro-organisms'.[9] However, the ELD does not describe nor list the substances and objects that can cause environmental damage.

Consistently with the principles of civil liability,[10] the ELD sets forth that the 'operator'[11] – that is to say the person or undertaking whose activity[12] caused an imminent threat of, or actual environmental damage[13] – is liable for preventing and remediating the environmental damage. European legislation,[14] as interpreted by the Court of Justice,[15] is based on the 'polluter pays' principle, on the precautionary principle and on the principles of preventive action, which first of all aim at *preventing* environmental damage, implying that the liability must act as a deterrent for future polluting activities. This function is fully fulfilled only when legislation imposes liability upon the operator whose activities caused the damage and only if the operator could take into account this potential liability in its cost-benefit analysis: only if polluters know that they are liable in full for damage, will they take the necessary preventive measures so that damage does not occur in the first place.[16] To adopt an economic terminology, operators are incentivized to internalize the environmental costs. For example, they may prefer to adopt an environmentally less risky technology: the potentially higher costs are

9 See ELD, Article 2, 1 c).

10 See on this Hinteregger, M. (ed.) (2008) 'Environmental Liability and Ecological Damage In European Law', Cambridge University Press.

11 See Article 2, 6, ELD.

12 See Article 3 ELD; Annex III lists the activities for which an operator is strictly liable. Among these are waste management operations.

13 The definition of environmental damage includes damage to protected species and natural habitats, water damage and land damage; see Article 2, 1, of the ELD.

14 See in particular Article 191, point two, of the Treaty of the Functioning of the European Union.

15 Joined cases C-378/08, C-379/08 and C-380/08, *Raffinerie Mediterranee (ERG) SpA v Ministro dello Sviluppo economico* (see in particular para. 57); Case C-534/13, *Ministero dell'ambiente e della tutela del territorio e del mare v. Fipa Group s.r.l.* (*Fipa Group*). In all the above mentioned cases, the Advocate General was *Kokott*; see also her final opinions about the cases available at curia.europa.eu. These two decisions have been commented on in various reviews and journals; see, in particular, concerning ERG cases: Pozzo, B. (2011) 'Note a margine delle recenti iniziative comunitarie in materia di responsabilità ambientale', Riv. quad. dir. amb., pp. 94 ff.; concerning *Fipa Group Case:* Pozzo, B. and B. Vanheusden and L. Bergkamp *et al.* (2015) 'The Remediation of Contaminated Sites and the Problem of Assessing the Liability of the Innocent Landowner: A Comparative Law Perspective', in ERPL, pp. 1071 ff.; Fogleman, V. (2015) 'Landowners' liability for remediating contaminated land in the EU: EU or national law?', *supra* note 9.

16 AG *Kokott* opinion in the *Fipa Group* Case, para. 55.

compensated for by the decreased possibility of being held liable for environmental damage.[17] From a juridical point of view, it follows that in order for the environmental liability mechanism to be effective and, in case of litigation, for the responsibility to be ascertained, it is necessary to establish a causal link between the activity of the operator and the environmental damage.[18]

Consequently, most national legislation considers and applies the so-called 'landowner defence'; according to this, the mere owner of a contaminated land is not liable for decontaminating the soil if his activity has not caused the contamination. Advocate General (hereinafter AG) *Kokott*, in a recent Opinion released on the occasion of the *Fipa Group Case*,[19] has argued that, causation of environmental damage being a prerequisite for the duties laid down in the ELD, mere owners of damaged sites, who are not responsible for the damage, play no part in the system of the ELD. After the *Fipa Group* Case, this interpretation has been confirmed by other judgments of the Court of Justice concerning similar cases.[20]

Article 16 of the ELD left the possibility to Member States to introduce or maintain 'more stringent provisions'[21] and in particular provisions that identify '*additional responsible parties*' (emphasis added); the Court of Justice, in the same decision *Fipa Group*, ruled that this article means that, regarding cases that are under the temporal scope of application of the Directive, the inclusion of the landowner among the 'responsible' parties is a discretional decision of Member States. Only the legislation of three Member States (Austria, Hungary and Poland)[22] contain provisions that impose liability for preventing and remediating contaminated land and other environmental damage on a landowner who did not cause the damage.

---

17 See ELD, Recital 2. See also on this AG *Kokott* Opinion in *Raffinerie Mediterranee (ERG)* case, para 94; and AG *Kokott* Opinion in the *Fipa Group* Case, para. 55 (about the principle of preventive action). See also OECD, Recommendation of the Council on Guiding Principles Concerning International Economic Aspects of Environmental Policies (C (72) 128, 1972), where the 'polluter pays' principle was set up in an international context for the first official time.

18 See the *Fipa Group* Case, para. 54. See also recently Case C-129/16, *Túrkevei Tejtermelő Kft.*, para. 48.

19 See AG *Kokott* opinion in the *Fipa Group Case*, in particular paras. 30, 33, 37, 45.

20 See Case C-156/14, *Tamoil*, and Case C-592/13, *Ediltecnica*, where the Court considered the question referred identical to that of the *Fipa Group* Case and confirmed the same ruling in application of Article 99 of the Rules of Procedure of the Court of Justice of the European Union.

21 On the meaning of "more stringent measures", see Jans, J.H. and L. Squintani *et al.* (2009) '"Gold plating" of European Environmental Measures?', JEEPL, Vol. 4, pp. 417-435, where the authors show that Member States only sparingly and incidentally use their power to lay down or maintain more stringent environmental standards after European harmonization. See also Anker, H.T. *et al.* (2015) 'Coping with EU environmental legislation: transposition principles and practices', Journal of Environmental Law, Vol. 27, No. 1, pp. 17-44.

22 See on this Fogleman, V. (2015) 'Landowners' liability for remediating contaminated land in the EU: EU or national law? Part I: EU law', *supra* note 8, p. 9.

In particular Hungarian Law, recently scrutinized and 'approved' by the Court of Justice,[23] provides that, in the absence of proof to the contrary, the persons who own or are in possession of the land 'on which the environmental damage or hazard occurred' are to be held jointly and severally liable; the owners can discharge themselves of their liability only if they can identify the actual user of the land and can prove that they did not cause the damage themselves. However, the ELD prohibits a Member State from identifying additional responsible parties to replace the polluter who was liable under the Directive; this in particular means that additional responsible parties may have only secondary liability.[24]

3. THE WFD AND 'OWNER' RESPONSIBILITY

Contrary to the ELD, which, as seen in the previous paragraph, aims to prevent environmental damage and founds its liability mechanism upon the causal link between an activity and the environmental damage, the WFD pivots on the notion of 'waste' and aims to provide the legislative framework for the collection, transport, recovery and disposal of waste.

The WFD defines 'waste' as 'any substance or object which the holder discards or intends or is required to discard' (Article 3(1) WFD).[25] The current interpretation, supported by the Court of Justice, describes waste as any substance or an object that is of no use for anybody, nor the owner, who indeed has decided to discard it, nor anybody else.[26] Literature and case law underline that, in order to conclude that a substance/object is waste, it is necessary that the substance/object: 1) is commonly regarded as waste; 2) has a low economic value; 3) is a production residue; 4) is a residue for which no use other than disposal can be envisaged; 5) is being transferred to a disposal or recovery operation; 6) is a residue whose composition is not suitable for the use made of it or where special

23 See Case C-129/16, *Túrkevei Tejtermelő Kft. V Országos Környezetvédelmi és Természetvédelmi Főfelügyelőség*, paras. 57, 63.

24 See AG *Kokott* opinion in the *Fipa Group* Case, paras. 48, 54. See also on this Pozzo, B. and B. Vanheusden and L. Bergkamp *et al.* (2015) 'The Remediation of Contaminated Sites and the Problem of Assessing the Liability of the Innocent Landowner: A Comparative Law Perspective', *supra* note 16; Fogleman, V. (2015) 'Landowners' liability for remediating contaminated land in the EU: EU or national law? Part I: EU law', *supra* note 8, p. 7.

25 As known, there is a list of waste that is constantly updated; however, the inclusion in or exclusion from the list is not decisive in classifying a substance or an object as waste. See 2014/955/EU, Commission Decision of 18 December 2014 amending Decision 2000/532/EC on the list of waste pursuant to Directive 2008/98/EC of the European Parliament and of the Council Text with EEA relevance (in force).

26 Here we are not referring to waste as a 'resource' or the circular economy, but to waste as something discarded by their holders and that must be recovered or disposed of in accordance with the specific rules adopted by EU legislation.

precautions must be taken when using it owing to the environmentally hazardous nature of its composition.[27]

In the WFD, the responsible[28] person for appropriate management and treatment is either the producer and/or the holder of the waste. It is interesting to note that from the perspective of property law and as confirmed by the Court of Justice in the *Van de Walle* Case,[29] the original waste producer is formally the *owner* of the waste. This is not surprising since in the European civil codes influenced by the German pandectists[30] there is a rule that provides that if a person transforms a substance and creates a new movable thing from the former one, he becomes the owner of the new thing. In the case of waste, the original owner of the thing (e.g. an apple), when he consumes it, usually transforms this thing into a new one that has a specific individuality (e.g. the peel) and consequently, according to this rule, becomes its owner. As we shall see later, the transfer of ownership of this new thing (the waste) can happen only if the owner transfers it to an undertaking that is authorized to take it.

The WFD thus appears to be based on a different approach than the ELD, since the criterion for establishing the responsibility for management and disposal of waste pivots on the material relationship between the property (waste) and the person who is considered responsible for its proper management and disposal. The WFD can thus be seen as imposing a true case of responsibility depending only on the mere fact of being the owner/holder of a property (the

27 See, among a significant number of contributions on the topic, Jones, Q.C., G. and S. Sackman (2016) 'Waste', in Waite, A. and G. Jones Q.C. and V. Fogleman (ed.), Waite and Jewell: Environmental Law in Property Transactions, p. 376; de Sadeleer, N. (2012) 'Scrap Metal Intended for Metal Production: The Thin Line between Water and Products', JEEPL, Vol. 9, No. 2, pp. 136-163; Cheyne I. and M. Purdue (1995) 'Fitting Definition to Purpose: the Search for a Satisfactory Definition of Waste', JEL, Vol. 7, No. 2, p. 149; Cheyne, I. (2002) 'Definition of Waste in EC Law', JEL, Vol. 14. No. 1, pp. 61-73; de Sadeleer, N. (2005) 'Rifiuti, Residui e Sottoprodotti: una trilogia ambigua', Rivista Giuridica dell'Ambiente; Kramer, L. (2003) 'The Distinction between Product and Waste in Community Law', Environmental Liability II: I, pp. 3-14; de Sadeleer, N. (2005) 'EC Waste Law or How to Juggle with Legal Concepts', JEEPL, Vol. 6, p. 458.

28 Regarding the difference between 'liability' and 'responsibility', see Fogleman, V. 'Landowners' liability for remediating contaminated land in the EU: EU or national law? Part I: EU law', *supra* note 8, pp. 8 and 18.

29 See para. 55. According to the Court of Justice (see Case C-113/12, *Brady*, para. 51 and Case C-188/07, *Commune de Mesquer*, para. 74), the person who is in fact in possession of products immediately before they become waste must be regarded as having 'produced' that waste and thus be categorized as its 'holder'.

30 See Section 950 BGB: Processing (1) A person who, by processing or transformation of one or more substances, creates a new movable thing acquires the ownership of the new thing, except where the value of the processing or the transformation is substantially less than the value of the substance. Processing also includes writing, drawing, painting, printing, engraving or a similar processing of the surface. (2) On the acquisition of ownership of the new thing, the existing rights in the substance are extinguished. See also Article 940 Italian civil code and, even if Switzerland is not part of the European Union, Article 726 Swiss civil code. In literature, see Gambaro, A. (1998), 'Specificazione', Digesto discipline privatistiche, Utet, Torino.

waste). This is a property-based responsibility and does not originate from the commission of an illegal act or omission and is not linked to an activity. According to case law and literature,[31] the mere fact of holding waste implies the duty not to abandon it and the duty to recover or dispose of waste in accordance with the provisions of EU legislation. In this case, the 'polluter pays' principle operates differently than in the ELD; according to the Court of Justice, responsibility for waste management is allocated to the waste producer (the owner) or to the current or previous waste holders[32] because these persons contributed to the 'creation of the waste and, in certain cases, to the consequent risk of pollution'.[33]

AG *Kokott* in her opinion in the *Van de Walle* Case as well as other scholars[34] comment that the concept of 'holder' is broader than that of 'owner', since it covers all the persons likely to get rid of the waste. According to this view, this concept is also autonomous from the traditional concept of holder for the purposes of private law. Indeed, in the WFD the 'holder' must, but also *can*, dispose of the waste, which implies that they have the power to extinguish the proprietary rights over the object.

This conclusion, at a closer view, seems not to be convincing. Let's think of the case in which the waste has a positive economic value, such as the gold or silver residue of jewel production. This, according to scholars and case law,[35] is technically waste and must be handled according to EU directives. If the gold residue is transferred to a holder without the specific instruction to get rid of it, it is hardly arguable that the holder has the power to dispose of the waste. Owners only can dispose of their property; the holder can be their representative and act on their behalf but cannot have the power to extinguish some else's proprietary right.

Article 15 of the WFD also sets out, even if not directly, how proprietary rights are transferred to different subjects. Indeed, according to this article, the responsibility for the proper handling of waste is extended to all persons from production to disposal; a person's responsibility extends beyond the point when they hand in the waste to another party, unless the consignee is legally authorized to take the waste and carry out recovery or disposal operations. This is confirmed

31 See in particular authors quoted at note 27; Case C-113/12, *Brady*, para. 74.

32 See the WFD, Article 14. Responsibility may be borne also by the producer of the product: so-called extended producer responsibility.

33 Case C-188/07, *Commune de Mesquer v Total France SA*, para. 77; Case C-254/08, *Futura Immobiliare srl Hotel Futura v. Comune di Casoria*, para. 45.

34 See de Sadeleer, N. (2006) 'Case C-1/03, *Paul Van de Walle*, Judgment of the Court (Second Chamber) of 7 September 2004', Common Market Law Review, 43, pp. 207-223, p. 217. See also AG *Kokott* in the opinion on *Van de Walle* Case, para. 56.

35 See on this de Sadeleer, N. (2005) 'EC Waste Law or How to Juggle with Legal Concept', JEEPL, Vol. 6, p. 464 and p. 467; Case C-359/88, *Vessoso and Zanetti*.

by the recent *Brady* case[36] where the Court of Justice, although discussing the interpretation of Articles 8 and 10 of Directive 75/442/EEC, stated that where a holder of waste has it handled by private or public waste collector or by an undertaking that obtained a permit from the competent authority to carry out waste recovery operations listed in Annex II B, the undertaking only, and not the earlier holder of that waste, is responsible for carrying out the recovery operations.

From the perspective of private law, Article 15 also means that only when the waste is handed in to an authorized establishment or undertaking, are proprietary rights and ownership transferred to that undertaking; there may be cases where the owner or the holder (on behalf of the owner) pays the person who is supposed to carry out the disposal or cases where the undertaking pays the holder/owner; in the latter case, it is likely to be a recovery operation.[37] By contrast, the contract between the owner and an establishment which is not authorized to take the waste does not transfer ownership and is void.

4. THE WFD AND THE CASE OF ACCIDENTAL POLLUTION

According to the so-called subjective approach to the notion of waste, its definition pivots on the notion of 'discard',[38] which usually implies a voluntary act.[39]

In 2004 the Case C-1/03, *Van de Walle*, has put into question this assumption for the first time. The Court argued that petrol accidentally spilled by a petrol station and mixed with soil, as well as the soil contaminated by it, were to be considered 'waste' and subject to the specific regulation of the WFD, which, as seen in the previous paragraph, imposes responsibility on the waste owners and holders. This interpretation has recently, on other occasions, been proposed

36 Case C-113/12, *Brady*; see in particular, paras. 80-81.

37 See on this de Sadeleer, N. (2005) 'EC Waste Law or How to Juggle with Legal Concept', JEEPL, Vol. 6, p. 475.

38 See on this, de Sadeleer, N. (2006) 'Case C-1/03, *Paul Van de Walle*, *supra* note 34, p. 213 (and their further references). On the meaning of 'discard', there are many judgments of the Court of Justice, which have been commented by scholars. See in particular Joined Cases C-206/88 and C-207/88, *Vessoso and Zanetti*; Case C-194/05, *Commission v Italy*, para. 32; Case C-188/07, *Commune de Mesquer*, para. 53; Case C-113/12, *Brady*, paras. 38-39. For further reference, see also de Sadeleer, N. (2012) 'Scrap Metal Intended for Metal Production: The Thin Line between Water and Products', p. 144.

39 See de Sadeleer, N. (2005) 'New Perspectives on the Definition of Waste in EC Law', JEEPL, Vol. 1, p. 55 and n. 58, where the author quotes the papers where it is argued that it was not possible to equate the abandonment of waste for the purposes of Article 4.2 of the Waste Directive with the accidental discharge of pollutant into the soil.

again[40] and may lead to attributing liability and responsibility to the owners of the contaminated soils, even if they did not contribute to the spillage and thus, technically speaking, are not the causer of the land damage.

In the *Van de Walle* Case an oil company (Texaco) leased buildings and premises from a public legal entity ('the landowner') in order to set up a service station; it then signed an operating agreement with an operator who would run the petrol station ('the operator'). According to the agreement, Texaco would provide the land, building and movable property to the operator as well as supply the oil. Afterwards, it was found that fuel had leaked from the service station's storage tanks, causing soil and groundwater contamination. Hydrocarbons were thus, and no question about that, spilled accidentally.

The Court of Justice ruled that the hydrocarbons were waste as was the soil contaminated by them; consequently the Court applied the directive on waste that was in force at that time (Directive 75/442/EEC as amended by Directive 91/156/EEC). In crucial passages, the judgment reads that 'it is clear that accidentally spilled hydrocarbons which cause soil and groundwater contamination are not a product which can be re-used without processing … those hydrocarbons are therefore substances which the holder did not intend to produce and which he discards, albeit involuntarily, at the time of the production or distribution operations which relate to them'.[41] In another paragraph, the Court stated that 'the hydrocarbons cannot be separated from the land which they have contaminated and cannot be recovered or disposed of unless that land is also subject to the necessary decontamination'.[42]

Both the oil company that supplied petrol to the service station as well as the manager/operator of the service station were judged liable: in particular, Texaco was considered the producer of the hydrocarbons and former holder of the waste and thus responsible according to Articles 8 and 15 of the Directive 75/442/EEC; the operator, as the service station's manager and buyer of the oil, was in possession of the hydrocarbons and had them in stock when they became waste, so he could be considered the person who 'produced' them according to Articles 1 and 15.[43]

The judgment also left room for attributing liability to the owner of the sites where the service station was built. Since the Court of Justice argued that the contaminated soil also can be classified as 'waste', it follows that the landowner could be considered 'holder' of waste; however, in the specific case, the landowner (a public legal entity) was not judged responsible. Other judgments of the Court of Justice and some passages of AG *Kokott*'s Opinions reached similar

40 See below.
41 Para. 47.
42 Para. 52.
43 Paras. 59-60.

conclusions, suggesting that the landowners could be considered responsible for soil decontamination as holders of waste.[44]

The *Van de Walle* ruling, jointly with other issues related to the protection of soil, triggered a debate about a new directive on soil. As mentioned in the introduction, on 22 September 2006 the Commission adopted the Thematic Strategy for Soil Protection (COM(2006) 231), which included a 'Proposal for a Directive of the European Parliament and of the Council establishing a framework for the protection of soil and amending Directive 2004/35/EC'. Unfortunately, the proposal was withdrawn in 2014.[45] Even if the debate did not flow into a new comprehensive directive, at least it led to the adoption of the soil exclusion from the WFD in 2008; in the words of the Directive, 'land (in situ) including unexcavated contaminated soil and buildings permanently connected with land' are excluded from the scope of the WFD.[46] This exclusion is convincing also because Article 3(1) of the WFD defines waste as a 'substance' or an 'object', which suggests that an immovable property (such an unexcavated contaminated soil is)[47] cannot be considered waste.

However, scholars[48] underline that this exclusion still raises many doubts and does not resolve all the possible overlaps between the two pieces of legislation; moreover, AG *Kokott* has recently suggested that, in the case of accidental pollution, even if claims must first be addressed against the causer of environmental damage, it does not appear to be impossible to make subordinate claims against otherwise uninvolved owners of polluted sites as holders of waste.[49] AG's argument focuses on the fact that 'if a polluting substance becomes waste as a result of the pollution, this property can hardly lapse just because it is mixed with the soil'. If applied extensively, as already observed, this conclusion may lead to attributing the responsibility for a soil decontamination to the current landowners even if they did not cause the contamination.

The abovementioned AG *Kokott's* statement is an *obiter dictum* inserted in an Opinion that she issued in relation to the *Fipa Group* case, already commented on in the previous paragraph; in this case the defendants were three landowners who

---

44 See Case C-252/05, *R (Thames Water Utilities Ltd) v Bromley Magistrates' Court*; Case C-188/07, *Commune de Mesquer v Total France SA*; AG *Kokott* Opinion, case C-378/08, *Erg and Others c. Italia*, paras. 130-138. See Fogleman, V. (2015), *supra* note 8, p. 15.

45 Regarding the debate about the possible exclusion of contaminated soil from the scope of application of the Waste Framework Directive, see also de Sadeleer, N. (2006), *supra* note 34, p. 219.

46 '*In situ*' means in the original position; it includes lands that have not been excavated. 'Contaminated soil' means, according to the Commission, a soil that 'exhibits any of the properties of waste which render it hazardous' as per Annex III to the WFD.

47 By contrast, excavated soil is capable of being waste. For an English case, see Waite and Jewell: Environmental Law in Property Transactions, p. 379.

48 See Fogleman, V. (2015), *supra* note 8, p. 16.

49 See AG *Kokott* Opinion in the *Fipa Group Case*, paras. 72, 76.

acquired polluted sites from the polluter himself. As discussed in the judgment at length, the landowners were surely not responsible for the soil contamination and maybe even 'innocent', in the sense that they did not know that the sites were polluted when they acquired them. Indeed, the polluter had already carried out some clean-up measures, and only afterwards it emerged that the decontamination had not been completely successful.[50] The question referred to the Court of Justice regarded the interpretation of the ELD and in particular of its Article 16, and did not mention the possible application of the WFD to the case; thus, this issue was not considered by the Court.

However, there are several considerations that should lead to the conclusion that in case of accidental pollution the causer of contamination only, and not the landowner, should be considered liable for decontamination.

First, from the perspective of private law, the reasoning by AG *Kokott* seems to overlook that when a substance is mixed with another one, the national civil codes provide rules about who becomes the owner of the mixed substance, but provides also that in certain cases the owner of the thing of less value must pay damages to the counterpart; this applies in particular when the union was not wanted by the owner of the principal thing (*invito domino*).[51] This is true with regard to Italian civil code,[52] the French civil code,[53] and the German BGB.[54] It follows that even if the landowners are considered responsible according to the WFD, they could then ask for being reimbursed by the operator whose activity caused the infiltration of the substance/waste into the soil. The ultimate liability, thus, is borne by the causer of the environmental damage, which is consistent with the 'polluter pays' principle as expressed in the ELD.

---

50 As it is well known in literature, the US federal legislation and in particular the Comprehensive Environmental Response Compensation Liability Act (CERCLA), as amended by the Small Business Liability Relief and Brownfields Revitalization Act in 2002, distinguishes the position of the 'innocent' landowner from that of the '*bona-fide*' purchaser of a contaminated land. The 'innocent landowner' is any natural or juridical person who acquires property and had no knowledge of the contamination at the time of purchase.

51 See on this for a perspective of private comparative law: Pozzo, B. (1999) 'Unione', Digesto discipline privatistiche, Utet, Torino.

52 Italian civil code, Article 939, last paragraph: Compensation for damage is also due in case of gross negligence.

53 French civil code, Article 577: Those who have made use of materials belonging to others, and without their knowledge, may also be ordered to pay damages, if there is occasion, without prejudice to criminal prosecution, if need be.

54 BGB Section 951, Compensation for loss of rights: (1) A person who, as a result of the provisions of sections 946 to 950, suffers a loss of rights may require from the person to whose benefit the change of rights occurs payment in money under the provisions on the return of unjust enrichment. The restoration of the former state cannot be required. (2) The provisions on the obligation to pay damages for torts and the provisions on the reimbursement of outlays made and on the right of removal of an installation are unaffected. In the cases of sections 946 and 947, the removal under the provisions applying to the right of removal of the possessor in relation to the owner is admissible even if the combination was not made by the possessor of the main thing.

Moreover, according to the principles of private law one acquires the status of 'holder' only when one takes delivery of the property, which implies the consent of both the consignor and the consignee; in case of accidental pollution, it is hard to see a 'delivery' of the waste from a previous holder to the current one. Equalizing the position of a voluntary holder to that of an involuntary one seems an interpretation that cannot be argued from the legislation in force. Consequently, in case of accidental contamination of soil, it cannot be argued that the landowner takes delivery of the 'waste' and apparently there is no room for application of the directives on waste management.

The case of illegal dumping of waste in someone else's land, recalled also by AG *Kokott,*[55] seems to be different. Of course, landowners are not obliged to fence their sites, but most of the time there are some precautions that landowners can and must take in order to avoid illegal deposit on their land; this is especially true when the illegal dumping is frequent in certain areas or is repeated several times. If landowners do not take any precautions and the waste is deposited in their land, they will then be obliged to manage (recover or dispose of) it according to the WFD. In any case, the landowners could then claim damages from the causer of the illegal dumping (if identifiable) according to the rules of civil liability or even ask for remedial measures according to the ELD itself, if applicable.

5. CONCLUSIONS

More than 10 years ago the *Van de Walle* Case triggered the debate about the possible overlap between environmental liability and waste responsibility. Considering contaminated soil as waste, the case also opened the discussion about the possibility of considering the landowner, in his capacity as holder of the waste, responsible for waste management and for soil decontamination in addition to (or even in substitution of) the causer of the contamination which led to the environmental damage, who would be liable according to the ELD. More recently, in her opinions, AG *Kokott* has underlined that when a substance is waste, it does not lose this quality just because it is mixed with soil; this again opens the door to claims against otherwise uninvolved owners of polluted sites as holders of waste in addition to claims against the polluter.[56]

The identification of liable/responsible party in case of soil contamination and in particular the question whether the landowner can be involved in the procedure of soil decontamination are urgent. As stated in various occasions by the institutions of the European Union and by the United Nations, soil

55 See AG *Kokott* Opinion in *Fipa Group Case*, para. 57.

56 AG Opinion *Fipa Group Case*, paras. 72, 76.

degradation has become a serious challenge and the remediation of contaminated sites and soil sustainable use is a priority.

As we have seen in this chapter, the application of the WFD to cases of polluted soils and the following allocation of responsibilities for remediating them to their owners, contradicts one of the key points of the liability system established by the ELD. According to this directive, a person or undertaking ('the operator') can be considered liable for environmental damages and under the duty to remediate it only if there is evidence of a causal link between an activity carried out by the operator and the environmental damage. AG *Kokott* in the *Fipa Group* case Opinion[57] argued that causation of environmental damage is a prerequisite for the duties laid down in the ELD and that mere owners of damaged sites, who are not responsible for the damage, play no part in the system of the ELD. Subsequent judgments of the Court of Justice, even recently, have confirmed this interpretation.[58] As scholars also have pointed out,[59] neither the ELD nor the WFD has priority over the other directive concerning the duty to remediate environmental damage, so it cannot be argued that the WFD must be applied even if it contradicts with the ELD.

This chapter also tries to argue that in case of accidental pollution, the WFD cannot be invoked since this directive regards the voluntary transfer of possession of the waste and its responsibility system, which allocates the responsibility to the owner and/or the holder of waste, to be justified only if the holder has accepted the possession of the waste voluntarily. Moreover, when a substance is mixed with another one and this union was not wanted by the owner of the thing that is more valuable, most national civil codes provide that the owner of the thing of lesser value must pay damages to the counterpart. This means that in case a substance (waste) is mixed with soil without the landowner's consent, the latter could ask for damages from the causer of the mixture. It follows that even if the landowner was considered holder of the waste, the ultimate liability would be borne by the causer of the contamination.

In conclusion, regarding environmental damage, the allocation of responsibilities to the landowners is possible only if specific national provisions establish this responsibility explicitly (this is the case in three Member States of the European Union and in particular in Hungary) and provided that, according to Article 16, these additional responsible parties are secondarily liable only. Regarding waste management, the related responsibilities lie with the waste owner or holder only if they accepted the possession of the waste voluntarily; 'unwanted' delivery is an issue that must be ruled according to civil liability principles.

---

57 See in particular paras. 30, 33, 37, 45.

58 See para. 3 in this chapter, in particular footnote 20.

59 See Fogleman, V. (2015), *supra* note 9, p. 21.

As mentioned in the opening of this chapter, a significant portion of the European territory still requires clean-up and remedial measures in order to halt health risks, loss of biodiversity as well and to guarantee a sustainable use of the soil for the future. However, it is necessary to allocate liability consistently with the EU principles and in particular with the 'polluter pays' principle and the principle of prevention of environmental damage, which implies that primary liability must be borne by the polluter whose activity caused the contamination and not by non-responsible landowners.

PART IV

ENVIRONMENTAL AND CLIMATE LITIGATION

CHAPTER 7

THE EUROPEAN COURT OF HUMAN RIGHTS: AN UNDERRATED FORUM FOR ENVIRONMENTAL LITIGATION

Natalia Kobylarz*

ABSTRACT

Since the 1960s, the ECHR organs have examined over 270 applications related to the protection or the degradation of the natural environment. This chapter offers a selective, systematised and up-to-date analysis of this vast body of case law and of applications pending the Court's examination. It explores the implications of the ECHR general principles for environmental litigation, in particular, the notions of "direct victim", "serious specific and imminent danger", "minimum level of disturbance", and "wide margin of appreciation". Whenever warranted, it applauds the Court's acceptance of surrogate protection of the environment through civil and political rights and the doctrine of positive obligations, or voices criticism of its conservative approach to giving precedence to economic considerations over the environmental harm. It then takes a forward-looking view on the work of the ECtHR, focusing on its dynamic and evolutive approach to the interpretation of the scope of the ECHR-protected rights and the cross-fertilisation of ideas which is occurring between the ECtHR and the IACtHR. Ultimately, it predicts that wise and widespread environmental litigation can

* The author holds a Master of Law degree from the University of Maria Curie-Sklodowska in Lublin, Poland and an LL.M. degree in International and Comparative Law from the Southern Methodist University in Dallas, United States (natalia.kobylarz@echr.coe.int). She works as a senior lawyer at the Registry of the ECtHR. She teaches an in-house Green Human Rights course and is the founder of the "Work Green" initiative, which aims at making the Council of Europe an environment-friendly workplace. In 2016 she was seconded to the Inter-American Court of Human Rights as adviser on the European human rights jurisprudence. The views expressed in this chapter are those of the author and do not necessarily represent the views of the ECtHR.

make the ECtHR start to employ ecological rationality in explaining the value of nature in cases in which its protection paradoxically seems to collide with conventionally-perceived anthropocentric rights.

1. INTRODUCTION

The European Convention on Human Rights ("the ECHR" or "the Convention") does not guarantee a substantive right to a healthy environment[1] and none of its provisions are specifically designed to ensure the general protection or the preservation of nature.[2] But the link between the environment and human rights intrinsically exists.

The theoretical bedrock of this assertion was laid down in the 1972 Stockholm Declaration on the Human Environment and was developed over the years by various authorities, including the Inter-American Court of Human Rights ("IACtHR") in its most recent Advisory Opinion on the Environment and Human Rights.[3] A thriving natural environment is, therefore, a precondition to the enjoyment of human rights; human rights law can be used as a tool to address environmental issues from both a substantive and procedural stance;[4] and both are necessary for sustainable development.[5]

This nexus is also clearly manifested in the practice of the ECHR organs which have regularly been seized to respond to grievances related to the

1 Recommendations have been made to the member states of the Council of Europe (via the Council of Europe's Committee of Ministers) that an additional protocol to the ECHR be drawn up to create the right to a healthy environment as a basic human right and to enhance the environmental protection through procedural rights as set out in the Aarhus Convention (see, Recommendations of the Council of Europe's Parliamentary Assembly nos. 1431 (1999); 1614 (2003), 1883 (2009) and 1885 (2009)). The Committee of Ministers has invariably considered such an additional protocol redundant since the ECHR system already indirectly contributes to the protection of the environment through existing Convention rights and their interpretation in the evolving case law of the ECtHR.

2 *Inter alia*, *X. v. Federal Republic of Germany* (dec.), no. 7407/76, 13 May 1976; *Kyrtatos v. Greece*, no. 41666/98, § 52, ECHR 2003-VI; *Hamer v. Belgium*, no. 21861/03, § 79, ECHR 2007-V (extracts); *Turgut and Others v. Turkey*, no. 1411/03, § 90, 8 July 2008; and *Dubetska and Others v. Ukraine*, no. 30499/03, § 105, 10 February 2011.

3 Corte Interamericana de Derechos Humanos, Opinión Consultiva OC-23/17 "Obligaciones estatales en relación con el medio ambiente en el marco de la protección y garantía de los derechos a la vida y a la integridad personal – interpretación y alcance de los Artículos 4.1 y 5.1, en relación con los artículos 1.1. y 2 de la Convención Americana Sobre Derechos Humanos, § § 47-70, del 15 de noviembre 2017.

4 Manual on human rights and the environment, 2nd edition, 2012, Council of Europe Publishing, p. 8.

5 Transforming our world: the 2030 Agenda for Sustainable Development, Resolution adopted by the General Assembly on 25 September 2015.

protection or the degradation of the natural environment. Since the 1960s,[6] the European Court of Human Rights ("the ECtHR" or "the Court") and the previously existing European Commission of Human Rights, have issued, by the author's count, approximately 270 such environment-related rulings. Some of these constitute foundational pronouncements of new principles which allow human rights law – which is traditionally ignorant of any environmental considerations – to address contemporary planetary conundrums.[7] Others are day-to-day decisions which test these legal precedents in a wide range of real-life circumstances and which offer solutions to often systemic or repetitive problems.[8] All in all, these environment-related rulings prove that the European system of human rights protection efficiently safeguards the environment by proxy of first-generation human rights, the scope of which is constantly evolving[9] and which

6 The first environment-related case, Schmidt v. Federal Republic of Germany (dec.), no. 715/60, was decided by the Commission on 5 August 1960.

7 *Inter alia*, *López Ostra v. Spain*, 9 December 1994, Series A no. 303-C, concerning lack of response to pollution caused by a waste-treatment plant operating without licence; *Guerra and Others v. Italy*, 19 February 1998, Reports of Judgments and Decisions 1998-I, concerning failure to provide local population with information about risks of accident at a nearby chemical factory and about possible emergency procedures; *Chassagnou and Others v. France* [GC], nos. 25088/94 and two others, ECHR 1999-III, concerning obligation of land-owners to allow hunting on their property and obligatory membership of hunting associations; *Hatton and Others v. the United Kingdom* [GC], no. 36022/97, ECHR 2003-VIII, concerning noise nuisance due to night flies operated at Heathrow Airport; *Öneryıldız v. Turkey* [GC], no. 48939/99, ECHR 2004-XII, concerning loss of life and property resulting from an accidental explosion at a rubbish tip close to illegal shanty town; *Taşkın and Others v. Turkey*, no. 46117/99, ECHR 2004-X, concerning pollution due to sodium cyanide leaching used for gold extraction from a mine located in an earthquake zone, operating under invalidated permit; *Fadeyeva v. Russia*, no. 55723/00, ECHR 2005-IV, concerning failure to resettle a family living in a severely polluted area and to design or apply effective measures to reduce industrial pollution; *Giacomelli v. Italy*, no. 59909/00, ECHR 2006-XII, 2 November 2006, concerning lack of prior EIA and failure to suspend unlawful operation of a waste plant generating toxic emissions; and *Tătar v. Romania*, no. 67021/01, 27 January 2009, concerning failure to assess risks and consequences of hazardous industrial activity of gold and silver mining with sodium cyanide and to keep the public informed.

8 *Inter alia*, *Nikas and Nika v. Greece*, no. 31273/04, 13 July 2006, concerning revocation of exemption from reforestation without summoning affected land owners of farming land unsuitable for forestation, implying prohibition of future construction, and lack of suspensive effect of judicial review; *Ledyayeva and Others v. Russia*, nos. 53157/99, 53247/99, 53695/00 and 56850/00, 26 October 2006, similar to *Fadeyeva*, cited above; *Şatır v. Turkey*, no. 36192/03, 10 March 2009, concerning revocation of title to private land without compensation on grounds that it was part of public forest estate; *Kolyadenko and Others v. Russia*, nos. 17423/05 and 5 others, 28 February 2012, concerning loss of home and property and risk to life resulting from a flash flood caused by opening, without warning, of reservoir during heavy rain; *Frank Eckenbrcht and Heinz Ruhmer v. Germany* (dec.), no. 25330/10, 10 June 2014, concerning noise nuisance from Lepizig Halle Airport; and *Cuenca Zarzoso v. Spain*, no. 23383/12, 16 January 2018, concerning noise and night-time disturbances from private bars in Valencia.

9 *Inter alia*, *Marckx v. Belgium*, 13 June 1979, § 41, Series A no. 31 and *Stafford v. the United Kingdom* [GC], no. 46295/99, § 68, ECHR 2002-IV.

are recognised as being interdependent and indivisible from economic and social rights.[10]

2. OVERVIEW OF THE ENVIRONMENT-RELATED CASE LAW OF THE ECtHR

The largest group of the environment-related judgments and decisions delivered by the ECHR organs, numbering nearly 110, concerns the balancing of states' ecologically sound policies with individuals' rights to the peaceful enjoyment of property or respect for home and private and family life. Cases in this group arose out of measures such as the expropriation of private land or the demolition of dwellings in areas of protected coastline in Turkey,[11] or in areas designated for reforestation in Greece.[12] They also concern restrictions put in place by the governments of various European states to ensure a sustainable use of natural resources[13] or the protection of endangered species[14] and biological diversity.[15]

The remaining cases illustrate the other side of the coin – that is to say, ecologically unfriendly operations and urban development resulting in pollution, environmental disasters, occupational illnesses or nuisance, in so far as they may threaten the right to life or the right to a respect for home and private and family life. Thus, the Court has ruled over forty times in respect of: toxic emissions caused by the operation of nuclear plants and power stations, for example, in Switzerland[16] and Georgia;[17] factories and smelters, mainly in Italy[18] and Romania;[19] gold and coal mines in Turkey[20] and Ukraine;[21] and of waste-

10 Separate opinion of Judge Pinto de Albuquerque in *Konstantin Markin v. Russia* [GC], no. 30078/06, ECHR 2012 (extracts), and IACtHR's OC 23-17, cited above § 57.

11 *N.A. and Others v. Turkey*, no. 37451/97, ECHR 2005-X.

12 *Papastavrou and Others v. Greece*, no. 46372/99, ECHR 2003-IV.

13 *Pindstrup Mosebrug A/S v. Denmark* (dec.), no. 34943/06, 3 June 2008.

14 Paratheristikos Oikodomikos Synetairismos Stegaseos Ypallilon Trapezis Tis Ellados v. Greece, No. 2998/08, 3 May 2011.

15 *Annika Jacobson v. Sweden* (dec.), no. 59122/08, 22 May 2012 and *Valle Pierimpiè Società Agricola S.P.A v. Italy*, no. 46154/11, 23 September 2014.

16 *Balmer-Schafroth e.a v. Switzerland* [GC], no. 22110/93, 26 August 1997 and *Athanassoglou and Others v. Switzerland* [GC], no. 27644/95, ECHR 2000-IV.

17 *Jugheli and Others v. Georgia*, no. 38342/05, 13 July 2017.

18 *Guerra and Others*, cited above and *Smaltini v. Italy* (dec.), no. 43961/09, 24 March 2015.

19 *Băcilă v. Romania*, no. 19234/04, 30 March 2010.

20 *Taşkın and Others*, cited above; *Öçkan and Others v. Turkey*, no. 46771/99, 28 March 2006; *Lemke v. Turkey*, no. 17381/02, 5 June 2007; and *Genç and Demirgan v. Turkey*, nos. 34327/06 and 45165/06, 10 October 2017.

21 *Dubetska and Others*, cited above.

treatment plants or dumpsters, in Italy,[22] Norway[23] and Spain.[24] One group of ten cases concerns environmental disasters – natural and man-made – such as flash floods[25] or the explosion of methane generated by decomposing refuse in a city landfill.[26] The Court has also examined eight applications brought by people from countries such as the United Kingdom, France and Malta who claimed to be the victims of nuclear or military gas tests,[27] or who worked with hazardous substances.[28] A group of close to sixty rulings concern nuisance (mainly noise, smell or general disturbance) resulting from urban development. These cases range from judgments on the inconveniences of large-scale airport traffic across Europe[29] to more trivial problems such as fireworks displays in Malta[30] or the operation of private night bars in residential areas in Spain.[31]

An analysis of the Court's environment-related case law would not be complete without the last group of over forty judgments and decisions concerning various forms of ecological activism. These were mainly argued under the right to exercise free speech,[32] or freedom of assembly[33] or under procedural rights to obtain information[34] or judicial review of policies threatening the environment.[35]

---

22 *Giacomelli*, cited above and related, *Di Sarno and Others v. Italy*, no. 30765/08, 10 January 2012.

23 *Moe and Others v. Norway* (dec.), no. 30966/96, 14 December 1999.

24 *López Ostra*, cited above.

25 *Murillo Saldias and Othes v. Spain* (dec.), no. 76973/01, 28 November 2006; *Kolyadenko and Others*, cited above and related, *Hadzhiyska v. Bulgaria* (dec.), no. 20701/09, 15 May 2012.

26 *Öneryıldız,* cited above.

27 *Tauria and 18 others v. France* (dec.), no. 28204/95, 4 December 1995; *McGinley and Egan v. the United Kingdom*, 9 June 1998, Reports of Judgments and Decisions 1998-III; *L.C.B. v. the United Kingdom*, 9 June 1998, Reports of Judgments and Decisions 1998-III; and *Roche v. the United Kingdom* [GC], no. 32555/96, ECHR 2005-X.

28 *Howald Moor and Others v. Switzerland,* nos. 52067/10 and 41072/11, 11 March 2014 and *Brincat and Others v. Malta*, nos. 60908/11 and 4 others, 24 July 2014.

29 *Inter alia*, *Hatton and Others*, cited above.

30 *Zammit Maempel v. Malta*, no. 24202/10, 22 November 2011.

31 *Inter alia*, *Moreno Gómez v. Spain*, no. 4143/02, ECHR 2004-X.

32 *Inter alia*, *Verein gegen Tierfabriken Schweiz (VgT) v. Switzerland* (no. 2) [GC], no. 32772/02, ECHR 2009.

33 *Inter alia*, *Zeleni Balkani v. Bulgaria*, no. 63778/00, 12 April 2007 and *Schneider v. Luxembourg*, no. 2113/04, 10 July 2007.

34 *Sdruzeni Jihoceske Matky v. the Czech Republic* (dec.) 19101/03, 10 July 2006 and *Guseva v. Bulgaria*, no. 6987/07, 17 February 2015.

35 *Štefanec v. the Czech Republic*, no. 75615/01, 18 July 2006; *Collectif national d'information et d'opposition à l'usine Melox – Collectif Stop Melox and Mox v. France*, no. 75218/01, 12 June 2007; *L'Erablière A.S.B.L. v. Belgium*, no. 49230/07, ECHR 2009 (extracts); *Lesoochranarske zoskupenie Vlk v. Slovakia* (dec.), no. 53246/08, 2 October 2012; and *Valentina Viktorovna Oglobina v. Russia* (dec.), no. 28852/05, 26 November 2013.

On top of this, about a dozen communicated applications concerning the environment are currently pending before the Court[36] and some 200, involving over 4,000 applicants, are awaiting processing. At the moment, Italy and Turkey are the two countries which face the most environmental litigation before the ECtHR in the form of the "class action" applications concerning pollution caused by waste disposal or mining and the steel industry.

How many of these 270 environment-related rulings were actually on nature's side can only be judged after a thorough analysis, not only of the operative part of each decision, but also of the reasoning in so far as it may contain newly formulated general principles - possibly leading to the evolution of the Court's own jurisprudence and inspiring the development of domestic case law. It is also equally important to study the process by which the relevant judgments were executed and to look beyond the particular circumstances of each case because the general measures, which are ordered for environmental human rights violations, benefit not only individual applicants but also other members of current and future generations.

3. IMPLICATIONS OF THE ECHR GENERAL PRINCIPLES FOR ENVIRONMENTAL LITIGATION

The Strasbourg system aims at ensuring the genuine and practical exercise of rights guaranteed by the Convention.[37] This is why the state parties must not only refrain from interfering with the exercise of these rights, but also (under the well-established and widely operating doctrine of positive obligations) take the necessary legal and/or practical measures to actively safeguard them.[38] Moreover, the protection of most Convention rights depends on the balancing of various interests which may be at stake in a democratic society. To this end, the ECtHR accepts that the protection of the environment is an increasingly important

36 *Ningur Noyanalpan and Others v. Turkey*, no. 26660/05; *Erol Cicek and Others v. Turkey*, no. 44837/07; *Locascia and Others v. Italy*, no. 35648/10; *Vecbaštika and Others v. Latvia*, no. 52499/11; *Ivan Kozul and Others v. Bosnia and Herzegovina*, no. 38695/13; *Cordella and Others v. Italy*, no. 54414/13; *Kapa and 3 others v. Poland*, no. 75031/13; *Aleksandar Mastelica and Others v. Serbia*, no. 14901/15; *Lina Ambrogi Melle and Others v. Italy*, no. 54264/15; *O'Sullivan Mc Carthy Mussel Development Ltd v. Ireland*, no. 44460/16.

37 *Case "relating to certain aspects of the laws on the use of languages in education in Belgium"* (merits), 23 July 1968, Series A no. 6; *Marckx*, cited above, § 31; and *X and Y v. the Netherlands*, 26 March 1985, § § 23, 24 and 27, Series A no. 91.

38 *Airey v. Ireland*, 9 October 1979, Series A no. 32, p. 17, § 32; *Guerra and Others*, cited above, § 60; and *Öneryıldız*, cited above, § § 89 and 90.

consideration in society[39] and that it should not be subservient to financial imperatives or, even to certain fundamental rights, such as ownership.[40] The rulings of the Convention organs, especially in the largest "balanced protection" category, clearly demonstrate – what may surprise the critics of the human rights approach to the protection of the environment – that, as much as the ECHR grants to humans a right to benefit from a decent environment, it also assigns ecological responsibilities to them. The Court will thus assent to conservation measures undertaken by states which otherwise interfere with someone's Convention rights, as long as they do not result in an excessive individual burden.[41]

To recapitulate, the ECtHR holds the states responsible if environmental harm is caused by the authorities' own actions, or – under the doctrine of positive obligations – by their omissions or by activities carried out by private parties (i.e. individuals or companies).[42] But the issue will only arise if such harm directly affects the applicant's Convention rights.[43] In the specific context of the right to respect for home and for private and family life, such harm would also have to interfere with the enjoyment of these rights to a distressing degree.[44]

The way in which the Convention organs have, over the years, understood these notions is often criticised as allegedly incompatible with what is necessary to defend ecological sustainability. I will now address these issues one by one – not as inherent and irreparable deficiencies, but rather as ideas which need reconditioning to fit the expectations and the needs of modern European societies in so far as they are affected by environmental pollution and climate change. I will also try to demonstrate that the ECHR system is readily equipped

39 *Inter alia*, *Fredin v. Sweden* (no. 1), 18 February 1991, § 48, Series A no. 192; *Fadeyeva*, cited above, § 103; *Hamer*, cited above, § 79; *Turgut and Others*, cited above, § 90; and *Rimer and Others v. Turkey*, no. 18257/04, § 38, 10 March 2009; *Ivan Atanasov v. Bulgaria*, no. 12853/03, § 66, 2 December 2010; *Matczyński v. Poland*, no. 32794/07, § 101, 15 December 2015; and *S.C. Fiercolect Impex S.R.L. v. Romania*, no. 26429/07, § 65, 13 December 2016.

40 *Hamer*, cited above, § 79; *Turgut and Others*, cited above, § 90; *Varnienė v. Lithuania*, no. 42916/04, § 54, 12 November 2013; and *S.C. Fiercolect Impex S.R.L.*, cited above, § 65.

41 *Inter alia*, *Muriel Herrick v. the United Kingdom* (dec.), no. 11185/84, 11 March 1985; *Philip and Annie Lay v. the United Kingdom* (dec.), no. 13341/87, 14 July 1988; *Matos e Silva, Lda., and Others v. Portugal*, 16 September 1996, Reports of Judgments and Decisions 1996-IV; *Bahia Nova S.A. v. Spain* (dec.), no. 50924/99, 12 December 2000; *Coster v. the United Kingdom* [GC], no. 24876/94, 18 January 2001; *Papastavrou and Others*, cited above; *Posti and Rahko v. Finland*, no. 27824/95, ECHR 2002-VII; *Coopérative des agriculteurs de la Mayenne and Coopérative laitière Maine-Anjou v. France* (dec.), no. 16931/04, 10 October 2006; *Valico S.R.L. v. Italy* (dec.), no. 70074/01, 21 March 2006; *Hamer*, cited above; *Depalle v. France* [GC], no. 34044/02, ECHR 2010; and *Matczyński*, cited above.

42 *Inter alia*, *Hatton and Others*, cited above, § 98; *Fadeyeva*, cited above, § § 89, 92 and 94; *Borysiewicz v. Poland*, no. 71146/01, § 51, 1 July 2008; and *Leon and Agnieszka Kania v. Poland*, no. 12605/03, § 100, 21 July 2009.

43 *Inter alia*, *Fadeyeva*, cited above, § 68; *Borysiewicz*, cited above, § 51; *Leon and Agnieszka Kania*, cited above, § 100.

44 *Inter alia*, *López Ostra*, cited above, para. 51.

to undertake a more significant role in the field of environmental litigation – even if, as in any other area of concern, it is not at all inclined to practice any strategic judicial activism.

3.1. DIRECT VICTIM REQUIREMENT VS. GENERAL INTEREST IN A HEALTHY ENVIRONMENT

The requirement that the harm complained of must have a direct effect on the alleged victim's Convention rights excludes from the Court's jurisdiction any *actio popularis*.[45]

This means that the Court refuses to examine the merits of any case that aims at defending the environment in general without specifying that there is an individual civil right at stake guaranteed by the Convention or its protocols. The ECtHR has admittedly rejected the argument, which was put forward in a number of public-interest applications, concerning illegal development of conservation areas or deforestation, that there was a civil right to an undisturbed panoramic view;[46] to private life in the surroundings of scenic beauty or wild habitats;[47] or to the peaceful enjoyment of one's possessions in a pleasant environment.[48] But the Court has entertained cases in which, in addition to a collective concern for the nature, applicants were also defending their specific interests in patrimony, in participation in a decision-making process or in gathering of information with a view to its subsequent provision to the public. Article 6 of the Convention can indeed guarantee the right to a fair judicial review of decisions concerning urban or industrial development, or the management of nature sites if it is shown, inter alia: (i) that the resulting loss of important features (such as a picturesque view) was likely to affect the applicant's economic interest (for example, to cause a drop in the market value of his or her real property);[49] and (ii) that the procedure of which the applicant complains could effectively bring about the restoration of the previous characteristics[50] or offer the applicant compensation.[51] A "civil right" (within the meaning of Article

45 *Klass and Others v. Germany*, 6 September 1978, § 33, Series A no. 28 and *Crash 2000 Ood and Others v. Bulgaria* (dec.), no. 49893/07, § 84, 17 December 2013.

46 *Ünver v. Turkey* (dec.), no. 36209/97, 26 September 2000.

47 *Kyrtatos*, cited above, § § 46 and 53 and *Valentina Viktorovna Oglobina*, cited above, § § 20-22 and 28.

48 *Ünver*, cited above.

49 *Dactylidi v. Greece* (dec.), no. 52903/99, 28 February 2002; *Sofia Kyrtatou and Nikos Kyrtatos v. Greece* (dec.), no. 41666/98, 13 September 2001; and *Karin Anderson and Others v. Sweden*, no. 29878/09, § § 46 and 47, 25 September 2014.

50 *Dactylidi*, cited above; *Sofia Kyrtatou and Nikos Kyrtatos*, cited above; *Gorraiz Lizarraga and Others v. Spain*, no. 62543/00, § § 46 and 47, ECHR 2004-III and, by contrast *Fotopoulou v. Greece* (dec.), no. 66725/01, 10 April 2003.

51 *Ivan Atanasov*, cited above, § § 94-96.

6 of the ECHR) can also exist irrespective of any pecuniary loss incurred. For example, in a case concerning lack of access to a court to challenge a permit to dump refuse on land adjacent to that on which the applicants lived and drew water from, the Court agreed that the ability to use water in the applicants' well for drinking purposes was one facet of their ownership right.[52] In another case, the ECtHR agreed that the applicant legal entity was entitled to the right to protect the quality of the private lives of its members, who resided in municipalities threatened by an allegedly harmful project. An important element of that case was that the association's statutory aim was limited (in space and in substance), to protecting the environment in the region concerned.[53]

The question of legal standing within the context of collective (and intergenerational) rights will soon be tackled again by the ECtHR in an important public-interest case concerning the archaeological site of Mesopotamia, the existence of which is threatened by the plan to construct a dam on the Tigris River.[54] The case was lodged by archaeologists, architects and historians who, in addition to common concern for cultural heritage, claim to have a personal interest in the preservation of the site under the right to respect for private life, the right to freedom of information and the right to education of future generations. The existence of the right to a cultural heritage as such has not been recognised under the ECHR. The link with the right to a healthy environment is thus more than apparent, starting with the procedural issue of *locus standi* and ending with the cardinal question of whether the Convention imposes on states a positive obligation to preserve heritage – whether cultural or natural –under, for example, the doctrine of public trust.

To hope for a breakthrough judgment in this case is not a wishful thinking. The ECtHR has always referred to the "living" nature of the Convention, which must be interpreted in the light of present-day conditions[55] and has considered that a failure on the part of the Court to maintain a dynamic and evolutive approach would risk rendering it a bar to reform or improvement.[56]

Moreover, the Court does not consider the provisions of the ECHR to constitute the sole framework of reference for the interpretation of the rights and freedoms enshrined in it. It takes into account elements of international law other than the Convention (including soft law) and it does not distinguish between sources of law on the basis of whether or not they have been signed or ratified by the respondent state in question.[57]

52 *Zander v. Sweden*, 25 November 1993, § § 26 and 27, Series A no. 279-B.
53 *L'Erablière A.S.B.L.*, cited above.
54 *Ahunbay and Others v. Turkey*, no. 6080/06, lodged on 3 March 2006; compare with *Syllogos v. the United Kingdom* (dec.), no. 48259/15, 31 May 2016.
55 *Marckx*, cited above, § 41 and Vo v. France [GC], no. 53924/00, § 82, ECHR 2004-VIII.
56 *Stafford*, cited above, § 68.
57 *Demir and Baykara v. Turkey* [GC], no. 34503/97, § § 76-84, ECHR 2008.

In the *Tigris Dam Case* (and in similar environment-related cases), the ECtHR can draw, among other sources, on the jurisprudence of the IACtHR which has expertly established a connection between individual and collective rights, and even acknowledged intergenerational rights in the context of ecological sustainability specifically defended through the assertion of the rights of indigenous communities.[58]

A general interest in having a healthy environment may also be defended under the ECHR through the proxy of participatory or procedural rights which have been taken up by the Court not only in respect of applicants with a personal interest,[59] in keeping with the 1998 Aarhus Convention.[60] Article 6 of the ECHR has therefore been applied to proceedings which were brought by environmental-protection associations to challenge the authorisation of activities dangerous to public health and the environment. In one such case, the Court held that, while the purpose of the impugned proceedings had fundamentally been to protect a general interest, there was a sufficient link between the "civil right" which the applicant association was claiming and its right to enable the public to be informed and to participate in the decision-making process.[61] Independently of Article 6, a general environmental interest often comes into play within the

58 Although the 1988 Additional Protocol to the American Convention on Human Rights in the Area of Economic, Social and Cultural Rights (known as the "Protocol of San Salvador") expressly recognises a right to a healthy environment, alleged violations of this right cannot not give rise to an individual petition governed by the American Convention. In result, there are no decisions of the American Convention organs making findings directly under the right to a healthy environment. The IACtHR has nevertheless found violations of the first-generation human rights guaranteed by the American Convention in relation to land grabbing linked to concessions for large-scale animal husbandry, mining, logging, construction of hydroelectric dam or for crude oil exploitation on the lands of indigenous and tribal peoples. The IACtHR has thus identified a whole panoply of rights of indigenous and tribal peoples that states must respect and protect when they undertake measures of economic development. Such rights include the right to a safe and healthy environment; the right to prior consultation and to free and informed consent; the right to derive reasonable benefit from development activities; and the right of access to justice and reparation. See, *inter alia*, *Mayagna (Sumo) Awas Tingni Community v. Nicaragua*, Judgment of August 31, 2001; *Moiwana Community v. Suriname*, Judgment of June 15, 2005; *Yakye Axa Indigenous Community v. Paraguay*, Judgment of June 17, 2005; *Sawhoyamaxa Indigenous Community v. Paraguay*, Judgment of March 29, 2006; *Claude-Reyes et al. v. Chile*, Judgment of September 19, 2006; *Saramaka People v. Suriname*, Judgment of November 28, 2007; *Xákmok Kásek Indigenous Community v. Paraguay*, Judgment of August 24, 2010; *Kichwa Indigenous People of Sarayaku v. Ecuador*, Judgment of June 27, 2012; *Kuna Indigenous People of Madungandí and the Emberá Indigenous People of Bayano and their members v. Panama*, Judgment of 14 October 2014; *Kaliña and Lokono Peoples v. Suriname*, Judgment of November 25, 2015; and the IACtHR's OC 23-17, cited above § 57.

59 *Inter alia*, *Guerra and Others*, cited above; *Taşkın and Others*, cited above; *Di Sarno and Others*, cited above.

60 Convention on Access to Information, Public Participation in Decision-Making and Access to Justice in Environmental Matters.

61 *Collectif national d'information et d'opposition à l'usine Melox – Collectif Stop Melox and Mox*, cited above; contrast with *Lesoochranarske zoskupenie Vlk*, cited above, § § 77, 78, and 88.

context of Article 10 of the ECHR which guarantees the freedom to impart and seek information,[62] and of Article 11 of the ECHR which grants the right to freedom of assembly.[63]

The "direct victim requirement" also implies that the ECtHR will not entertain applications in which a legal entity relies on a Convention right, such as to respect for private life or for home, which is inherently attributable to natural persons only.[64] However, the Court may readily grant victim status to people directly threatened by an environmentally harmful project, even if they defended their interests before national courts not personally but instead through an intermediary of an environmental-protection association that was set up for the specific purpose of protecting its members from the consequences of the project in question.[65] The Court thus acknowledges the important role of non-governmental organisations in environmental litigation. The underlying premise is that "in modern-day societies, when citizens are confronted with particularly complex administrative decisions, recourse to collective bodies such as associations is one of the accessible means, sometimes the only means, available to them whereby they can defend their particular interests effectively".[66]

3.2. SERIOUS SPECIFIC AND IMMINENT DANGER REQUIREMENT VS. PRECAUTIONARY PRINCIPLE

Irrespective of the above considerations, the doctrine of "direct harmful effect" can also appear to hinder the operation of the precautionary principle of international environmental law, in so far as it requires a direct and immediate link between the impugned situation and somebody's Convention right,[67] or, within the context of Article 6, that the applicants concerned be personally

62 *Appleby and Others v. the United Kingdom*, no. 44306/98, ECHR 2003-VI; *Animal Defenders International v. the United Kingdom* [GC], no. 48876/08, ECHR 2013 (extracts); *VgT Verein gegen Tierfabriken v. Switzerland*, no. 24699/94, ECHR 2001-VI; *Verein gegen Tierfabriken Schweiz (VgT)* (no. 2), cited above; and *Guseva*, cited above.

63 *Chassagnou and Others*, cited above; *Geert Drieman and Others v. Norway* (dec.), no. 33678/96, 4 May 2000; *Zeleni Balkani*, cited above; and *Costel Popa v. Romania*, no. 47558/10, 26 April 2016.

64 *Federation of Heathrow Anti-noise Group v. the United Kingdom*, (dec.), no. 9310/81, 15 March 1984; *Association des Résidents du Quartier Pont Royal, la commune de Lambersart and Others v. France* (dec.), no. 18523/91, 8 December 1992; *Asselbourg and 78 others and Greenpeace Association-Luxembourg v. Luxembourg* (dec.), no. 29121/95, ECHR 1999-VI; *Aly Bernard and 47 others and Greenpeace – Luxembourg v. Luxembourg* (dec.), no. 29197/95, 29 June 1999; *L'Association des Amis de Saint-Raphael et de Frejus and Others v. France*, no. 45053/98, 29 February 2000; and *Greenpeace e. V. and Others v. Germany* (dec.), no. 18215/06, 12 May 2009

65 *Gorraiz Lizarraga and Others*, cited above, § 39.

66 Ibid., § 38.

67 *Ivan Atanasov*, cited above, § 66 in fine.

exposed to a serious, specific and imminent danger.[68] Such stringent tests, especially if taken against the Court's own observation that the exercise of the right of individual petition cannot have the aim of preventing a violation of the Convention,[69] led to scholarly disapproval of international human rights litigation in the field of environmental protection, as being deprived of the essential preventive and, even less so, precautionary character.[70] The "serious, specific and imminent danger" requirement under Article 6, which came to be known as the "Balmer test", was even criticised by some of the Court's own judges, as unattainable.[71]

The Court has indeed emphasised that it is only in wholly exceptional circumstances that the risk of a future violation may confer the status of "victim" on an applicant. It is only if the applicant produces reasonable and convincing evidence of the probability of the occurrence of a violation concerning him or her personally. Mere suspicions or conjectures are not enough for the Court in this respect.[72] But when stripped of all wording aimed at posing a deterrent, what rests is the principle that the Court will examine the merits of cases in which applicants can assert, arguably and in a detailed manner, that for lack of adequate precautions taken by the authorities their Convention rights are at, not too remote, risk of being harmed.[73]

The case record shows that, on the one hand, the ECtHR will dismiss applications if it considers that the risks invoked in them are too unspecific or too remote to justify the applicants' assertion that they are the victims of a violation of the Convention. Such were the risks which were supposed to be inherent in, for example, the production of steel from scrap iron even before the steelworks in question had been built[74] or in the undetermined consequences to health of electromagnetic emissions caused by a mobile phone antenna.[75] In sum, the Court does not require scientific certainty but it does require a degree of validation of a claim that a particular activity threatens the environment and

68 *Balmer-Schafroth e.a*, cited above, § 40; *Tauria and 18 others*, cited above; *Asselbourg and 78 others and Greenpeace Association-Luxembourg*, cited above; *Athanassoglou and Others*, cited above, § 51.

69 *Tauria and 18 others*, cited above and *Aly Bernard and 47 others and Greenpeace – Luxembourg*, cited above.

70 Boyle, Alan: Human Rights and the Environment: Where Next? in the European Journal of International Law, Vol. 23, No. 3, 2012, pp. 613-642.

71 Dissenting opinion of Judge Petiti and six other judges in *Balmer-Schafroth e.a.*, cited above and dissenting opinion of Judge Costa and four other judges in *Athanassoglou and Others*, cited above.

72 *Tauira and 18 others*, cited above; *Asselbourg and 78 others and Greenpeace Association-Luxembourg*, cited above; and *Centre for Legal Resources on behalf of Valentin Câmpeanu v. Romania* [GC], no. 47848/08, § 101, ECHR 2014.

73 *Asselbourg and 78 others and Greenpeace Association-Luxembourg*, cited above.

74 Ibid. and *Aly Bernard and 47 others and Greenpeace – Luxembourg*, cited above.

75 *Luginbühl v. Switzerland* (dec.), no. 42756/02, 17 January 2006.

somebody's Convention rights. The ECtHR was very much divided on this issue when the "Swiss nuclear plants cases" were the first to develop and to fail the "*Balmer* test" on the grounds that the risks of the use of nuclear energy were only hypothetical.[76] In all such cases, the Court still engaged in a multifaceted analysis of the case material and the applicants' arguments. For example, in the steelworks cases mentioned above and in the most recent "nuclear" case against the Czech Republic,[77] it carefully looked at the conditions of operation imposed by the authorities and only then concluded that the norms dealing with the discharge of air-polluting wastes or the risk of a nuclear accident, respectively, did not appear to be so inadequate as to constitute a serious infringement of the principle of precaution.

On the other hand, the Court does not eschew the precautionary environment rulings if the alleged future or potential harm is rendered less speculative. State responsibility under the ECHR was very well engaged where the dangerous effects of an activity to which the individuals were likely to be exposed had been determined as part of an environmental impact assessment procedure in such a way as to establish a sufficiently close link with a Convention-protected right.[78] This was also the case where the absence of any such internal document or decision confirming the risk was counterbalanced by a record of a relatively recent incident on the site which had caused environmental harm.[79] It is also important to bring up the case in which the Court defied the "Balmer test" altogether. This case concerned the non-enforcement of a judicial order to stop the activities of thermal power plants, which had been proved to be causing hazardous emissions.[80] The applicants, however, lived at a great distance from the source of the pollution, and even though it was confirmed that their homes were in the affected zone, there were no specific emissions indicators for their home region. The ECtHR nevertheless held that the right to the protection of the applicants' physical integrity was brought into play, despite the fact that the risk which they ran was not as serious, specific and imminent as that run by those living in the immediate vicinity of the plants. To justify this conclusion, the Court attached importance to the fact that the applicants had standing before the domestic court; that the domestic court had ruled in their favour on the merits; and that the national constitution provided for the right to a healthy and balanced environment.

76 *Balmer-Schafroth e.a.*, cited above, § 40 and *Athanassoglou and Others*, cited above, § 51.

77 *Folkman and Others v. the Czech Republic* (dec.), no. 23673/03, 10 July 2006.

78 *Taşkın and Others*, cited above, § 113; *Öçkan and Others*, cited above; *Lemke*, cited above; *Hardy and Maile v. the United Kingdom*, no. 31965/07, 14 February 2012; and *Genç and Demirgan*, cited above.

79 *Tătar*, cited above, § § 93-97; contrast with *Tauria and 18 others*, cited above.

80 *Okyay and Others v. Turkey*, no. 36220/97, ECHR 2005-VII.

The analysis of the above cases leads to the following conclusions. Firstly, the Court's understanding of the precautionary principle (the substance of which is altogether very much debatable) certainly does not reflect its soft law/activist variant, which endorses a lower threshold for its applicability, namely that of "potential adverse effects."[81] It does not, however, differ from the most common and most authoritative definition under the Rio Declaration[82] or the case law of the International Court of Justice,[83] which unequivocally enshrine the serious and irreversible nature of environmental damage into the elements of the precautionary principle. Secondly, the ECtHR's applicability tests have, in practice, become more relaxed, which may open the door for human rights rulings which are more preventative. And thirdly, the Court does not apply these tests summarily and will always look at all the circumstances of a case. With the current progress in the field of science and with domestic regulations ensuring better access to information and requiring environmental impact assessments, it is becoming easier for applicants to submit convincing causality arguments and for the Court, to undertake legitimate risk assessments in precautionary-type of cases.

3.3. MINIMUM LEVEL OF DISTURBANCE REQUIREMENT VS. LESSER ENVIRONMENTAL HARM

Article 8 of the ECHR protects the right to respect for one's home, which in the context of environmental degradation or nuisance has been interpreted by the Court as closely interconnected with the notions of private and family life. The right to a home guarantees not just the right to the use of the actual physical area concerned, but also to the enjoyment of that area without disturbance. Such disturbance includes noise, emissions, smells or other forms of nuisance if they prevent people from enjoying the amenities of their homes. The adverse effects of environmental pollution must attain a certain minimum level of disturbance if they are to fall within the scope of this provision.[84] This means that – sometimes, disastrously for the environment – the ECHR will only be triggered when the level of environmental protection falls below that necessary to maintain any of the guaranteed rights while lesser violations of human rights go unscrutinised. But the notion of minimum threshold is also present in international environmental law. There is a vast consensus that harm which does not amount

81 1982 United Nations World Charter for Nature.

82 1992 Rio Declaration on Environment and Development, Principle 15 and also, the 1992 United Nations Framework Convention on Climate Change, Article 3(3).

83 *Gabčíkovo-Nagymaros Project Case* (*Slovakia v. Hungary*), ICJ Judgment of 25 September 1997 and *Pulp Mills on the River Uruguay Case* (*Argentina v. Uruguay*), ICJ Judgment of 20 April 2010.

84 *López Ostra*, cited above, § 51.

to a significant or "appreciable" degree should be tolerated, for example, in a liability regime or that a general obligation of prevention arises only in respect of activities that entail the risk of substantial harm.[85] In the ECHR system, an important safeguard in this respect lies in the Court's practice of assessing that minimum threshold of disturbance in the light of all the circumstances of the case, such as the intensity and duration of the nuisance in question, and its physical or mental effects on the individual's health or quality of life.[86] The ECtHR will take account of the general context of the environment and in principle, no issue will arise if the detriment complained of is negligible in comparison with the environmental hazards inherent to life in every modern city.[87] On the other hand, a case will not be dismissed on the sole grounds that the pollution or other nuisance in question does not produce a serious health impact or is not life threatening.[88] Another advantage for applicants is that, in establishing the particulars of each case, the Court is not bound by any strict evidentiary rules. The Court has generally applied the very high standard of proof "beyond reasonable doubt". It is nevertheless accepted that such proof may follow from the coexistence of sufficiently strong, clear and concordant inferences or of similar unrebutted presumptions of fact, and it has been the Court's practice to allow flexibility in that respect, taking into consideration the nature of the substantive right at stake and any evidentiary difficulties involved.[89] The ECtHR, in its free assessment of evidence, will thus rely, *inter alia*, on the findings of the domestic courts and other competent authorities; environmental standards under domestic law; relevant scientific studies (whether commissioned by state authorities or private entities); and the applicant's medical certificates and personal accounts of event.[90]

It is noteworthy that the ECtHR considered that, for example, in the "pollution" category, the minimum disturbance threshold had been met and the ECHR had been breached in nineteen (i.e. in almost half) of such cases examined by the Court.[91] Three additional pollution cases were found to have violated Article 6 only on account of the non-enforcement of a judicial decision to stop

85 Barboza, J. (2011) The Environment, Risk and Liability in International Law, Martinus Nijoff Publishers, pp. 10, 11, 14 and 15; see also, Trail Smelter Case (United States, Canada), 16 April 1938 and 11 March 1941, Reports of International Arbitral Awards, Vol. III, p. 1965.

86 *Fadeyeva*, cited above, § § 68-69.

87 Ibid., § 69; *Mileva and Others v. Bulgaria*, nos. 43449/02 and 21475/04, § 90, 25 November 2010; and *Marchiş and Others v. Romania* (dec.), no. 38197/03, § 33, 28 June 2011.

88 Among others, *López Ostra*, cited above, § 51; *Taşkın and Others*, cited above, § 113; *Marchiş and Others*, cited above, § 28; and *Brânduşe v. Romania*, no. 6586/03, § 67, 7 April 2009.

89 *Fadeyeva*, cited above, § 79.

90 *Dubetska and Others*, cited above, § 107.

91 *Inter alia*, *López Ostra*, cited above; *Guerra and Others*, cited above; *Taşkın and Others*, cited above; *Fadeyeva*, cited above; *Öçkan and Others*, cited above; *Ledyayeva and Others*, cited above; *Giacomelli*, cited above; *Lemke*, cited above; *Tătar*, cited above; *Brânduşe*, cited above; *Băcilă*, cited above; *Deés v. Hungary*, no. 2345/06, 9 November 2010; *Dubetska and Others*, cited above;

the hazardous activities in question.[92] In these judgments the ECtHR ordered the states concerned to pay compensation to the individual victims. Moreover, in the course of the implementation of these judgments by the Committee of Ministers (the supervisory mechanism of execution of judgments of the Council of Europe), additional obligations were imposed on the respective states requiring them to undertake the legal and practical measures (whether individual or general) necessary to ensure the ending of the situation that gave rise to a violation – if that was necessary in the circumstance of the case – and that similar violations were prevented in the future. Such measures included orders to: enforce outstanding judicial decisions;[93] assess environmental risks and develop practices aimed at the rapid provision of adequate information regarding environmental hazards;[94] reduce and control traffic;[95] set up a general framework for protection against industrial pollution, the rehabilitating polluting sites, creating sanitary zones around them, and resettling victims;[96] reform the legal system in order to ensure effective judicial review;[97] remove any aerials causing radiation;[98] shut down polluting mines;[99] lower levels of toxic emissions by making technical improvements to thermal plants, installing filters, or operating them at minimum capacity;[100] improve the waste management;[101] and monitor

Grimkovskaya v. Ukraine, no. 38182/03, 21 July 2011; *Di Sarno and Others*, cited above; *Dzemyuk v. Ukraine*, no. 42488/02, 4 September 2014; *Otgon v. the Republic of Moldova*, no. 22743/07, 25 October 2016; *Jugheli and Others*, cited above; and *Genç and Demirgan*, cited above.

92 *Zander*, cited above; *Okyay and Others*, cited above; *Iera Moni Profitou Iliou Thiras v. Greece*, no. 32259/02, 22 December 2005.

93 Interim Resolution CM/ResDH(2007)4 adopted by the Committee of Ministers on 14 February 2007 in respect of the judgment in the case of *Okyay and Others*, cited above.

94 Resolution CM/ResDH (2002)146 adopted by the Committee of Ministers on 17 December 2002 in respect of the judgment in the case of *Guerra and Others*, cited above and Resolution CM/ResDH(2016)349 adopted by the Committee of Ministers on 8 December 2016 in respect of judgments in the cases of *Tătar* and *Băcilă*, both cited above.

95 Action Plan submitted by Hungary on 15 June 2012 in respect of the judgment in the case of *Deés*, cited above.

96 Report CM/Inf/DH (2007)7 submitted by Russia on 13 February 2007 in respect of the judgments in the cases of *Fadeyeva* and *Ledyayeva and Others*, both cited above.

97 Resolution adopted by the Committee of Ministers on 21 March 1994 in respect of the judgment in the case of *Zander*, cited above.

98 Resolution CM/ResDH (2010)193 adopted by the Committee of Ministers on 2 December 2010 in respect of the judgment in the case of *Iera Moni Profitou Iliou Thiras*, cited above.

99 Action Plan submitted by Turkey on 20 April 2012 in respect of the judgments in the case of *Taşkın and Others*, *Öçkan and Others*; and *Lemke v. Turkey*, all cited above.

100 Interim Resolution CM/ResDH (2007)4 adopted by the Committee of Ministers on 14 February 2007 in respect of the judgment in the case of *Okyay and Others*, cited above.

101 Decision DH-DD (2016)507 adopted by the Supervision of the Execution of the Court's judgments on 8 June 2016 and Action Plan submitted by Italy on 14 May 2014 in respect of the judgment in the case of *Di Sarno and Others*, cited above.

the conformity of a polluting plant with environmental requirements.[102] These examples demonstrate that the enforcement of the ECtHR's judgments facilitates general changes in the behaviour of public bodies and may thus lead to overall environmental improvements.[103]

3.4. WIDE MARGIN OF APPRECIATION VS. ENVIRONMENTALLY HARMFUL POLICY DECISIONS

The last contentious issue revolves around the wide "margin of appreciation"[104] that the Court affords national authorities – for example under Article 8 of the ECHR and Article 1 of Protocol No. 1 to the ECHR (right to property) in determining their best environmental policies and in choosing between different ways and means of meeting their international obligations. This doctrine is based on the assumptions that domestic authorities have direct democratic legitimacy and that, in view of the difficulty implicit in the social and technical aspects of environmental issues, they are better placed than an international court to decide what exactly should be done to stop or reduce environmental harm or nuisance.[105] Similarly, under the positive limb of Article 2 of the ECHR (right to life), the ECtHR has held that an impossible or disproportionate burden must not be imposed on the authorities without consideration being given, in particular, to the operational choices which they must make in terms of priorities and resources.[106] But even with this approach, the Court can compare particular national choices with the European consensus or with international trends,[107] and can still review the merits of authorities' decision in order to ensure that they had not acted in an arbitrary manner or committed a manifest error of judgment in weighing the competing interests of the individual and of the community as a whole.[108] The doctrine of the margin of appreciation is also counterbalanced by the ECtHR's practice of scrutinising the domestic procedure with a view to verifying whether the public authorities were independent, diligent and (under

102 Action Report submitted by Italy on 1 August 2014 and Resolution CM/Res/DH (2014)214 adopted by the Committee of Ministers on 12 November 2014 in respect of the judgment in the case of *Giacomelli*, cited above.

103 Pedersen, O.W. (2010) The Ties that Bind: The Environment, the European Convention on Human Rights and the Rule of Law, in European Public Law, Vol. 16, No. 4, p. 571, 2010.

104 *Handyside v. the United Kingdom*, 7 December 1976, § § 48-50, Series A no. 24.

105 *Powell and Rayner v. the United Kingdom*, no. 9310/81, § 44 in fine, 21 February 1990; *Hatton and Others*, cited above, § 97; *Giacomelli*, cited above, § 80; and *Mileva and Others*, cited above, § 98.

106 *Öneryıldız*, cited above, § 71 and *Budayeva and Others v. Russia*, nos. 15339/02, 21166/02, 20058/02, 11673/02 and 15343/02, § 128, ECHR 2008 (extracts).

107 *Tănase v. Moldova* [GC], no. 7/08, § 176, ECHR 2010; *Kiyutin v. Russia*, no. 2700/10, § 65, ECHR 2011 and *Christine Goodwin v. the United Kingdom* [GC], no. 28957/95, § 85, ECHR 2002-VI.

108 *Hatton and Others*, cited above, § § 98 and 99.

Articles 8 or 1 of Protocol No. 1) they took all the competing interests into consideration.[109] In fact, the Court will usually start with an examination of the quality of the decision-making process; then, if necessary, it will also review the material conclusions of the domestic authorities.[110] Inspecting the procedures at issue, the ECtHR will examine whether the authorities have conducted sufficient studies to evaluate the risks of a potentially hazardous activity;[111] whether, on the basis of the information available, they have developed adequate policy *vis-à-vis* polluters; and whether all necessary measures have been taken to enforce this policy in good time.[112] The Court will likewise examine the extent to which the individuals affected by the policy at issue were able to contribute to the decision-making, including access to the relevant information[113] and their ability to challenge the authorities' decisions in an effective way.[114] As the Convention is intended to protect effective rights, not illusory ones, a fair balance between the various interests at stake may be upset not only where the regulations to protect the guaranteed rights are lacking, but also where they are not duly complied with.[115] The procedural safeguards available to the applicant may be rendered inoperative and the state may be found liable under the ECHR where a decision-making procedure is unjustifiably lengthy or where a decision taken as a result remains for an important period unenforced.[116] Overall, the onus is on the state to justify, using detailed and rigorous data, a situation in which certain individuals bear a heavy burden on behalf of the rest of the community.[117]

Even bearing the wide margin of appreciation in mind, the ultimate question before the Court remains whether a state has succeeded in striking a fair balance between the competing interests of the individuals affected and the community as a whole without imposing an excessive burden on the applicant.[118] The ECtHR has undertaken that proportionality test in respect of over one hundred environment-related applications, with different outcomes.

In the light of the growing number of national law suits regarding air quality in Europe's larger cities, it is important to note the "margin of appreciation" rulings in which the ECtHR has been called on to weight the effects of heavy aeroplane or car traffic on individual residents against the economic interests of the country as a whole.

---

109 *Fadeyeva*, cited above, § 128 and *Hatton and Others*, cited above, § 99.
110 Ibid., § 105
111 *Hatton and Others*, cited above, § 128 and *Giacomelli*, cited above, § 86.
112 *Ledyayeva and Others*, cited above, § 104 and *Giacomelli*, cited above, § § 92 and 93.
113 *Öneryıldız*, cited above, § 108.
114 *Guerra and Others*, cited above, § 60; *Hatton and Others*, cited above, § 127; and *Taşkın and Others*, cited above, § 119.
115 *Moreno Gómez*, cited above, § § 56 and 61.
116 *Taşkın and Others*, cited above, § § 124 and 125.
117 *Fadeyeva v. Russia*, cited above, § 128.
118 *Hatton and Others*, cited above, § § 100, 119 and 123.

The Court has, for the most part, declined to find violations in cases concerning aircraft traffic that were argued not in relation to any exhaust fumes pollution but with reference to noise nuisance caused to the residents of areas near various airports.[119] The Court usually reasoned that: the level of discomfort was not high; there was no disparity with domestic law; the individuals concerned had a real choice of leaving the area in question; noise-mitigating measures and compensation schemes had been put in place by the authorities; and the authorities were monitoring the situation.[120] The Court has also expressed the view, which has not resonated well with environmentalists, that no exception to the doctrine of wide margin of appreciation is warranted in environmental cases; it has attached great importance to the consideration that the intensified operation of airports, including at night, contributes to the general economy.[121]

In relation to road traffic, the ECtHR has so far been presented with four applications. In the case which was brought against Germany by Greenpeace together with individual residents of Hamburg,[122] the proportionality test was favourable to the state. The Court accepted that soot and respirable dust particles could have a serious detrimental effect on health – particularly in densely populated areas with heavy traffic. The case-file demonstrated, however, that the authorities had attended to the problem, having taken a series of reasonable and potentially efficient measures to curb emissions by diesel vehicles. The Court concluded that the authorities had not erred in refusing to order the compulsory installation of filters in diesel vehicles, which the applicants recommended as the most effective measure. The importance of the principles established by the ECtHR in this case in respect of the victim status and the minimum level of disturbance takes precedence over the finding of "no violation" under the proportionality test. Notably, violations were found in cases that were to some extent linked, which were brought by a Hungarian living near a motorway toll gate[123] and a Ukrainian who had a motorway re-routed through her street.[124] Lastly, an important application concerning noise and exhaust fumes emissions

119 *Arrondelle v. the United Kingdom* (dec.), 7889/77, 15 July 1980; *Baggs v. the United Kingdom* (dec.), 9310/81, 14 October 1985; *Powell and Rayner*, cited above; *Hatton and Others*, cited above; *Ashworth and Others v. the United Kingdom* (dec.), no. 39561/98, 20 January 2004; *Balzarini and 435 others v. Italy* (dec.), no. 3717/03, 28 October 2004; *Giani v. Italy* (dec.), no. 77633/01, 28 October 2004; *Nasalli Rocca v. Italy* (dec.), no. 8162/02, 31 March 2005; *Flamenbaum and Others v. France*, nos. 3675/04 and 23264/04, 13 December 2012; *Frank Eckenbrcht and Heinz Ruhmer v. Germany* (dec.), no. 25330/10, 10 June 2014; and *Elżbieta Płachta and 3 others v. Poland* (dec.), no. 25194/08, 25 November 2014.

120 *Hatton and Others*, cited above, § § 118, 120, 123, 125, 127 and 128.

121 Ibid., § § 122 and 126.

122 *Greenpeace e. V. and Others*, cited above.

123 *Deés*, cited above.

124 *Grimkovskaya*, cited above.

stemming from heavy day and night motorway traffic in Poland is currently pending examination before the ECtHR.[125]

4. CONCLUSION

Faced with a large number of environment-related cases, the ECHR organs have gradually expanded the protection of the civil and political human rights to encompass various forms of environmental risk and harm. Nowadays, the system efficiently safeguards the natural environment, albeit in a surrogate and somewhat covert manner, through the rights of humans to the environment. Regarding the balancing of community and personal interests, it recognises the growing importance of obligations of states and individuals to preserve the natural environment for current and future generations. Through the procedural rights and duties that are considered essential for the practical realisation of substantive rights, European human rights law reinforces the fundamental principles and concepts of international and community environmental law, such as citizens' participation in a decision-making process, access to information and justice, environmental impact assessment and good governance. Within this procedural context, it sometimes becomes indirectly involved in public-interest campaigns for the defence of non-human species, ecological processes and lesser threats to humans. The ECtHR is a readily operative and effective last-resort mechanism for redressing environmental damage, halting ecologically unsound projects, and deterring environmentally unfriendly policies.

It is, nevertheless obvious that the ECHR has its limits in that it does not stipulate a substantive right to a healthy environment and thus does not provide the Court with infinite jurisdiction over anything from the ozone layer to the Siberian tiger.[126] But this anthropocentric and restrained protection of the environment is not deficient simply because it cannot serve all purposes. The direct protection of the environment's components (other than humans), lies primarily within the realm of environmental law. It is therefore wrong to diminish the role of human rights law only because it cannot wholly incorporate environmental protection.[127]

125 *Kapa and 3 others*, cited above, communicated to the parties in December 2017.

126 On environmental goods, Miller, D. (1999) Social Justice and Environmental Goods, in Fairness and Futurity. Dobson, A. (ed.) Essays on Environmental Sustainability and Social Justice, Oxford University Press, pp. 152-153.

127 Donald A.K. and Shelton, L. Dinah (2011) Environmental Protection and Human Rights, Cambridge University Press, p. 130

Nature may well have a value in and of itself and giving it rights may no longer be a fanciful legal notion.[128] It still cannot practically be protected independently of a human being, if only because of the fact that at the centre of the cause and of the solution of the problems such as pollution, climate change and deforestation are individuals with legal standing and with substantive rights guaranteed by national and international law (and with obligations derived therefrom).[129] The natural environment thus needs the agency of a human, whether as its guardian *ad litem*[130] or to defend it through the exercise of his or her own rights. Moreover, to leave the rights with the people is not to say that they should have supremacy over the natural environment. Human rights law could, both conceptually and practically, redefine human self-interest in view of the environmental necessity of modern times, and make this interest rational and intergenerational. Human rights law could therefore become eco-centric and no longer give precedence to economic considerations over the environmental damage.[131]

Such a paradigm shift could be achieved by the ECtHR, not through a single giant leap, but through incrementalism – its usual practice of muddling through various legal problems – in a way, forced on its judges by applicants. Wise and widespread environmental litigation is therefore essential in making the Court employ ecological rationality in explaining the value of nature in cases in which its protection paradoxically seems to collide with conventionally-perceived individual rights. Just as much as the environmental law suffers from a lack of coherence and is immature,[132] "green" human rights case law is also a work in progress – it is sometimes encouraging and sometimes deceiving. But the Court's jurisprudence is dynamic and susceptible to change because the notion that the ECHR is a living instrument is firmly established and because the cross-fertilisation of ideas is definitely occurring between the different human rights

128 For example, Constitution of Ecuador, Articles 10 and 71-74 and *Wheeler c. Director de la Procuraduria General Del Estado de Loja*, Juicio No. 11121-2011-0010, for review in English: The Ecuadorian Exemplar: The First Ever Vindications of Constitutional Rights of Nature, Erin Daly, Review of European Community & International Environmental Law, Volume 21, Issue 1, pages 63–66, April 2012, and New Zealand's Te Awa Tupua (Whanganui River Claims Settlement) Act 2017, Public Act 2017 No 7, 20 March 2017, Article 14.

129 Donald A.K. and Shelton, L. Dinah (2011) Environmental Protection and Human Rights, Cambridge University Press.

130 New Zealand's Te Awa Tupua (Whanganui River Claims Settlement) Act 2017, Public Act 2017 No 7, 20 March 2017, Article 18 (2) "Te Pou Tupua is to be the human face of Te Awa Tupua and act in the name of Te Awa Tupua."

131 Hiskes, R.P. (2008) The Human Right to a Green Future, in Environmental Rights and Intergenerational Justice, Cambridge University Press.

132 Pedersen, O.W. (2013) Modest Pragmatic Lessons for a Diverse and Incoherent Environmental Law, Oxford Journal of Legal Studies, Vol. 33, Issue 1, pp. 103-131.

systems.[133] For all these reasons, notwithstanding the limits of the human rights law and the importance of other platforms of ecological justice, environment cases should continue to be brought before the European Court of Human Rights.

133 The development of international human rights law through the activities and case law of the European and the Inter-American Courts of Human Rights, Speech given by Judge Antonio A. Cançado Trinidade, then President of the IACtHR on the occasion of the opening of the judicial year of the ECtHR, 22 January 2004.

CHAPTER 8

A NATURAL RESOURCE BEYOND THE SKY: INVOKING THE PUBLIC TRUST DOCTRINE TO PROTECT THE ATMOSPHERE FROM GREENHOUSE GAS EMISSIONS

Samvel VARVAŠTIAN*

ABSTRACT

The persisting absence of comprehensive climate change legislation in the United States has long resulted in the ever-growing number of climate-related lawsuits. Litigation has been used in various ways, for example, by requesting the regulating bodies to introduce new air quality standards, or by targeting specific individual greenhouse gas emissions sources. In the last few years, climate plaintiffs have increasingly relied on common law public trust doctrine and constitutional provisions granting rights to natural resources in an attempt to force the government to take decisive climate change mitigation measures. The latter line of climate cases, also known as atmospheric trust litigation, is the result of a nationwide campaign, which seeks judicial recognition of the fact that the planet's atmosphere is a natural resource; thus, its protection from dangerous greenhouse gas emissions is an essential obligation of the government. This chapter explores how United States courts have interpreted the public trust doctrine with regard to the atmosphere.

* Mykolas Romeris University (sam.vasti@gmail.com). I am grateful to the 2017 EELF Conference participants for their helpful comments, particularly to Robin Kundis Craig and Valerie Fogleman. I am also grateful to Helle Tegner Anker and Birgitte Egelund Olsen for their careful editorial work and anonymous peer reviewers for their valuable feedback.

1. INTRODUCTION

Climate change presents a global problem, critically affecting many regions on the planet and jeopardizing both the environment and human communities. The impact of climate-related extremes, including heat waves, droughts, wildfires, weather anomalies, sea level rise, disrupted hydrological cycles, and ocean acidification is taking its toll on lives and livelihoods as well as ecosystems.[1] Unsurprisingly, climate change has been recognized as adversely affecting a whole spectrum of human rights, most notably the right to life, health, housing, and food and water.[2]

The legal response to climate change, developed over nearly the last three decades, has been multi-level. Global climate deals, regional action and national climate legislation as well as action by non-state actors have all been used in a complex way to mitigate climate change and adapt to its impact.[3] The existing policies, however, have not yielded any decisive results.[4] The reasons behind this are many,[5] but in a general sense, the failure to achieve the required climate goals is attributable to poor policy implementation or the lack of such a policy altogether.

The United States (US), unfortunately, has long demonstrated a lacklustre approach, when it comes to climate policy. Being among the top climate polluters,[6] the country has failed to develop any comprehensive federal climate policy.[7] Starting from the early 1990s, this regulatory void has gradually been filled with litigation.[8] The chapter focuses on a specific type of litigation,

1 See, in general, IPCC, 2014: Climate Change 2014: Synthesis Report. Contribution of Working Groups I, II and III to the Fifth Assessment Report of the Intergovernmental Panel on Climate Change [Core Writing Team, R.K. Pachauri and L.A. Meyer (eds.)]. IPCC, Geneva, Switzerland, p. 151 ff.

2 Understanding Human Rights and Climate Change. Submission of the Office of the High Commissioner for Human Rights to the 21st Conference of the Parties to the United Nations Framework Convention on Climate Change, 26 November 2015. http://www.ohchr.org/Documents/Issues/ClimateChange/COP21.pdf (accessed on 8 February 2018).

3 See Bodansky, D., J. Brunnée and L. Rajamani (2017) International Climate Change Law, Oxford University Press; Chan, S., R. Falkner, M. Goldberg, and H. van Asselt (2018) 'Effective and geographically balanced? An output-based assessment of non-state climate actions', Climate Policy, 18(1), pp. 24-35; Wirth, D. A. (2015) 'The International and Domestic Law of Climate Change: A Binding International Agreement Without the Senate or Congress?', Harvard Environmental Law Review 39(2), pp. 515-566.

4 Thus, recent anthropogenic GHG emissions are the highest in history. *Supra* note 1, p. 44.

5 See Lazarus, R.J. (2009) 'Super Wicked Problems and Climate Change: Restraining the Present to Liberate the Future', Cornell Law Review 94(5), pp. 1153-1233.

6 Boden, T.A., G. Marland and R.J. Andres (2017) National CO2 Emissions from Fossil-Fuel Burning, Cement Manufacture, and Gas Flaring: 1751-2014, Carbon Dioxide Information Analysis Center, Oak Ridge National Laboratory, U.S. Department of Energy.

7 Peel, J. and H.M. Osofsky (2015) Climate Change Litigation: Regulatory Pathways to Cleaner Energy, Cambridge University Press, pp. 62-63.

8 Ibid., p. 19.

developing since 2011, in which plaintiffs have relied on common law public trust doctrine and constitutional provisions granting rights to natural resources in an attempt to force the government to take decisive climate change mitigation measures. The latter line of climate cases, also known as atmospheric trust litigation, is the result of a nationwide campaign,[9] which seeks judicial recognition of the fact that the planet's atmosphere is a natural resource – just like air, water and soil – thus its protection from dangerous greenhouse gas (GHG) emissions is an essential obligation of the government.[10]

2. ATMOSPHERIC TRUST CASES AND THEIR PLACE IN CLIMATE CHANGE LITIGATION

Scholarly studies have identified and classified the body of climate change litigation based on various criteria.[11] To date, the most prominent categories of climate cases include litigation revolving around the environmental impact assessment legislation and air quality legislation.[12] Such litigation has been used with mixed success, mostly to challenge the authorization of fossil fuel development and operations as well as action with regard to GHG emissions standards.[13] Albeit instrumental in targeting local activities, these types of climate cases have not put the climate regime to the test on a broader scale. With action being scattered across different regions and targeting individual decisions and entities, the question arises whether it could be possible to make a sweeping challenge to governmental policy and take on climate change inaction in a comprehensive way.

This approach is exactly what lies at the core of atmospheric trust litigation. These cases are not based on environmental impact assessment or air quality legislation but rather on constitutional provisions and common law. Notably, both constitutional and common law claims have been explored in climate

9 All atmospheric trust cases have been brought by children plaintiffs supported by various non-profits, including Our Children's Trust, Wildearth Guardians, etc.

10 See Wood, M.C. and C.W. Woodward IV (2016) 'Atmospheric Trust Litigation and the Constitutional Right to a Healthy Climate System: Judicial Recognition at Last', Washington Journal of Environmental Law & Policy 6(2), pp. 634-684.

11 See Markell, D. and J.B. Ruhl (2012) 'An Empirical Assessment of Climate Change in the Courts: A New Jurisprudence or Business as Usual?', Florida Law Review 64(1), pp. 15-86; Lin, J. (2012) Climate change and the courts, *Legal studies*, 32(1), pp. 35-57; Peel, J. and H.M. Osofsky (2013) 'Climate Change Litigation's Regulatory Pathways: A Comparative Analysis of the United States and Australia', Law and Policy 35(3), pp. 150-183.

12 Ibid.

13 Varvaštian, S. (2018) 'Access to Justice in Climate Change Litigation from a Transnational Perspective: Private Party Standing in Recent Climate Cases', in J. Jendrośka and M. Bar (eds), Procedural Environmental Rights: Principle X of the Rio Declaration in Theory and Practice, Intersentia, pp. 481-502.

change litigation before;[14] however, the atmospheric trust litigation has so far been the only line of climate cases systematically exploring these legal avenues. Plaintiffs in the atmospheric trust litigation invoke the common law public trust doctrine, which grants rights to certain natural resources,[15] thus representing a rights-based approach to climate change litigation.[16]

The public trust doctrine derives from ancient Roman law, finding its way into English common law in the Middle Ages and eventually settling in American common law.[17] The doctrine, being based on the antimonopoly notion,[18] requires the government to hold vital natural resources in trust for the public beneficiaries, thus protecting those resources from monopolization or destruction by private interests.[19] In its traditional application throughout the 19th century, the doctrine was limited to navigable and tidal waters and the land submerged beneath them for the purposes of navigation, commerce and fishing.[20] Such application of the doctrine was dictated by the paramount importance of waterways to economic activities at that time.[21]

However, the public trust doctrine has not remained static. In the 20th century, many US courts started expanding it to protect wildlife, ecosystems, non-navigable waters, parks and beaches for the purposes of recreation as well as ecological preservation.[22] At the same time, the doctrine traditionally developed at the state level[23] and the developments in relevant jurisprudence in some states did not necessarily extend to other states.[24] The expansion of the public trust doctrine to the atmosphere – as the key natural resource polluted by GHG

14 For example, plaintiffs in the renowned cases *American Electric Power Co. v Connecticut*, *Comer v Murphy Oil USA, Inc.* and *Native Village of Kivalina v ExxonMobil Corp.* have all brought public nuisance and other common law claims. For a detailed account of these cases see Peel, J. and H.M. Osofsky, *supra* note 7.

15 See Sax, J.L. (1970) 'The Public Trust Doctrine in Natural Resource Law: Effective Judicial Intervention', Michigan Law Review 68(3), pp. 471-566.

16 See Peel, J. and H.M. Osofsky (2018) 'A Rights Turn in Climate Change Litigation?', Transnational Environmental Law 7(1), pp. 37-67.

17 Abate, R. S. (2016) 'Atmospheric Trust Litigation in the United States: Pipe Dream or Pipeline to Justice for Future Generations?' in R. S. Abate (ed.) Climate justice: case studies in global and regional governance challenges, Environmental Law Institute, pp. 548-552.

18 Blumm, M.C. and A.P. Moses (2017) 'The Public Trust as an Antimonopoly Doctrine', Boston College Environmental Affairs Law Review 44(1), pp. 1-54.

19 Wood, M.C. and C.W. Woodward IV, *supra* note 10, pp. 647-648.

20 Craig, R.K. (2009) 'Adapting to Climate Change: The Role of State Common-Law Public Trust Doctrines', Vermont Law Review 34(4), p. 784.

21 Blumm, M.C. and A.P. Moses, *supra* note 18, p. 8.

22 Ibid., pp. 31-43.

23 Ryan, E. (2015) 'The Public Trust Doctrine, Private Water Allocation, and Mono Lake: The Historic Saga of *National Audubon Society v Superior Court*', Environmental Law 45(2), pp. 573-574.

24 See: Craig, R.K. (2007) 'A Comparative Guide to the Eastern Public Trust Doctrines: Classifications of States, Property Rights, and State Summaries', Penn State Environmental Law Review 16(1), pp. 1-113; Craig, R.K. (2010) 'Comparative Guide to the Western Public Trust

emissions, which in turn is the main cause of anthropogenically-driven climate change – has been advocated by law professor *Mary Christina Wood*, whose works have been instrumental in shaping the atmospheric trust litigation.[25]

The atmospheric trust litigation makes sweeping challenges to governmental climate policy at state and/or federal level, and as the public trust doctrine is in some cases enshrined in constitutional law,[26] its interpretation with regard to the atmosphere may often have constitutional ramifications. Ultimately, atmospheric trust litigation envisions taking multi-pronged political action on climate, including, for instance, removing subsidies to fossil fuel industry and active phase-out of such fuels and equipment dependent on them, actively promoting renewable energy, preparing and implementing plans to remove GHGs from the atmosphere, etc.[27] Given the complex nature of climate change and the factors underlying it, such an approach may be the only viable solution to solve the problem. At the same time, it seems that the federal US government is unwilling to make the necessary policy shift.[28]

3. FEDERAL ATMOSPHERIC TRUST LITIGATION

As of today, the federal atmospheric trust litigation is comprised of two cases directed against the federal government – *Alec L. v Jackson*[29] and *Juliana v United States.*[30] The first case was decided a few years ago and resulted in a decision unfavourable to the plaintiffs. The second one, however, is ongoing and has so far demonstrated viability. Since the case is targeting federal policy, it is of nationwide importance and, if successful, it could have an impact not only on the US, but could also have repercussions throughout the rest of the world. This section now turns to discussing both cases in detail.

Doctrines: Public Values, Private Rights, the Evolution toward an Ecological Public Trust', Ecology Law Quarterly 37(1), pp. 53-197.

25 See: Goodwin, A.T. (2015) 'A Wake-Up Call for Judges', Wisconsin Law Review 2015(4), pp. 785-788; Boudreau, T. (2017) 'The Earth's Atmosphere As A Global Trust: Establishing Proportionate State Responsibility To Maintain, Restore And Sustain The Global Atmosphere', Environmental and Earth Law Journal 7(1), p. 68.

26 See Klass, A.B. (2015) 'The Public Trust Doctrine in the Shadow of State Environmental Rights Laws: A Case Study', Environmental Law 45(2), pp. 431-462; Kalen, S. (2016) 'An Essay: An Aspirational Right to a Healthy Environment', UCLA Journal of Environmental Law and Policy 34(2), pp. 156-195.

27 See Blumm, M.C. and M.C. Wood (2017) 'No Ordinary Lawsuit: Climate Change, Due Process, and the Public Trust Doctrine', American University Law Review 67(1), p. 20.

28 Ibid., pp. 4-5.

29 *Alec L. v Jackson*, 863 F.Supp.2d, p. 11 (D.D.C. 2012).

30 *Juliana v United States*, 217 F.Supp.3d, p. 1224 (D. Or. 2016).

3.1. ALEC L. v JACKSON

In *Alec L. v Jackson*, the youth plaintiffs alleged that several federal US agencies 'have violated their fiduciary duties to preserve and protect the atmosphere as a commonly shared public trust resource under the public trust doctrine.'[31] For that purpose, the plaintiffs asked the court to issue the following declarations: 1) that the atmosphere is a public trust resource and that the federal government, as a trustee, has a fiduciary duty to refrain from taking actions that waste or damage it; 2) that the defendants have violated their fiduciary duties by contributing to and allowing unsafe amounts of GHG emissions into the atmosphere.[32] Specifically with regard to the latter point, the plaintiffs asked the court to define such duties by declaring that the defendants have to 'reduce global atmospheric carbon dioxide levels to less than 350 parts per million during this century.'[33] To ensure the implementation of this, the plaintiffs asked the court to issue an injunction directing the above-mentioned federal agencies to take all necessary actions to enable carbon dioxide emissions to peak by December 2012 and decline by at least 6 per cent yearly beginning in 2013 and to order them to submit various documents (including annual US GHG reports, a climate recovery plan, etc.) for the court's approval.[34]

Notably, the plaintiffs did not allege violation of any federal legislation or constitutional provision, but invoked the federal public trust doctrine.[35] The defendants moved to dismiss the claim, arguing that the plaintiffs' complaint was grounded in state common law but did not raise a federal question, thus failing to invoke a federal court's jurisdiction.[36]

The court granted the defendants' motions. The court's assessment of the applicability of federal jurisdiction in the context of the public trust doctrine was based on the Supreme Court's decision in the non-climate case *PPL Montana, LLC v Montana*.[37] In that case, the Supreme Court distinguished the public trust doctrine from another legal principle – the equal footing doctrine – by stating that 'the public trust doctrine remains a matter of state law' and that 'the States retain residual power to determine the scope of the public trust'.[38] Furthermore, the court in *Alec L. v Jackson* referred to yet another non-climate case, where the Court of Appeals for the District of Columbia Circuit (D.C. Circuit) observed that '[i]n this country the public trust doctrine has developed almost exclusively

31 *Alec L. v Jackson*, 863 F.Supp.2d, p. 12 (D.D.C. 2012).
32 Ibid., pp. 13-14.
33 Ibid., p. 14.
34 Ibid.
35 Ibid., p. 12.
36 Ibid., pp. 12-13.
37 *PPL Montana, LLC v Montana*, 565 U.S., p. 576 (D. Mont. 2012).
38 Ibid., p. 603.

as a matter of state law',[39] while a federal common-law public trust doctrine would possibly be displaced by federal statutes.[40]

Upon the appeal, the D.C. Circuit affirmed the position of the lower court, by holding that the Supreme Court in *PPL Montana* 'directly and categorically rejected any federal constitutional foundation for [the public trust] doctrine, without qualification or reservation.'[41] In other words, in this case, the question whether the atmosphere is a natural resource protected by this doctrine at the federal level practically remained unanswered because the courts rejected the very idea of the federal public trust doctrine.

3.2. JULIANA v UNITED STATES

In August 2015, a group of minors from across the US filed a new federal atmospheric trust lawsuit in the District Court for the District of Oregon against the US President and a number of federal agencies. The lawsuit challenged numerous decisions taken by the defendants, such as 'whether and to what extent to regulate [carbon dioxide] emissions from power plants and vehicles, whether to permit fossil fuel extraction and development to take place on federal lands, how much to charge for use of those lands, whether to give tax breaks to the fossil fuel industry, whether to subsidize or directly fund that industry, whether to fund the construction of fossil fuel infrastructure such as natural gas pipelines at home and abroad, whether to permit the export and import of fossil fuels from and to the US, and whether to authorize new marine coal terminal projects.'[42]

According to the plaintiffs, the defendants have known for more than fifty years that carbon dioxide produced by burning fossil fuels was destabilizing the climate system, significantly endangering the plaintiffs, yet despite that knowledge, they exercised the sovereign authority over the country's atmosphere and fossil fuel resources in such a way that permitted, encouraged, and enabled continued exploitation, production and combustion of fossil fuels, thus deliberately allowing atmospheric concentrations of carbon dioxide to escalate to unprecedented levels.[43] The plaintiffs asserted that the defendants' decisions have substantially caused the planet to warm and the oceans to rise, thus drawing a direct causal line between defendants' policy choices and floods, food shortages, destruction of property, species extinction, and various other harms.[44] Accordingly, the plaintiffs based their lawsuit on constitutional grounds as well as the public trust doctrine. The defendants moved to dismiss the claims, just like in

39 *District of Columbia v Air Florida, Inc.*, 750 F.2d 1077, p. 1082 (D.C. Cir. 1984).
40 Ibid., p. 1085 n. 43.
41 *Alec L. ex rel. Loorz v McCarthy*, 561 Fed.Appx. 7, p. 8 (D.C. Cir. 2014).
42 *Juliana v United States*, 217 F.Supp.3d, p. 1234 (D. Or. 2016).
43 Ibid., p. 1233.
44 Ibid., p. 1234.

the first federal atmospheric trust case, challenging, *inter alia*, the application of the federal public trust doctrine.

The magistrate judge *Coffin* recommended denying the motions to dismiss, holding that the plaintiffs' public trust and other claims may proceed. The judge emphasized that the invoked public trust doctrine 'is directed against the United States and its unique sovereign interests over the territorial ocean waters and atmosphere of the nation',[45] observing that 'the complaint touches upon protected areas (territorial ocean waters at a minimum) impacted by the government's alleged conduct and harm to many plaintiffs given the alleged sea level rise, ocean acidification, and atmosphere change.'[46] Notably, the judge disagreed that the federal public trust doctrine and, therefore, its application to the atmosphere was foreclosed by cases referred to in *Alec L. v Jackson*, since the legislative and executive branches' control over the territorial sea is arguably not absolute and constrained by the public trust doctrine under the Constitution.[47] At any rate, the judge held that the matter should be further developed before the court could adjudicate.

This position was subsequently endorsed by district judge *Aiken*. The judge referred to the seminal work within this field by *Joseph Sax*, who highlighted three types of restrictions imposed by the public trust doctrine on the government: 1) the property subject to the trust must not only be used for a public purpose, but it must be held available for use by the general public; 2) the property may not be sold, even for a fair cash equivalent; 3) the property must be maintained for particular types of uses.[48] In light of this, judge *Aiken* stated that atmospheric trust lawsuits:

> '... depart from the "traditional" public trust litigation model, which generally centers on the second restriction, the prohibition against alienation of a public trust asset. Instead, plaintiffs assert defendants have violated their duties as trustees by nominally retaining control over trust assets while actually allowing their depletion and destruction, effectively violating the first and third restrictions by excluding the public from use and enjoyment of public resources.'[49]

Although the judge did not find it necessary to address the question of whether the atmosphere is a public trust natural resource at that particular point, she referred to the roots of the doctrine as well as its further interpretation by courts

45 *Juliana v United States*, Order and Findings & Recommendation, 6:15-cv-01517-TC, p. 20 (D. Or. 2016).
46 Ibid., p. 21.
47 Ibid., pp. 21-23.
48 *Juliana v United States*, 217 F.Supp.3d, p. 1254 (D. Or. 2016) (citing Sax J. L., *supra* note 15, p. 477).
49 Ibid.

and legal scholarship, which suggests that the answer may be positive.[50] Furthermore, she essentially reiterated the magistrate judge's view by holding that 'because a number of plaintiffs' injuries relate to the effects of ocean acidification and rising ocean temperatures, they have adequately alleged harm to public trust assets.'[51] Finally, the judge disagreed with the court's reasoning in *Alec L. v Jackson*, regarding the applicability of the federal public trust doctrine, by declining to interpret the doctrine as purely a matter of state law[52] and concluding that the 'federal government, like the states, holds public assets – at a minimum, the territorial seas – in trust for the people.'[53] The case was pending before the Ninth Circuit Court of Appeals at the time of writing; ultimately, the above-mentioned questions, including the applicability of the federal public trust doctrine, will likely be addressed by the Supreme Court.

4. STATE ATMOSPHERIC TRUST LITIGATION

While the application of the public trust doctrine at the federal level may be contentious, atmospheric trust litigation at the state level could have been conspicuously within the grasp of the judiciary, since the doctrine has been prolifically interpreted in state jurisprudence. This, however, is not exactly so. Although atmospheric trust lawsuits have already been filed in many state courts across the US, only a handful of courts have actually gone as far as to explicitly address the question of whether the atmosphere is a natural resource covered by the public trust doctrine.

4.1. DECLINING TO RECOGNIZE THE ATMOSPHERE AS A NATURAL RESOURCE

In the two early cases, *Aronow v State* and *Filippone v Iowa Department of Natural Resources*, the state courts in Minnesota and Iowa merely concluded that the public trust doctrine in the respective states does not apply to the atmosphere.[54] Notably though, in a concurring opinion one of the judges in the latter case expressed that there was 'a sound public policy basis' for extending the public trust doctrine to the atmosphere in Iowa by referring to relevant statutes, which

50 Ibid., p. 1255, fn 10.
51 Ibid., p. 1256.
52 Ibid., pp. 1256-1259.
53 Ibid., p. 1259.
54 See *Aronow v State*, A12-0585, 2012 WL 4476642, p. 3 (Minn. Ct. App. 2012); *Filippone ex rel. Filippone v Iowa Dept. of Natural Resources*, 829 N.W.2d 589, p. 2-3 (Iowa Ct. App. 2013).

included air as a natural resource to be protected for public benefit.[55] However, the same judge felt reluctant to have the court in the present case rule in a different manner.[56]

Meanwhile, in another early case *Svitak v State*, the Court of Appeals of Washington stated that declaring the atmosphere a public trust natural resource would 'create a new judicial cause of action [that] would necessarily involve resolution of complex social, economic, and environmental issues', which is inappropriate under common law 'because it invades the prerogatives of the legislative branch, thereby violating the separation of powers doctrine'.[57] The court concluded that '[b]ecause [...] state constitution does not address state responsibility for climate change, it is up to the legislature, not the judiciary, to decide whether to act as a matter of public policy.'[58]

A similar position was expressed by the Circuit Court of Oregon in *Chernaik v Kitzhaber*.[59] On the appeal, though, the Court of Appeals of Oregon held that a declaration on the atmosphere is justiciable and would not violate the separation of powers principle, meaning that the 'plaintiffs are entitled to a judicial declaration of whether [...] the atmosphere "is a trust resource" that the State of Oregon, as a trustee, has a fiduciary obligation to protect [...] from the impacts of climate change'.[60] On remand, the court of first instance explicitly shied away from recognizing the atmosphere as a natural resource protected by the state public trust doctrine. The court held that although the atmosphere 'perhaps may be said to fall within this broad definition of "resource", [it] does not fit into the structure and legal reasoning which underpins Oregon's public trust doctrine' for the following reasons: 1) unlike the submerged and submersible lands and the waters of the State, the State does not hold title to the atmosphere, as the latter 'is not acquired and sold or traded for economic value and hence is not a commodity' 2) the atmosphere does not present the concern of being 'exhaustible and irreplaceable' in nature, as it 'is not the type of resource that "can only be spent once," although it certainly can be polluted or otherwise changed'.[61] It remains to be seen though, whether such an interpretation is endorsed in the future.[62]

55 *Filippone ex rel. Filippone v Iowa Dept. of Natural Resources*, 829 N.W.2d 589, pp. 3-4 (Iowa Ct. App. 2013).
56 Ibid.
57 *Svitak ex rel. Svitak v State*, 2013 WL6632124, p. 2 (Wash. App. Div. 2013).
58 Ibid.
59 *Chernaik v Kitzhaber*, No. 16-11-09273, 2012 WL 10205018 (Or. Cir. Ct. 2012).
60 *Chernaik v Kitzhaber*, 328 P.3d 799, p. 808 (Or. Ct. App. 2014).
61 *Chernaik v Brown*, No. 16-11-09273, 2015 WL 12591229, pp. 10-12 (Or. Cir. Ct. 2015).
62 The case was on appeal at the time of writing.

4.2. LEAVING THE QUESTION OPEN

In *Kanuk v Alaska* the youth plaintiffs alleged that the defendant, the state Department of Natural Resources breached its public trust obligations stemming from the state constitution by failing 'to protect and preserve the atmosphere as a public trust resource'.[63] The plaintiffs asked the court to declare the atmosphere a public trust resource under the state constitution and 'to declare that the parameters of the [s]tate's duty to protect the atmosphere are [...] "dictated by the best available science", which required carbon dioxide emissions to peak in 2012 and be reduced by at least 6 % each year until 2050'.[64]

The Superior Court of Alaska dismissed the case as non-justiciable by observing, *inter alia*, that even if it 'were to declare the atmosphere a public trust resource [...], it would still have to determine whether the defendant breached its fiduciary duty to protect and preserve the atmosphere under the public trust doctrine', which would necessarily involve 'a policy determination about how the state should "fulfill" its fiduciary duty under the public trust doctrine.'[65] This position was reiterated by the Supreme Court of Alaska,[66] which, however, held that the plaintiffs' public trust and constitutional claims regarding the recognition of the atmosphere as a natural resource were justiciable, because they implied the judicial interpretation of the state constitution.[67]

In light of this, the court observed that although the state constitution does not explicitly create a public trust, it is applied to describe the nature of the state's duties with respect to wildlife and other natural resources meant for common use.[68] However, the court stopped short at recognizing the atmosphere as such a resource. For one, it held that the plaintiffs' request for a judgment that the state 'has failed to uphold its fiduciary obligations' concerning the atmosphere cannot be granted, since the court has declined, on political question grounds, to determine precisely what those obligations entail.[69] Second, the court held that although the state legislature 'has already intimated that the state acts as trustee with regard to the air just as it does with regard to other natural resources', the 'past application of public trust principles has been as a restraint on the state's ability to restrict public access to public resources, not as a theory for compelling regulation of those resources'.[70] Finally, the court judged that:

63 *Kanuk ex rel. Kanuk v State Dep't of Nat. Res.*, 335 P.3d 1088, p. 1091 (Alaska 2014).
64 Ibid.
65 *Kanuk v State of Alaska, Department of Natural Resources*, 3AN1107474, 2012 WL 8262431, p. 4 (Alaska Super. 2012).
66 *Kanuk ex rel. Kanuk v State Dep't of Nat. Res.*, 335 P.3d, p. 1097.
67 Ibid., p. 1099.
68 Ibid.
69 Ibid., p. 1101.
70 Ibid., p. 1102.

'Although declaring the atmosphere to be subject to the public trust doctrine could serve to clarify the legal relations at issue, it would certainly not "settle" them. It would have no immediate impact on greenhouse gas emissions in Alaska, it would not compel the State to take any particular action, nor would it protect the plaintiffs from the injuries they allege in their complaint. Declaratory relief would not tell the State what it needs to do in order to satisfy its trust duties and thus avoid future litigation; conversely it would not provide the plaintiffs any certain basis on which to determine in the future whether the State has breached its duties as trustee.'[71]

In the end, though, the court took an optimistic course of view, emphasizing that if the plaintiffs are able to bring forward justiciable claims in the future, they have a basis to proceed 'even absent a declaration that the atmosphere is subject to the public trust doctrine.'[72] This is so because the plaintiffs' complaint alleged 'that the atmosphere is inextricably linked to the entire ecosystem, and that climate change is having a detrimental impact on already recognized public trust resources such as water, shorelines, wildlife, and fish.'[73] The court thus concluded that the alleged breach of the state's duties with regard to the management of these resources does not depend on a declaratory judgment about the atmosphere.[74]

To a similar effect was another state atmospheric trust case *Foster v Ecology*, where the youth plaintiffs requested the government of the Washington state to implement rules that would ensure carbon dioxide emissions are reduced to levels scientifically required to protect the oceans from acidification and the climate system from further disruption.[75] The plaintiffs based their claims on the public trust doctrine under the state constitution.[76] Although judge Hill of the Superior Court of Washington did not explicitly expand the state public trust doctrine to encompass the atmosphere, she did nonetheless rebuke the agency's argument that 'since the public trust doctrine has not been expanded by the courts beyond protection of navigable waters it cannot be applied to protection of the "atmosphere."'[77] Specifically, the judge observed that such argument 'misses the point since current science makes clear that global warming is impacting the acidification of the oceans to alarming and dangerous levels, thus endangering the bounty of [...] navigable waters.'[78]

71 Ibid.
72 Ibid., p. 1103.
73 Ibid.
74 Ibid.
75 *Foster v Wash. Dep't of Ecology*, No. 14-2-25295-1 SEA, 2015 WL 7721362, p. 1 (Wash. Super. Ct. 2015).
76 Ibid., pp. 3-4.
77 Ibid., p. 4.
78 Ibid.

In other words, in this case the link between the state of the atmosphere and ocean acidification was once again critical in addressing the former's pollution with GHG emissions, with judge Hill emphasizing that:

> '… the navigable waters and the atmosphere are intertwined and to argue a separation of the two, or to argue that GHG emissions do not affect navigable waters is nonsensical. Therefore, the public trust doctrine mandates that the State act through its designated agency to protect what it holds in trust. The Department of Ecology is the agency authorized both to recommend changes in statutory emission standards and to establish limits that are responsible.'[79]

The judge, referring to the state constitution as well as the agency's own regulations, concluded that 'if ever there were a time to recognize through action [the] right to preservation of a healthful and pleasant atmosphere, the time is now.'[80]

In contrast, in another state atmospheric trust case *Funk v Wolf*, the Commonwealth Court of Pennsylvania left the question of whether the atmosphere is a natural resource virtually unaddressed, by merely observing that the requested declaration on the atmosphere would have no practical effect.[81] The unwillingness of the court in Pennsylvania to recognize the atmosphere as a public trust natural resource, or even address the question altogether, seemed strange due to the recognition of the public trust doctrine in the state constitution, granting environmental human rights and the existing state jurisprudence related to it.[82]

4.3. RECOGNIZING THE ATMOSPHERE AS A NATURAL RESOURCE

In *Butler v Brewer* the Court of Appeals of Arizona declared that courts have never 'determined that the atmosphere, or any other particular resource, is *not* a part of the public trust'.[83] Although the court stated that the present case 'does not address the measures by which a resource may be determined to be a part of the public trust or a framework for analyzing [whether] the public trust applies to the atmosphere with respect to GHG emissions and climate change', it 'assume[d] without deciding that the atmosphere is a part of the public trust'.[84]

---

79 Ibid.

80 Ibid.

81 *Funk v Wolf*, 144 A.3d 228, p. 251 (Pa. Cmwlth. 2016).

82 For a detailed analysis of this case see Varvaštian, S. (2017) 'Climate Change and the Constitutional Obligation to Protect Natural Resources: The Pennsylvania Atmospheric Trust Litigation', Climate Law 7(2-3), pp. 209-226.

83 *Butler ex rel. Peshlakai v Brewer*, Not Reported in P.3d (Ariz. Ct. App. 2013).

84 Ibid.

Meanwhile, the District Court of Texas in *Bosner-Lain v State Commission on Environmental Quality* and the Court of Appeals of New Mexico in *Sanders-Reed v Martinez* went even further, recognizing that the public trust doctrine and constitutional law in the respective states protect the atmosphere as a natural resource. Thus, the court in Texas ruled that:

> '... the public trust doctrine includes all natural resources of the State including the air and atmosphere. The public trust doctrine is not simply a common law doctrine but was incorporated into the Texas Constitution [...], which states: "The conservation and development of all of the natural resources of this State, [...] and the preservation and conservation of all such natural resources of the State are each and all hereby declared public rights and duties; and the Legislature shall pass all such laws as may be appropriate thereto."'[85]

Similarly the New Mexico court agreed that the state constitution 'recognizes that a public trust duty exists for the protection of New Mexico's natural resources, including the atmosphere, for the benefit of the people of this state.'[86]

Ultimately, however, despite recognizing the atmosphere as a public trust natural resource, the state courts in all three above-mentioned cases dismissed them on various other grounds.[87]

5. CONCLUDING REMARKS

So far, US courts have not demonstrated unity with regard to recognition of the atmosphere as a natural resource protected by the common law public trust doctrine. While some state courts have explicitly rejected the idea, or left the question open, others have been more willing to adapt the doctrine to the pressing needs of this century, recognizing its relevance to the relationship between atmospheric pollution with GHG emissions and climate change. Furthermore, it is still unclear whether the doctrine proves viable at federal level. Meanwhile, at state level, there are still many jurisdictions that have not tackled the question altogether.

Although putting the atmosphere on the map of natural resources is instrumental in recognizing that it could be damaged by GHG emissions, the discussed jurisprudence indicates that a bare declaration on the atmosphere

85 Bonser-Lain v Texas Com'n on Environmental Quality, 2012 WL 3164561 (Texas Dist. Ct. 2012).

86 *Sanders-Reed ex rel. Sanders-Reed v Martinez*, 350 P.3d 1221, p. 1225 (N.M. Ct. App. 2015).

87 For instance, the court in New Mexico concluded that the state constitution delegates the implementation of specific duties to the legislature; therefore, 'the courts cannot independently intervene to impose a common law public trust duty upon the State to regulate greenhouse gases in the atmosphere.' (*Ibid.*, pp. 1225-1227).

might have little practical effect; it is more rational to link it to other resources. Thus, it is important to stress the interaction between the atmosphere and water resources, which offers a novel angle to the application of the public trust doctrine, while building on the established traditional interpretation of it by courts all across the US. This way, plaintiffs in future atmospheric trust litigation could avoid the pitfalls faced by their predecessors and present much more viable claims. Regardless of whether such claims would target action at federal or state level, their successful exploration would be crucial as, despite all the setbacks, it has long been perceived that no step is too small to take in addressing climate change.

PART V

ECOSYSTEM APPROACHES AND ADAPTIVE MANAGEMENT

CHAPTER 9

MANAGING ENVIRONMENTAL UTILISATION SPACE IN THE DUTCH ENVIRONMENT AND PLANNING ACT

Lolke S. Braaksma and Kars J. de Graaf*

ABSTRACT

This chapter analyses how the environmental utilisation space concept is implemented in the upcoming Dutch Environment and Planning Act and to what extent this concept contributes to the goal of sustainable development. It first studies the origins and application of the environmental utilisation space concept in Dutch environmental law and its relationship with sustainable development and the ecosystem approach. The chapter continues with an analysis of the implementation of this concept by the Dutch legislator in the Crisis and Recovery Act of 2010 and the future Environment and Planning Act, with an emphasis on the role of municipalities in managing environmental utilisation space in environmental plans and the implementation of a programmatic approach. The chapter finishes with a summary of the obstacles and incentives relevant when implementing the environmental utilisation space concept in the future Environment and Planning Act.

---

* Lolke S. Braaksma, LLM is a PhD candidate within the Research Programme Law on Energy and Sustainability at the University of Groningen (L.S.Braaksma@rug.nl); Kars J. de Graaf is Associate professor with a chair in Public Law and Sustainability, University of Groningen (K.J.de.Graaf@rug.nl).

1. INTRODUCTION

The current legal framework in the Netherlands is considered insufficient to provide the government with the instruments needed to actively work towards a sustainable society while allowing for economic development.[1] One of the main reasons is the lack of an integral and coherent approach for regulating the physical environment that people live in. Environmental principles, standards and values are spread across many different legislative acts and provisions focus either on a particular subject or address one particular environmental issue.[2] The Dutch legislator therefore adopted the Environment and Planning Act (EPA) – which is anticipated to come into force in 2021 – in which environmental, spatial planning and nature conservation acts are integrated into one act.[3] The EPA incorporates existing legal instruments, and adds new elements, striving towards a sustainable society.[4] It also aims to provide more effective and efficient tools to implement EU environmental law in the Dutch legal order.

One of the guiding concepts for the EPA is the (environmental) utilisation space concept, which functions as a general notion for the legislator as well as the public administration when designing environmental legislation and policies. Utilisation space is defined in the Explanatory Memorandum of the EPA as the '*the legal leeway that exists in a specific area to allow for the realisation of (economic) activities*'. According to the legislator, it has a slightly broader meaning than the term *environmental* utilisation space, which refers to the legal leeway that exists only in relation to the existing legal requirements to protect the environment.[5] The government chose to use the term utilisation space as it is more appropriate because of the broad scope of the EPA.

The EPA restructures practically all regulation concerned with the physical environment, which includes nature, water, infrastructure, housing, parking, recreation and mobility. The Netherlands is densely populated and the physical environment is therefore intensively used.[6] In the future EPA, the Environmental Utilisation Space Concept (EUS concept) is connected both to the legal leeway within binding environmental standards and to the actual quality of the physical environment in a certain area. The implementation of this concept can lead to

1 See *Parliamentary Papers II* 2013/14, 33 962, No. 3, pp. 6-10.
2 See for example: Platjouw, F.M. (2016) '*Environmental Law and the Ecosystem Approach. Maintaining ecological integrity through consistency*', Routledge, p. 146.
3 *Parliamentary Papers II* 2013/14, 33 962, No. 3, p. 6.
4 Ibid., pp. 7-8.
5 Ibid., see the attached appendix, pp. 388-389.
6 Borgers, H.C. and N.C.M. Fikke (2016) 'Verdeling van gebruiksruimte met de Omgevingswet: Devide et empira – slim en samenhangend sturen op de benutting en bescherming van de leefomgeving', *Bouwrecht*, Vol. 9, No. 66, p. 1.

more coherent ways to strive towards a sustainable use of ecosystems while maintaining ecological integrity.

This chapter analyses to what extent the EUS concept, as set out in theory, is implemented in the EPA. Although the entire act itself could be seen as an implementation of this concept, this chapter focuses on two specific legal instruments within the EPA: municipal environmental plans and the programmatic approach. In doing so, we emphasize the relationship between the EUS concept and the notions of sustainable development and the ecosystem approach. We have structured our views as follows. The next section starts by describing the origins of the EUS concept and continues to analyse the differences between the legal- and the ecologic/economic definitions of this concept and how it relates to sustainable development and the ecosystem approach. After that, an analysis will be presented in section 3 on how the EUS concept is implemented throughout the EPA and in particular with regard to two legal instruments: the municipal environmental plans and the programmatic approach. The chapter finishes in section 4 with conclusions, in which a summary will be given of the obstacles and the incentives when implementing the EUS concept in environmental legislation and policies.

2. ENVIRONMENTAL UTILISATION SPACE: THE CONCEPT

The implementation of the EUS concept allows for a coherent way to balance the use or exploitation of ecosystems while maintaining the ecological integrity of those ecosystems. To clarify this, we will provide a general overview of the origins of this concept, as it was introduced originally as an economic theory (section 2.1). After that, we will identify the applications of this concept. It will be shown that the EUS concept has different applications in environmental policies and that it is often linked to the notion of sustainable development and the ecosystem approach (section 2.2).

2.1. ORIGINS

The EUS concept was originally developed by Siebert in 1982 and was introduced in the Netherlands by Opschoor in 1987.[7] Opschoor defines environmental utilisation space as: '*the locus of all feasible combinations of environmental services that represent steady states in terms of levels of relevant environmental quality and*

7 Siebert, H. (1982) 'Nature as a life support system: renewable resources and environmental disruption', *Journal of Economics*, Vol. 42, No. 2, pp. 133-142.

stocks of renewable resources'.[8] With this definition in mind, the EUS concept reflects the (limits of the) services provided by the Earth's ecosystems such as renewable, semi-renewable and non-renewable resources and the capacity to absorb waste and pollution. The concept was innovative, as it focuses on the reason why these limits exist in the first place, namely that the physical (ecological) environment is only capable of maintaining human exploitation to a certain extent.[9] This means that there are limits to the amount of environmental pressure that the earth's ecosystems can take without damaging these systems or the life support processes that they enable.[10] According to Sips et al. the environment satisfies human needs in two main ways: firstly, by supplying raw materials and energy as inputs to the economic systems, and secondly, by collecting and regenerating waste and emissions on the output side of the economic system.[11] Therefore, environmental utilisation space is related to the environmentally relevant material aspects of economic activity.[12]

2.2. RELATED CONCEPTS FOR DESIGNING ENVIRONMENTAL LEGISLATION AND POLICY

Sustainable development and an integral approach in policies to regulate the environment are notions that are often linked with the EUS concept.[13] With the publication of the report 'Our Common Future' (WCED) in 1987, the notion of sustainable development gained considerable attention worldwide.[14] Sustainable development is defined here as '*(...) paths of human progress that meet the needs and aspirations of the present generation without compromising the ability of future generations to meet their needs*'.[15] This definition implies that a balance has to be achieved between the quality of the physical environment (planet), the economy (profit) and the social aspects (people), because ultimately, the goal of the sustainable development concept is to provide a foundation for environmental

8 Opschoor, J.B. and R. Weterings (1994) 'Environmental utilisation space: an introduction', *Tijdschrift voor Milieukunde*, Vol. 9, No. 5, p. 199.

9 United Nations World Commission on Environment and Development, '*Our Common Future*', 1987, p. 30.

10 Opschoor, J.B. and R. Weterings (1994) 'Environmental utilisation space: an introduction', *Tijdschrift voor Milieukunde*, Vol. 9, No. 5, p. 198.

11 Sips, H. *et al.* (1994) 'Environmental utilisation space and Dutch environmental policy', *Tijdschrift voor Milieukunde*, Vol. 9, No. 5, p. 208.

12 Opschoor, J.B. and R. Weterings (1994) 'Environmental utilisation space: an introduction', *Tijdschrift voor Milieukunde*, Vol. 9, No. 5, p. 204.

13 For example by Opschoor, J.B. and R. Weterings (1994) 'Environmental utilisation space: an introduction', *Tijdschrift voor Milieukunde*, Vol. 9, No. 5, p. 199.

14 United Nations World Commission on Environment and Development, '*Our Common Future*', 1987. In this report the interaction between economic growth and the environment is indicated. It shows that economic growth can be ecologically unsustainable.

15 Ibid., p. 29.

legislation and policy that is ecologically justifiable. The definition and the implications of the concept itself have been debated but the elements of the original formulation of the sustainable development concept 'remain sufficient, valid and instructive'.[16] Here we would like to emphasize – with Gaines – that ecological sustainability is the indispensable requirement for sustainable development.[17]

Another concept related to the EUS concept is the so-called ecosystem approach. Since the 1980s the understanding for the need of a more holistic approach had been set in motion through the recognition that permits for different human activities, such as industrial activities and infrastructure construction were inadequate to face the challenges ahead.[18] The idea of an ecosystem approach has specifically been relevant in nature conservation and the management of protected areas. There is no universally shared definition that encapsulates this concept in its totality.[19] Nevertheless, Trouwborst argues that the ecosystem approach has three core elements that are substantially agreed upon by scholars.[20] When applying the ecosystem approach, it entails: (i) a holistic management of human activities, (ii) based on the best available knowledge on the components, structure and dynamics of ecosystems, (iii) and aimed at satisfying human needs in a way that does not compromise the integrity, or health, of ecosystems.[21] The ecosystem approach is a concept for a governance approach that focuses on the operationalisation of the EUS concept and works towards a sustainable use of ecosystems that aims to maintain the ecosystem integrity.[22]

---

16 Sustainable development can be achieved through a holistic analysis, equity, adaptability, and multi-level governance, see: Squintani, L. and H.H.B. Vedder with M. Reese and B. Vanheusden (eds.) (2014) '*Sustainable Energy United in Diversity: Challenges and Approaches in Energy Transition in the EU*', European Environmental Law Forum, Vol. 1, p. 1; in essence these criteria are substantially equal to the theory as presented by Opschoor, thus connecting the EUS concept to sustainable development.

17 Gaines, S.E. (2014) 'The energy revolution as sustainable development', in: L. Squintani and H.H.B. Vedder with M. Reese and B. Vanheusden (eds.), '*Sustainable Energy United in Diversity: Challenges and Approaches in Energy Transition in the EU*', European Environmental Law Forum, Vol. 1, p. 10.

18 See Kidd, S., A. Plater and C. Frid (2011) '*The Ecosystem Approach to Marine Planning and Management*', Earthscan, p. 1; Platjouw, F.M. (2016) '*Environmental Law and the Ecosystem Approach. Maintaining ecological integrity through consistency*', Routledge, p. 30.

19 Ibid., pp. 30-31.

20 Trouwborst, A. (2009) 'The Precautionary Principle and the Ecosystem Approach in International Law: Differences, Similarities and Linkages', *Review of European Community and International Environmental Law*, Vol. 18, Issue 1, pp. 26-28.

21 A report by the United Nations General Assembly describes seven core elements of the ecosystem approach: UNGA, Report on the work of the United Nations Open-ended Informal Consultative Process on Oceans and the Law of the Sea at its seventh Meeting (17 July 2006) A/61/156, para. 6.

22 Platjouw, F.M. (2016) '*Environmental Law and the Ecosystem Approach. Maintaining ecological integrity through consistency*', Routledge, p. 32. The ecosystem approach is also the primary

The implementation of the ecosystem approach in environmental policies will result in different assessment frameworks being integrated into one through the development of a general criterion. With this criterion, it is possible to create an integral assessment framework to assess individual permit applications. A difficulty of the ecosystem approach is to develop this integral assessment framework, because of the complexity and uncertainties of appreciating the (true) value of ecosystem services.[23] To appropriately balance the conservation of the structure and functioning of ecosystems while allowing ecosystems to provide services for human purposes, it is necessary to operationalize the concept of the ecosystem approach. This can be done through different methods, which we will not discuss in this chapter.[24]

A couple of remarks can be made when comparing the concepts of sustainable development and the ecosystem approach with the EUS concept. Implementing the EUS concept in environmental legislation and policy is, for example, rather difficult because of uncertainty about the functioning of ecosystems in general and the adaptability of such systems in a specific situation. The same difficulty is relevant when governments implement the concepts of sustainable development and the ecosystem approach; it is not easy to ensure that all elements are sufficiently taken into account and a proper balance between those elements is struck. At the core, however, the EUS concept and the ecosystem approach seem to be focused even more on the ecological validity of policies and regulations than sustainable development. Other interests, such as the need for economic development and social wellbeing are also taken into account in the latter concept. Nevertheless, the *utilisation space concept*, as well as the ecosystem approach do take into account interests like public participation in decision-making processes as well as legal protection.[25] This is of course the result of the need to translate these concepts into legal instruments and binding regulations that are agreed upon within a political arena.

---

framework for action under the Convention on Biological Diversity (CBD) since the seventh Conference of the Parties (COP 7, Decision VII/11) and describes it as a strategy for the integrated management of land, water and living resources that promotes conservation and sustainable use in an equitable way.

23 See: Tolsma, H.D. (2010) 'Integrated environmental permitting', *Environmental Law Network International*, pp. 81-87; Tolsma also describes other difficulties when implementing an integral assessment framework (model 4), such as legal uncertainties and a lack of judicial control.

24 See: Sukhdev, P. (ed.) (2008) '*The Economics of Ecosystems and Biodiversity: Ecological and Economic Foundations*', European Communities; Platjouw, F.M. (2016) '*Environmental Law and the Ecosystem Approach. Maintaining ecological integrity through consistency*', Routledge.

25 Lang, H. (2014) '*Public Participation in Environmental Decision-Making in China: Towards an Ecosystem Approach*', PhD thesis, University of Groningen, p. 24 ff., see also the Convention of Biological Diversity, '*Decision V/6: Ecosystem Approach*', Fifth Ordinary Meeting of the Conference of the Parties (COP 5), 2011.

3. THE EUS CONCEPT AND THE FUTURE ENVIRONMENT AND PLANNING ACT

In this section, we will start with an overview of the EUS concept in the Crisis and Recovery Act of 2010, as this is the first legislative act in the Netherlands that explicitly mentions the term 'environmental utilisation space' (section 3.1). After that, we analyse to what extent the implementation of the EUS concept in the future Dutch EPA is in accordance with the ideas set out in the previous section (section 3.2). Finally, we will discuss two key legal instruments that can be applied to influence the distribution of environmental utilisation space: the municipal environmental plan that implements area-specific environmental quality standards (section 3.3) and the programmatic approach (section 3.4).

3.1. DEVELOPMENT OF THE EUS CONCEPT IN DUTCH ENVIRONMENTAL LAW

The EUS concept has been discussed in the Netherlands for over 30 years, but was not explicitly mentioned in binding environmental regulations until the recent Crisis and Recovery Act (CRA) of 2010 came into force.[26] The term 'environmental utilisation space', however, has been used frequently in environmental policies before that.[27] Environmental utilisation space is not exclusively used for the environment either, as issues such as nature conservation, energy transition and managing natural resources are also regulated on the basis of this concept. In a report from the Scientific Council for Government Policy in 1994, a couple of reasons are presented for not implementing the EUS concept directly into binding regulations. The main reasons are the uncertainty about the possibility to objectively measure environmental utilisation space and the fact that it is unknown what elements of ecosystems contribute to sustainable development because of the versatility of ecosystems.[28]

Nevertheless, the CRA explicitly mentions environmental utilisation space in one of its provisions. Article 2.1 CRA stipulates that environmental utilisation space is: '*the margin within a development area between the existing environmental quality and the applicable environmental quality standards, which is available to realize activities detrimental to the environment*'. The legislator allows the government to experiment with the EUS concept to stimulate (sustainable) economic development within existing urban areas, existing businesses and the

26 Since the Brundtland report in 1987, different reports, like the report '*Duurzame risico's: een blijvend gegeven*', from the Netherlands Scientific Council for Government Policy (1994) refer to this concept.

27 *Parliamentary Papers II* 2013/14, 33 962, No. 3, p. 286.

28 Report 'Duurzame risico's: een blijvend gegeven', The Netherlands Scientific Council for Government Policy (1994), pp. 36-37.

enlargement of the Port of Rotterdam, but only for a period less than ten years.[29] The aim is to provide local governments with an instrument to create environmental utilisation space that will allow for economic development.[30] The term 'environmental utilisation space' can also be found in other legislation, such as in aviation law.[31] Here, it refers to the space or leeway that is available within the applicable environmental standards, mostly concerned with noise pollution. If there is any environmental utilisation space, it can be used to allow for new economic developments.

3.2. THE ENVIRONMENT AND PLANNING ACT

Before discussing the implementation of the EUS concept in the EPA, we want to note that all government bodies have to keep in mind the key objective of the EPA when using the legal instruments that are provided. Article 1.3 EPA stipulates that: '*With a view to ensuring sustainable development, the habitability of the country and the protection and improvement of the living environment, this Act aims to achieve the following interrelated objectives: a. to achieve and maintain a safe and healthy physical environment and good environmental quality, and b. to effectively manage, use and develop the physical environment in order to perform societal needs.*'[32] In Dutch legislative acts, this provision is the first in which the concept of sustainable development is explicitly mentioned. The meaning of the concept is further clarified in the Explanatory Memorandum of the EPA. A reference is made here to the Brundtland report, as the definition given there is accepted worldwide.[33] The EPA and the legal instruments it provides are aimed at achieving sustainable development, for instance by allowing the government to set targets to achieve (EU) environmental quality standards and providing for specific obligations to provide (local) governments with information on how to achieve them.[34]

Most environmental standards are not stipulated by the EPA itself but are implemented by delegated legislation such as governmental decrees.[35] In the

29 See Article 2.2 Crisis and Recovery Act.

30 Boeve, M.N. (2017) '*Het omgevingsrecht van de compacte stad: Het omgevingsrechtelijk instrumentarium voor verdichting en functiemenging in het stedelijk gebied*', (diss. UvA), UvA-DARE, pp. 17-18.

31 Aanhef Wijzigingswet Wet luchtvaart, *Government Gazette*, 2008, 561.

32 See also De Graaf, K.J., F.M. Platjouw and H.D. Tolsma (2017) 'The future Dutch Environment and Planning Act in light of the ecosystem approach', *Ecosystem Services*, Vol. 23, PART A, p. 11.

33 *Parliamentary Papers II* 2013/14, 33 962, No. 3, p. 12.

34 Ibid., p. 281.

35 De Graaf, K.J., F.M. Platjouw and H.D. Tolsma (2017) 'The future Dutch Environment and Planning Act in light of the ecosystem approach', *Ecosystem Services*, Vol. 23, PART A, p. 9; the relevant governmental decrees are the 'Besluit activiteiten leefomgeving (Bal.)' and the 'Besluit kwaliteit leefomgeving (Bkl.)'.

Explanatory Memorandum of the EPA, the term (environmental) utilisation space is mentioned regularly and is mostly linked to the discretionary powers of the municipal council to manage the quality of the (local) physical environment by implementing area-specific environmental quality standards in an environmental plan and also to the possibility of government bodies to introduce a plan- or programmatic approach to achieve goals concerned with the quality of the physical environment.[36] The re-introduction of environmental utilisation space can be seen as a progressive understanding of the usefulness of this concept.[37] It does seem, however, that the government tries to avoid putting too much emphasis on the interest of protecting the environment by introducing and referring primarily to the term 'utilisation space' instead of 'environmental utilisation space' in the Explanatory Memorandum of the EPA. Perhaps the legislator intends to relate the concept more to economic development, rather than its original purpose: ecological sustainability.

For some human activities – like those that have a relevant spatial implication – the limits of the utilisation space are set mainly through the public processes that lead to amendments to environmental plans, projects decisions or permits. For human activities – like those that have a serious detrimental consequence for any of the compartments of the environment – limitations will be imposed by adopting (area-specific) environmental quality standards (for noise, air quality or smell), general rules and instructions adopted by a higher tier of government which are binding for decentralized governments.[38] For the Dutch legislator, the EUS concept offers an instrument to achieve balance and consistency between the exploitation of the environment for economic activities and protecting of the same environment against the effects of those activities. Instead of restricting the use of the EUS concept to so-called development areas, as Article 2.1 Crisis and Recovery Act does, it will introduce a generic basis for the balancing of different interests when making decisions about the permissibility of human activities in the physical environment.

From the use of the EUS concept in the Explanatory Memorandum of the EPA , it can be concluded that mentioning the EUS concept there only refers to the available *legal space*. Fikke and Borgers argue, in this context, that the distribution of environmental utilisation space for human activities is not merely a policy choice between combinations of the exploitation and the protection of

36 *Parliamentary Papers II* 2013/14, 33 962, No. 3, pp. 286/287; see also: Groothuijse, F.A.G., R. Uylenburg and M.N. Boeve (2010) 'Het omgevingsrecht geprogrammeerd, Verkenning van de juridische mogelijkheden voor het ontwikkelen en harmoniseren van een programmatische aanpak in het omgevingsrecht', *STEM*, p. 19.

37 Borgers, H.C. and N.C.M. Fikke (2016) 'Verdeling van gebruiksruimte met de Omgevingswet: Devide et empira – slim en samenhangend sturen op de benutting en bescherming van de leefomgeving', *Bouwrecht*, Vol. 9, No. 66.

38 *Parliamentary Papers II* 2013/14, 33 962, No. 3, p. 286.

the environment.[39] A thorough (scientific) assessment of the existing environmental quality and the consequences of human activity in a particular situation is required, as well as a decision to establish the carrying capacity of the physical environment in order to balance conflicting interests. These conflicting interests can consist of safety, economy, health and the interest of economic development. This indicates that the EUS concept in the EPA does not correspond exactly with the original concept as described by Opschoor in 1987. Although the concept definitely has its roots in the original EUS concept, there is also the recognition that the available environmental space will not completely be determined by environmental concerns, such as the regenerative capacity of ecosystems. The balance between the need for economic development (exploitation of ecosystems) and the protection of the environment for future generations will be struck in the political arena. The EPA itself is considered 'colourless' on how this balance has to be struck by (local) government(s) in practice, leaving the risk that other interests are favoured at the expense of environmental protection.[40]

3.3. AREA-SPECIFIC ENVIRONMENTAL QUALITY STANDARDS IN ENVIRONMENTAL PLANS

With the future EPA, municipalities will be obliged to adopt a single environmental plan in which all (local) regulations concerned with the physical environment in their territory are stipulated (Article 2.4 EPA). This includes assessment criteria for decentralized permit systems, and environmental quality standards, resulting in an integrated regulatory environmental plan.[41] The idea is that environmental plans enable an integrated approach to regulating the physical environment. The environmental plan, therefore, has a remarkably broad scope in which the local public authority also has to weigh and balance all relevant interest when allocating functions to locations (Article 4.2 EPA), like in a zoning plan on the basis of spatial interests. When allocating functions to locations, the local public authority enjoys a wide margin of discretion.[42]

A specific element of environmental plans will be the possibility to manage the environmental quality of specific areas by setting local area-specific environmental quality standards. Environmental quality standards, in general, are

---

39 Borgers, H.C. and N.C.M. Fikke (2016) 'Verdeling van gebruiksruimte met de Omgevingswet: Devide et empira – slim en samenhangend sturen op de benutting en bescherming van de leefomgeving', *Bouwrecht*, Vol. 9, No. 66.

40 See for example: Backes, Ch.W. (2017) 'De kleur van de Omgevingswet', *Tijdschrift voor Omgevingsrecht*, No. 2, pp. 68-74.

41 De Graaf, K.J., F.M. Platjouw and H.D. Tolsma (2017) 'The future Dutch Environment and Planning Act in light of the ecosystem approach', *Ecosystem Services*, Vol. 23, PART A, p. 12.

42 Ibid., p. 12, this discretion is restricted by both national and EU environmental quality standards.

important in multiple ways, one of which is to serve as a reference framework for the government when distributing environmental utilisation space, as it clarifies the state or quality that parts of the physical environment must have within a specific time frame.[43] The goal can either be stipulated in legally binding terms or in a best efforts obligation, with the date of commencement and the locations specified. The competent public authority to establish these local area-specific environmental quality standards is the municipal council, unless another (higher) tier of government has already set specific standards.

The Explanatory Memorandum of the EPA describes various types of such local environmental quality standards, e.g. the maximum concentration of substances in the environment (water, soil or air) and the average probability that a certain level will be exceeded in a given year.[44] The reason for allowing many different sorts of environmental quality standards is to offer '*the possibility to adopt tailor-made approaches that will adhere closely to the requirements of the EU directives (such as the Water Framework Directive, the Air Quality Directive and the National Emission Ceilings Directive).*'[45] Furthermore, in light of the relevant governmental decree, local governments are able to 'tune' the local area-specific environmental standards to be appropriate for area-specific features and qualities of the local environment.[46] This means the municipal council can determine the desired or permissible environmental quality levels for various components, such as noise, safety, air, vibration, soil pollution and odour. In order to clarify this idea, the Explanatory Memorandum of the EPA compares the role of the municipal council in setting environmental quality standards with the role of a professional DJ that uses his audio mixer (*mengpaneel*) to manage different sounds to allow for the most appropriate mix for the occasion. The municipal council sets environmental quality standards that are tailor-made for the local physical environment and provides the legal framework that will be decisive to allow or refuse specific human activities within that area. These quality levels are the prerequisites for economic development, and will therefore determine the environmental utilisation space available in that specific area.

The municipal council determines the appropriate quality standards per component (noise, external safety, air, vibration, odour, soil pollution and light), but it is possible to involve the desired quality of other sectoral components when determining standards to create a more coherent legal framework of area-specific environmental values.[47] This discretionary power can, however, also result in municipalities creating environmental plans in which the environmental quality

---

43 Ibid., p. 19.

44 *Parliamentary Papers II* 2013/14, 33 962, No. 3, pp. 20-21.

45 Ibid., p. 20.

46 See the Explanatory Memorandum of Order of Council the 'Besluit kwaliteit leefomgeving'.

47 Brans, M.C. (2016) 'Flexibiliteitsmogelijkheden in de Omgevingswet; de AMvB's verkend (deel 2)', *Bouwrecht*, Vol. 96, Afl. 12, p. 652.

standards are fixed on the absolute minimum, resulting in more environmental utilisation space at the expense of the environment. With regard to air quality and external safety, it is not possible to determine less strict values than the standard values stated in national or EU regulations. For sound, vibration and odour, it is possible to 'tune' the environmental values according to the limits set out in the appendix of the corresponding Order of Council. This means that municipalities are to a large extent responsible for regulating human activities with local environmental effects and thus for determining the appropriate environmental utilisation space, based on those local environmental effects. It is questionable whether local governments will be sufficiently encouraged and able to put environmental protection above local economic development when using the environmental plan to manage the environmental utilisation space in their municipality.

3.4. THE PLAN OR PROGRAMMATIC APPROACH

Another relevant instrument specifically introduced in Dutch environmental law to create and manage environmental utilisation space in a specific area is the plan- or programmatic approach.[48] Such an approach is used increasingly in Dutch environmental law, as well as on the European level.[49] A distinction can be made between sectoral plans or programmes that try to create utilisation space relating to a specific environmental compartment and a generic approach. Sectoral approaches focus on specific segments of the environment, such as air quality, water quality or nitrogen deposition.[50] Generic approaches allow for coordination between all sorts of sectoral provisions when trying to create utilisation space in a specific area. An example is the previously mentioned instrument of Article 2.1 of the Crisis and Recovery Act, which allows government to put in place regulation for different aspects of the environment in a development area simultaneously. The idea of a plan- or programmatic approach is that the assessment whether an environmental quality standard can be achieved or maintained does not take place on the level of granting or denying an individual permit, but at the plan- or programme level. Sectoral objectives and goals like environmental quality standards are managed on the plan- or programme level in order to both achieve the goal within the set time frame and

48 Boeve, M.N. (2017) 'Het omgevingsrecht van de compacte stad: Het omgevingsrechtelijk instrumentarium voor verdichting en functiemenging in het stedelijk gebied', (diss. UvA), UvA-DARE, p. 268 ff.

49 See: Squintani, L. and H.F.M.W. van Rijswick (2016) 'Improving Legal Certainty and Adaptability in the Programmatic Approach', *Journal of Environmental Law*, Vol. 28, No. 3. pp. 443-470.

50 Ibid., p. 269; for example the National Cooperation Air quality (NSL) and the Dutch implementation of the Water Framework Directive (2000/60/EG).

provide for environmental utilisation space to allow for new economic development.

A special programme under the EPA will be a programme with a so-called programmatic approach. This type of programme provides public authorities with the competence to implement a programme that provides an alternative assessment framework for deciding on permit applications, project decisions or about amendments to the environmental plan.[51] This alternative assessment framework entails that competent local authorities will have to implement a program which contains specific measures for the development, use, management, protection or maintenance of the physical environment, which have to be realized within a certain time frame.[52] The Dutch Government already gained notable experience with the programmatic approach resulting in the National Co-operation Programme on Air Quality' (*Nationaal Samenwerkingsprogramma Luchtkwaliteit*) and the Programmatic Approach to Nitrogen (*Programmatische aanpak Stikstof*).[53]

The programmatic approach functions as a framework for the assessment and permissibility of activities in a specific area. In the EPA the programmatic approach is introduced as an instrument, which instructs local governments to assess the permissibility of activities in accordance with the applicable programme(s).[54] The goal of any programmatic approach is to achieve environmental quality standards or other objectives within a certain time frame, established either by the competent local public authorities or imposed by EU secondary legislation.[55] To that end, the programme will most likely introduce measures and regulation that are specifically aimed to achieve that goal. Simultaneously, the programmatic approach allows for new economic development because environmental utilisation space is created by the programme. A potential risk for environmental protection occurs when activities that are detrimental to the quality of the environment are permitted at a moment when the (positive) results of the measure stipulated in the programme are not yet or only partly available.[56]

---

51 *Parliamentary Papers II* 2013/14, 33 962, No. 3, p. 17.

52 Article 3.15 EPA ff; De Graaf, K.J., F.M. Platjouw and H.D. Tolsma (2017) 'The future Dutch Environment and Planning Act in light of the ecosystem approach', *Ecosystem Services*, Vol. 23, PART A, p. 13.

53 Ibid., p. 14. For an introduction into the Dutch programmatic approach, see: Boeve, M.N. and B. van den Broek (2012) The Programmatic Approach; A Flexible and Complex Tool to Achieve Environmental Quality Standards, *Utrecht Law Review*, Vol. 8, No. 3, pp. 74-85.

54 *Parliamentary Papers II* 2013/14 33 962, No. 3, p. 34.

55 Ibid., p. 34.

56 At this time the Netherlands is waiting on a preliminary ruling by the ECJ about the Dutch programmatic approach to Nitrogen as there are several questions whether the programme is contrary to the European Habitats Directive. For potential shortcomings of this approach see: H. Schoukens (2017) 'Habitats Restoration Measures as Facilitators for Economic Development within the context of EU Habitats Directive: Balancing No Net Loss with the Preventive

Another risk when using a programme is the amount of discretion given to public authorities. In general, a programme allows public authorities to balance the detrimental consequences of economic development or human activity for the environment with the measures intended to relieve the pressure on the environment and achieve a specific environmental quality standard (or another objective relating to the physical environment). It is questionable to what extent public authorities use this discretion set out in the assessment framework to work towards sustainable development.[57]

4. CONCLUDING REMARKS

The EUS concept is closely related to the concepts of sustainable development and the ecosystem approach and has been used in Dutch environmental policies for over 30 years. In 2010 it has explicitly been used in the legal provisions of the Crisis and Recovery Act in order to stimulate sustainable economic development. The concept has proven to be useful when there is a desire to create environmental utilisation space in order to allow for economic development. It is therefore not surprising that the EUS concept, although not explicitly mentioned in the text of the future EPA itself, is an important, underlying and guiding concept for the application of all legal instruments introduced and that is connected to the concept of sustainable development. When the EPA comes into force, the notion of environmental utilisation space, sustainable development and the ecosystem approach appear to gain relevance. The implementation of the EUS concept, however, does not correspond in its entirety with the original idea of Opschoor in 1987, as multiple interests are taken into account when the environmental quality standards are adopted and – understandably – political arguments will play a role as well. The environmental utilisation space is therefore not (only) linked to the ecosystems within the environment and the services they provide, but also to other interests, such as health and economic development, with the risk that the concern for environmental protection becomes less important to the benefit of economic development.

For at least two of the instruments provided in the future Dutch EPA, the legislator has explicitly indicated that they have an important role to play in determining and adopting binding boundaries for the availability of environmental utilisation space. In particular the environmental plan grants the

Approach?, *Journal of Environmental Law*, Vol. 29, No. 1, pp. 47-73 and chapter 10; also see the opinion of Advocate General Kokott delivered on 25 July 2018 in joined cases C-293/17 and C-294/17, ECLI:EU:C:2018:622.

57 De Graaf, K.J., F.M. Platjouw and H.D. Tolsma (2017) 'The future Dutch Environment and Planning Act in light of the ecosystem approach', *Ecosystem Services*, Vol. 23, PART A, p. 14.

municipal council the possibility to adopt local area-specific environmental quality standards that allow these authorities – like DJs with an audio mixer – to 'tune' those environmental values in such a way that they are appropriate for the specific area on the basis of an assessment of the carrying and the regenerative capacities of the local environment, including the inhabitants, is closely related to the environmental utilisation space concept. Although it must be said that these environmental quality standards are based on *local* (negative) environmental consequences only. When tuning the environmental quality values in environmental plans, municipalities will enjoy a considerable discretion, limited by legislative standards. The exact degree of discretion varies between the different components. For air quality and external safety, there are European and national provisions that limit discretion for local authorities. But for odour, noise and vibrations the local authorities have a large degree of discretion.

The Dutch legislator has also indicated that the so-called plan- or programmatic approach is an important instrument that governments can use to create environmental utilisation space. The programmatic approach is an example of an approach that allows governments to assess whether environmental quality values will be met or achieved on the 'higher' level of the programme instead of at the level of individual permits. The idea is that the programme introduces (legal) measures that will create environmental utilisation space to allow further (economic) development while achieving the desired environmental quality within the set time frame.

The obstacles or threats lie in the (potential) danger that the discretion awarded to the local authorities will allow these actors to adopt less strict environmental quality standards than is appropriate with a view to the carrying and regenerative capacity of the local environment. Local authorities have to find a balance between the interests of the planet, the people and profit. Ultimately, it comes down to our understanding of ecosystems, a valuation of the services they provide to us and political choices at the EU and the national level when adopting environmental quality standards and the way those choices are implemented and achieved in practice. The EPA itself is 'colourless' on how these interests are supposed to be assessed in relation to each other.

CHAPTER 10

RECONCILING ADAPTIVE MANAGEMENT STRATEGIES WITH THE EU NATURE DIRECTIVES: THE UNFORTUNATE CASE OF THE DUTCH INTEGRATED APPROACH TO NITROGEN

Hendrik SCHOUKENS*

ABSTRACT

The concept of adaptive management is generally defined as a flexible decision-making process that can be adjusted in the face of uncertainties as outcomes of management actions and other events become better understood. One notable application of adaptive management in the context of EU protected nature is the Dutch Integrated Approach to Nitrogen (*Programma Aanpak Stikstof – PAS*), which entered into force in 2015 and puts forward a more reconciliatory and integrated approach towards permitting additional nitrogen emissions in the vicinity of Natura 2000 sites. In this paper, the Dutch PAS is used as a benchmark to explore the margins available within the EU Nature Directives to implement more flexible adaptive management strategies. The paper concludes that the Dutch PAS is not to be approached as an illustration of an effective adaptive management strategy since, amongst others, it stands at odds with the preventative underpinnings of the EU Nature Directives.

* Hendrik Schoukens (email: hendrik.schoukens@ugent.be), postdoc researcher, Department of Public International Law, Ghent University (Belgium).

1. INTRODUCTION

Nitrogen deposition impact describes the input of reactive nitrogen from the atmosphere to the biosphere both as gas, dry deposition, and in precipitation as Fwet deposition.[1] Since the start of the 20th century, the sharp increase in human-induced nitrogen emissions, prompted by the rise of industrial agriculture, has significantly altered the natural nitrogen cycle. Recent research has depicted that human activities currently contribute twice as much terrestrial nitrogen fixation as natural resources.[2] As far as the environmental impact of elevated nitrogen deposition is concerned, it has been firmly established that it leads to eutrophication of ecosystems, which in turns causes an increased availability of nitrogen and subsequent exclusion of other species by more nitrophilous plants.[3] According to the findings of the European Environmental Agency (EEA), approximately 50 per cent of all vulnerable natural or semi-natural habitats in the EU are expected to be at risk of excessive nitrogen deposition in 2020.[4]

In the search for more sustainable management practices for natural ecosystems within the European Union, a proliferation of adaptive and/or programmatic approaches is to be noted. Since such strategies allow for a more flexible and adaptive approach to permitting policies, they are increasingly favoured by government agencies over more static, *ad hoc*-approaches to decision-making schemes in the context of degraded ecosystems.[5] This has also been the case in the context of the management of nitrogen deposition loads in vulnerable ecosystems. As of today, the Dutch Integrated Approach to Nitrogen (in Dutch: *Programma Aanpak Stikstof* – PAS)[6] probably represents one of the most interesting illustrations of this recent shift towards adaptive management strategies in the specific context of EU nature conservation law.[7] It is one of the

1 Bobbink, R. *et al.* (2010) 'Global Assessment of Nitrogen Deposition Effects on Terrestrial Plant Diversity: a synthesis', Ecological Applications, pp. 30-59.

2 Canfield, D.E. *et al.* (2010) 'The Evolution and Future of Earth's Nitrogen Cycle', Science, pp. 192-196.

3 See e.g. Bobbink, R. *et al.* (1998), 'The effect of air-borne nitrogen pollutants on species diversity in natural and semi-natural European vegetation', J. Ecol., 86, pp. 717-738.

4 European Environment Agency, Effects of air pollution on European ecosystems. Past and future exposures of European freshwater and terrestrial habitats to acidifying and eutrophying air pollutans, 2014.

5 Squitani, L. and H. van Rijswick (2016) 'Improving Legal Certainty and Adaptability in the Programmatic Approach', Journal of Environmental Law, pp. 443-470.

6 Dutch Ministry of Economic Affairs and Ministry of the Environment (2015) Programmatic Approach to Nitrogen (Programma Aanpak Stikstof).

7 For an extensive overview, see Schoukens, H. (2017) 'Nitrogen deposition, habitat restoration and the EU Habitats Directive: moving beyond the deadlock with the Dutch Nitrogen Approach', Biol. Conserv., 212, pp. 484-492. See also de Heer, M. *et al.* (2017) 'The Integrated Approach to Nitrogen in the Netherlands: A preliminary review from a societal, scientific, juridical and practical perspective, Journal for Nature Conservation', 35, pp. 101-111.

most comprehensive attempts to balance out economic interests, such as the continuation of intensive agriculture and livestock activities, with international and EU conservation commitments. However, at the same time the Dutch PAS is also one of the most contested examples of adaptive management, with myriad proceedings before national and EU courts. For, in order to be considered viable within the context of environmental stressors impacting EU protected ecosystems, such novel sustainable management approaches need to adhere to the substantive criteria set out by Council Directive 92/43/EEC of 21 May 1992 on the conservation of natural habitats and of wild fauna and flora (Habitats Directive).[8] Often portrayed as the cornerstone of EU environmental policy, the Habitats Directive aims to promote the maintenance and recovery of biodiversity, taking account of economic, social, cultural and regional requirements. As accumulated excessive levels of nitrogen deposition represent one of the major obstacles for achieving resilient natural habitats, permitting new or even ongoing economic activities, such as dairy farming or road construction works, has become an increasingly complicated matter.[9] In the course of the past decade, reconciling the economic interests tied to the continued emissions of nitrogen by industry, agriculture and public transportation with the Member States' restoration pledges under the Habitats Directive has grown into one of the most prominent regulatory challenges in several EU Member States, such as the Netherlands, Germany, Denmark, and Belgium (Flemish Region).[10]

This paper analyses the extent to which the Dutch integrated approach to nitrogen can be treated as a successful implementation of adaptive management in the context of Natura 2000 management. Since the Dutch Council of State has recently decided to refer several legal questions concerning the compatibility of the PAS with the EU Nature Directives to the Court of Justice of the EU (CJEU), appropriate emphasis is placed upon the recent case law developments at EU level concerning the precautionary principle and adaptive management. In a first section, the main outline of the Dutch PAS is sketched out against the backdrop of the principle of adaptive management, whereas the Dutch integrated approach is subsequently reviewed in the light of the recent evolutions in the case law of the CJEU. The main conclusions as regards the compatibility of the Dutch integrated

8 Directive 92/43/EEC on the Conservation of Natural Habitats and Wild Fauna and Flora, OJ L 206, 22 July 1992. For an elaborate discussion of the legal implications of the protection and restoration duties contained by the Habitats Directive, see C.H. Born *et al.* (eds.), (2015) The Habitats Directive in its EU Environmental Law Context. European Nature's Best Hope?

9 For an overview, see Schoukens, H. (2015) 'Atmospheric nitrogen-deposition and the Habitats Directive: Tinkering with the law in the face of the Precautionary Principle', Nordic Environ. Law J., pp. 25-57.

10 For an overview of the regulatory state of affairs concerning nitrogen deposition and Natura 2000 sites, see Backes, C.W. *et al.* (2011) Stikstofdepositie en Natura 2000. Een rechtsvergelijkend onderzoek, Universiteit Maastricht/Alterra.

approach to nitrogen with EU nature conservation law are bundled in the final section of this paper.

2. ADAPTIVE MANAGEMENT AND THE DUTCH PAS: PUTTING THEORY INTO PRACTICE?

2.1. THE BIRTH OF A NOVEL MANAGEMENT TECHNIQUE

The term 'adaptive management' was first coined by *Holling* and *Walters* in the late 1970s and early 1980s as an alternative to the conventional management methods, such as the newly emerged environmental impact assessment, which was found to stand at odds with the emerging model of ecosystem dynamics.[11] At the time, the establishment of a more dynamic approach to management was deemed essential in view of the dynamic and unpredictable nature of many ecosystems.[12] Instead of tackling environmental stressors in a piecemeal and reactive fashion, the new adaptive management technique approaches the conservation of vulnerable natural resources in a more flexible, integrated and reiterative manner, with more room for discretion and deliberation. Whereas a multitude of definitions of adaptive management have been put forward over time,[13] one of the key determinations underpinning adaptive management is the idea that planned experimentation should be used as a means to overcome the overly static 'predicative' approaches to environmental impact assessments which dominated environmental decision-making at the time.[14] As a result, adaptive management is often summarized with reference to the mantra 'learning while doing',[15] which appears to go against the 'front-end' approach prevailing in many environmental decision-making procedures, which grant the power to authorize harmful activities 'for once and for all' to specialized governmental agencies based upon prior impact assessments, evaluation of the available alternatives as well as expert-opinions.[16] Sensing an opportunity to bolster a more reconciliatory

---

11 Holling, C.S. (1978) Adaptive environmental assessment and management; Walters, C.J. (1986) Adaptive management of natural resources.

12 For more background on the genesis of the notion of 'adaptive management', see Ruhl, J.B. and R.L. Fischman (2010) 'Adaptive Management in the Courts', Minnesota Law Review, pp. 429-432.

13 See, amongst others, Allen, G.M. and E.M. Gould Jr. (1986) 'Complexity, wickedness and public forests', J For., 84, pp. 20-23.

14 Ruhl & Fischman, *supra* note 12, pp. 429-442.

15 Doremus, H. (2007) 'Precaution, Science and Learning While Doing in Natural Resource Management', Wash. L. Rev., 82, pp. 547-553.

16 Ruhl & Fischman, *supra* note 12, p. 442.

take on the protection of ecosystems, adaptive management techniques increasingly have moved to the centre of the regulatory debate.

2.2. ADAPTIVE MANAGEMENT ON THE GROUND: THE TWOFOLD RATIONALE OF THE PAS

Previously a fringe issue, adaptive management was taken to the front stage by the Dutch government in its dealing with the formidable threat posed by accumulated nitrogen deposition in EU protected Natura 2000 sites. With their choice of an integrated and adaptive management approach to the nitrogen deposition, the Dutch government decisively aimed to solve the recurrent conflict between the strict nature protection rules on the one hand and economic interests linked to nitrogen emitting projects on the other hand.[17] The stringent application of the precautionary principle in the context of individual permit applications prone to affect already degraded Natura 2000 sites had placed the Dutch government in a precarious position. This eventually resulted in the above-mentioned integrated and programmatic approach to nitrogen, which came into effect on 1 July 2015 and was subsequently partly revised in 2015 and 2017.[18] In terms of material scope, the PAS applies to 117 of the 160 Natura 2000 sites in the Netherlands. To accomplish its ambitions, the PAS, which takes into account an expected economic growth by 2.5 %, includes binding agreements on remedial measures at the Natura 2000 sites and on reduction of the nitrogen load. It is an integral programme of the Dutch government and the joint provinces. Accordingly, the PAS has a wide range since it integrates all activities that generate nitrogen-related effects in the Netherlands. Whereas the PAS primarily aims for the 2015-2021 time period, it has a total duration of 18 years.

The added value of the PAS is primarily grounded on its twofold objective. On the one hand, the integrated approach seeks to ensure immediate compliance with the protection duty included in Article 6(2) (*standstill*) and, in the long run, to contribute to Article 6(1) of the Habitats Directive (achieving the favourable conservation status). On the other hand, though, the PAS purports to create additional leeway for economic development and facilitate permitting procedures. Pursuant to *de Heer et al.*, the creation of 'room of economic development' can be aligned with the concept of a safe operating space for humanity within planetary boundaries,[19] as put forward by *Rockström*.[20]

The direct trade-off between future reduction and restoration measures and room for economic development lies at the heart of the Dutch integrated

17 PAS, *supra* note 7, pp. 14-15.

18 The PAS has last been revised on 15 December 2017, in order to take account of the most recent data that have been made available through the AERIUS tool.

19 de Heer *et al.*, *supra* note 8, p. 102.

20 Rockström, J. *et al.* (2009) 'A safe operating space for humanity', Nature, pp. 472-475.

approach. It is of crucial importance to take into consideration that the PAS no longer primarily aims to achieve nitrogen deposition levels below the critical loads in the affected Natura 2000 sites. This is based on the presupposition that more resilient habitats would be able to thrive in the long run, even if the critical loads for nitrogen are still exceeded. Likewise, the competent Dutch authorities were of the opinion that major cuts in the level of nitrogen emissions would have met with societal resistance and thus could not be presented as a realistic policy objective.[21] In exchange for the reductions and restoration measures integrated into the PAS, project developers and dairy farmers are thus offered more flexibility when applying for new permits. To be more precise, 50 per cent of the additional reductions generated by the agricultural sector will be returned to economic operators as so-called 'room for deposition/development', granting them the possibility to operate in situations where, in the absence of an integrated approach, no further room for development would be at their disposal.[22] In doing so, the integrated approach avoids more drastic solutions that would result in a rethinking of current Dutch livestock practices. The restoration efforts that are to be implemented at site-level should in turn guarantee that the authorised nitrogen emitting activities do not lead to a further deterioration and ensure, in the long run, that the applicable conservation objectives are achieved.[23] Given the presence of AERIUS, an impressive online calculation tool[24] measuring the dispersion and emission of nitrogen, and several monitoring/adjustments clauses,[25] it is not hard to understand why the Dutch PAS is often presented as a remarkable example of adaptive management in the context of Natura 2000 sites.

2.3. ENVIRONMENTAL EVALUATION, OPINIONS AND CONSULTATIONS

The adoption of the PAS did not happen overnight. It was preceded by years of intense negotiations, with all relevant societal actors, including both economic partners, farming associations as well as several environmental NGOs.[26] Finally, it was agreed that the integrated approach would reduce the average nitrogen deposition by 10 per cent over 18 years, as opposed to by a mere 8 per cent if no additional measures were taken. In itself, this already illustrates the rather limited

21 de Heer et al., *supra* note 7, p. 106.
22 PAS, *supra* note 6, pp. 28-29.
23 *Ibid.*, pp. 22-27.
24 The AERIUS Calculation tool can be consulted at: https://www.aerius.nl/nl/over-aerius/producten/calculator (accessed on 20 April 2018).
25 PAS, *supra* note 6, pp. 47-60.
26 de Heer *et al.*, *supra* note 7, p. 104.

policy ambitions of the PAS in terms of nature conservation.[27] The legal basis for the integrated approach is provided by the 1998 Dutch Nature Conservation Act, which was explicitly modified in order to accommodate the integrated approach to nitrogen related nature permit applications. The procedural guarantees for the wider public have also been integrated into this approach. A plethora of comprehensive impact assessments have been carried out.[28] The environmental impacts and effects of the solutions and measures put forward by the PAS were evaluated in more detail in a comprehensive strategic environmental assessment (SEA)[29] as well as an appropriate assessment.[30] As far as the former is concerned, it is useful to point out that the SEA looked into the societal acceptability and feasibility of various levels of ambition for the PAS, taking into account several alternative scenarios.[31] The so-called reference scenario ('zero-alternative') was closely studied as well.[32] As far as the required consideration of more environmentally friendly scenarios was concerned, the outcome of the SEA seemed to curb the expectations. While some alternatives which offered less room for economic development (e.g. alternative 2) or relied on more ambitious national reduction targets (e.g. alternative 3) might succeed in achieving more ambitious environmental gains and reduced deposition levels, all of them would still give rise to additional exceedances of the critical loads in many nitrogen-vulnerable natural habitats according to the SEA.[33] The existence of AERIUS, which includes a combination of deposition maps and habitat maps, was indispensable for setting up an effective integrated approach. This online tool is for example used for calculating nitrogen emissions from economic activities and their deposition in Natura 2000 sites when granting permits, but also for monitoring purposes.[34]

27 Schoukens, *supra* note 7, p. 487. See more extensively Van der Feltz, G.C.W. (2015) 'Programma aanpak stikstof ter inzage. Spanning tussen natuur en economie', Tijdschrift Omgevingsrecht, pp. 50-65.

28 Leneman, H. *et al.* (2013) Sociaaleconomisch perspectief van de PAS: sociaaleconomische effecten van het PAS, 2013 (LEI-nota, 13-041, Den Haag).

29 Ministry of Economic Affairs and Ministry of the Environment (2015) Plan-MER over het programma aanpak stikstof 2015-2021.

30 Ministry of Economic Affairs and Ministry of the Environment (2015) Passende beoordeling over het programma aanpak stikstof 2015-2021.

31 SEA, *supra* note 29, pp. 41-50.

32 *Ibid.*, pp. 39-40.

33 *Ibid.*, pp. 99-100.

34 PAS, *supra* note 6, pp. 81-83.

2.4. THE CORE OF THE DUTCH INTEGRATED APPROACH: ADDITIONAL SOURCE-BASED REDUCTION ACTIONS AND RESTORATION MEASURES

In order to achieve a further reduction of the nitrogen deposition level, the PAS puts forward two types of distinct measures. First and foremost, the integrated approach includes a list of source-related generic measures that are applicable in the whole of the Netherlands.[35] The PAS puts forward additional reduction measures to be carried out by the Dutch agricultural sector, which is singled out as one of the major inhibitors for achieving favourable conservation status in said Natura 2000 sites. Taken together, these measures should enable a further reduction of agricultural emissions by at least 10 kt/yr by 2030 versus the 2013 baseline. In addition to the source-based measures included in the annexes to the PAS, the bulk of which has been translated into binding legislation, voluntary measures have been put forward and partly translated in covenants with several relevant stakeholders.

Secondly, ecological restoration constitutes the common denominator of the nature-related measures included in the integrated approach to nitrogen. In response to the strict application of the protection duties laid out by the EU Nature Directives, additional actions were necessary to ensure the long-term resilience of the affected ecosystems. Measures aimed at hydrological restoration have gained a prominent place within the recently established recovery strategies.[36] Given the many uncertainties surrounding the effectiveness of habitat recovery strategies in the context of nitrogen deposition, the purported restoration strategies have been internationally reviewed.[37] To be sure, this research held that the presented restoration measures are, generally speaking, capable of avoiding and, if necessary, offsetting the adverse effects related to elevated nitrogen levels in Natura 2000 areas. Evidently, this finding would turn out to be crucial in view of the protection duties set out by Article 6 of the Habitats Directive. Furthermore, each separate Natura 2000 site has been the subject of a tailor-made site analysis which enumerates the concrete challenges and possible restoration and management measures.[38] In turn, each site-specific analysis has also been subjected to an additional prior appropriate assessment.

---

35 Ibid.

36 Ibid., pp. 20-21.

37 Review Committee (2014) Restoration strategies for nitrogen-sensitive habitats in Natura 2000 areas – Herstelstrategieën stikstofgevoelige habitats in Natura 2000, Derde Reviewronde.

38 Smits, N.A.C. *et al.* (2014) Herstelstrategieën stikstofgevoelige habitats. Ecologische onderbouwing van de Programmatische Aanpak Stikstof (PAS). Deel I: Algemene Inleiding herstelstrategieën: beleid, kennis en maatregelen; Deel II: Herstelstrategieën voor stikstofgevoelige habitats, Alterra Wageningen UR & Programmadirectie Natura 2000 van het Ministerie van Economische Zaken.

Furthermore, the analysis explicitly specifies the exact possibilities for additional nitrogen deposition.

2.5. ADMINISTRATIVE BURDEN RELIEF: ROOM FOR ADDITIONAL NITROGEN EMISSIONS AND ECONOMIC DEVELOPMENT

Another key feature of the adaptive management approach underpinning the PAS is the facilitation of the permitting procedures for new emissions of nitrogen. Taken together with the future recovery strategies focused on rendering the affected habitats more resilient, the additional reduction measures aim to create 'room for nitrogen deposition' (in Dutch: '*depositieruimte*') for new economic development in the vicinity of nitrogen-sensitive Natura 2000 sites.[39] The first type is room for autonomous development, which encompasses general economic activities, such as increasing electricity consumption linked to population growth and the increase in traffic density over the coming years.[40] The remainder of the room for deposition will be available for the so-called priority projects and other economic activities. This is referred to as 'room for development' (in Dutch: '*ontwikkelingsruimte*') under the PAS terminology, since it encompasses the additional margin provided for new development in the context of nitrogen-sensitive Natura 2000 sites. Provided that the purported project developments fall within the scope of the room for economic development which has been included in the recovery strategies, the PAS will then serve as appropriate assessment for these projects, thereby significantly alleviating the administrative burden for new plans and projects. There is no concrete hierarchy to be observed in this regard. In principle, the room for development is distributed on the basis of a 'first come, first served' approach.[41]

2.6. ADAPTIVE MANAGEMENT TOOLS: MONITORING AND ADJUSTMENT

In order to further bolster its adaptive management aspirations, the Dutch PAS also includes a chapter on monitoring and adjustment, which is deemed essential to underpin the ecological and scientific premises of the integrated approach.[42] The monitoring rules, which are seminal in view of the adaptive management approach aimed for, allow the competent authorities to continuously monitor the progress of the implementation of the recovery and reduction measures. Both the

39 PAS, *supra* note 6, pp. 28-29.
40 Id., pp. 29-30.
41 Ibid.
42 de Heer *et al.*, *supra* note 7, p. 104.

effectiveness of source-related deposition and the effectiveness of restoration measures at site level are continuously monitored through the AERIUS calculation tool. If the monitoring results reveal that the deterioration of a Natura 2000 site continues in spite of the implemented measures, the competent authorities are required to revise these measures, contemplate additional source-based or restorative measures or temporarily adjust the room for development that had been allocated for future economic activities.[43]

3. DISCUSSION: THE DUTCH INTEGRATED APPROACH TO NITROGEN REVIEWED IN THE LIGHT OF THE EU NATURE DIRECTIVES

In view of the preceding analysis, it is not hard to understand why the PAS is sometimes presented as a textbook example of integrated and adaptive management of a relevant environmental stressor.[44] However, the question now arises whether its concrete application supports this praise. For one, the EU Nature Directives set out the clear-cut substantive duties to be observed when establishing adaptive management approaches, even when this is preceded by numerous consultation and assessment procedures. In 2016, several environmental NGOs that were openly dissatisfied with the limited level of ambition of the PAS challenged hundreds of permit decisions that were based upon the integrated approach. The Dutch Council of State has not definitively rejected any of those permits so far. However, in May 2017, it referred numerous preliminary questions pertaining to the alignment of the integrated approach with the EU Nature Directives to the CJEU.[45] Even while the Dutch Council of State still seemed to side with the Dutch government on several points in its interlocutory decisions of May 2017,[46] it pointed to several scientific inconsistencies regarding the scientific robustness of the integrated approach.[47] Whereas the final ruling of the CJEU on the compliance of the PAS with the principles underpinning Article 6 of the Habitats Directive was not yet available at the time of writing this chapter, the major substantive legal pitfalls to be

43 PAS, *supra* note 6, pp. 52-59.

44 See also in this respect: de Heer *et al.*, *supra* note 7, pp. 109-110.

45 There are currently two cases pending before the CJEU, in which partly overlapping questions are posed, see Case C-293/17, *Coöperatie Mobilisation for the Environment UA et al.* and Case C-294/17, *Stichting Behoud Werkgroep de Peel.* For an extensive overview, see: Frins, R. (2017) 'PAS op de plaats … en nu? Deel I & Deel II', Tijdschrift voor Bouwrecht, 2017 pp. 586-595 and pp. 727-740.

46 Decision of the Dutch Council of State, 17 May 2017, ECLI:NL:RVS:2017:1259 (Stichting Werkgroep Behoud De Peel); Decision of the Dutch Council of State, 17 May 2017, ECLI:NL:RVS:2017:1260 (Coöperatie Mobilisation for the Environment UA).

47 See e.g. Dutch Council of State (De Peel), *supra* note 46, paras. 14 to 27.

avoided by the Dutch PAS can already be outlined. Below, the legal obstacles are discussed more into detail against the backdrop of the most recent jurisprudential developments at EU level.[48]

3.1. ADAPTIVE MANAGEMENT IN TIMES OF NON-COMPLIANCE AND BIODIVERSITY DECLINE: GENUINE RECOVERY MEASURES OR MERE TRADE-OFFS?

When adaptive management strategies are implemented in the context of EU protected sites, the intersection with the existing conservation duties, amongst others the recovery imperative present in Article 6(1) of the Habitats Directive, remains crucial. Most importantly, it needs to be guaranteed that the benefits created by the novel approaches are not merely used to comply with existing restoration obligations. If that were to be the case, the adaptive management approaches would merely be regarded as a justification of a 'business as usual'-approach. In the context of the Habitats Directive, this implies that account is to be taken of the autonomous conservation and recovery duties set out by Article 6(1) and 6(2) of the Habitats Directive. Pursuant to Article 6(1) of the Habitats Directive, Member States are under an obligation to positively conserve natural habitats, meaning that they are required to take the conservation measures necessary to ensure continuation of the habitat types and species present on sites listed for protection in Annexes I and II of the Directive.[49] As to the compatibility of the Dutch integrated approach with the first mentioned provision, it needs to be reiterated that, as such, Article 6(1) of the Habitats Directive does not put forward a strict deadline and/or timescale in terms of reaching favourable conservation status. In this respect, the EU Nature Directives clearly distinguish themselves from other EU environmental directives such as the Water Framework Directive, which explicitly sets forth when its environmental objectives need to be met.[50] Furthermore, favourable conservation status of natural habitats does not necessarily have to be met at specific site level.[51]

However, even when the overall favourable conservation status is to be reached at European and/or national level, the concept still needs to be translated into site-specific conservation objectives, which have to put forward ambitious

48 Due to a lack of space I cannot elaborate on the questions raised by the Dutch Council of State as regards the exemption of certain projects from a prior evaluation by the Dutch PAS.

49 European Commission (2000) Managing Natura 2000 Sites, The Provisions of Article 6 of the 'Habitats' Directive 92/43/EEC, p. 16.

50 Directive 2000/60/EC of the European Parliament and the Council of 23 October 2000 establishing a framework for Community action in the field of water policy, OJ L 371, 22 December 2000.

51 See most recently Case C-281/16, *Vereniging Hoekschewaards Landschap*.

recovery targets whenever the overall status of the natural habitats at issue needs to be improved. To be more precise, whenever the nitrogen-sensitive habitats are at risk of disappearance and/or degradation at site level and specific recovery objectives have been established, it is fair to conclude that a binding restoration duty rests upon the shoulders of the Member State in question.[52] Yet, instead of putting forward comprehensive restoration as its primary objective, the Dutch integrated approach to nitrogen is primarily concerned with halting the ongoing degradation, as is required by Article 6(2) of the Habitats Directive.[53] The latter provision basically requires Member States to take appropriate steps to avoid the deterioration of natural habitats and the disturbance of species. Not unsurprisingly, this non-regression principle plays an increasing role in determining how much room for manoeuvre Member States have when, for instance, contemplating adaptive management strategies, amongst others in the context of ongoing nitrogen emitting activities, such as industrial activities, livestock activities and intensive agriculture. In recent years, Article 6(2) of the Habitats Directive has been strictly enforced by the CJEU, even in cases where the ongoing deterioration might give rise to restoration duties.[54]

In this light, it is as such not surprising to note that the Dutch government prioritized the non-regression approach over a more progressive pathway to comprehensive restoration in the short run. Even more so, the additional delay was said not to be problematic since the integrated approach would still contribute to the achievement of favourable conservation status in the long run.[55] The lack of an explicit timeframe in the Habitats Directive was used as default position by the Dutch government in this regard. However, even if there is no clear-cut deadline to achieve favourable conservation status, the case law clearly acknowledges the duty to at least implement conservation measures no later than six years after the designation of a Natura 2000 site on the list of sites of EU importance.[56] Granted, one might claim that forestalling the achievement of the favourable conservation status is in itself not at odds with the wording of the Habitats Directive. Other EU environmental directives, such as the Water Framework Directive, even include exemption clauses which allow a Member State to postpone the achievement of the environmental objectives or at least grant some leeway for a phased recovery approach. Some may contend that part of the prioritization exercise has already taken place when Member States such as the Netherlands have designated their most valuable natural habitats as part of

52 Schoukens, *supra* note 9, pp. 29-30.
53 PAS, *supra* note 6, pp. 14-15.
54 For an overview, see Schoukens, H. (2017) Non-Regression clauses in Times of Ecological Restoration Law: Article 6(2) of the Habitats Directive as an unusual ally to restore Natura 2000, Utrecht Law Review, pp. 124-154.
55 See e.g. Stichting Werkgroep Behoud De Peel, *supra* note 46, para. 8.
56 Case C-90/10, *Commission v Spain*, para. 64.

the Natura 2000 Network. However, Natura 2000 sites are to be treated as the European Union's common natural heritage[57] unless the Member States can bring forth conclusive scientific evidence that the site, due to natural developments, is no longer suitable for attainment of favourable conservation status at national level.[58] By granting economic developers even more 'room for development' in the context of already overburdened Natura 2000 sites, the Netherlands could be accused of deliberately prolonging a non-compliance scenario.[59]

Regardless of the precise material and temporal scope of the imperative of restoration, the compatibility of the PAS with Article 6(1) and 6(2) of the Habitats Directive will also indirectly have to be addressed by the CJEU. The way the Dutch government addresses the legal qualification of restoration actions also gives rise to discussion. For one, the CJEU is asked by the Dutch judges in both preliminary reference procedures to shed light on the relationship between Article 6(1) and 6(2) of the Habitats Directive on the one hand, and Article 6(3) of the Habitats Directive on the other.[60] While the Dutch Council of State accepted that the source-based actions and restoration measures could indirectly also be used in the context of the appropriate assessment for the PAS even if their effects had not fully materialised at the time of conducting the evaluation, it still wanted to obtain validation of its understanding of the Habitats Directive by the CJEU. The chances are limited that the PAS would survive a strict judicial review in this respect. Interestingly, the CJEU recently had the opportunity to shed its light on the 'double use' of conservation measures in a landmark ruling on integral planning linked to harbour extension plans in the port of Antwerp.[61] In *Orleans*, the CJEU held that proactive habitat restoration measures which fall within the scope of the applicable conservation objectives at site level cannot be used in part as offsets for the destruction of protected nature. Given their double purpose, these measures were no longer eligible as 'conservation measures' within the framework of Article 6(1) of the Habitats Directive, nor could they be considered as protection measures under Article 6(2) of the Habitats Directive according to the EU judges.[62]

---

57 Case C-441/17, *Commission v Poland*, para. 208.

58 Vereniging Hoekschewaards Landschap, *supra* note 51, para. 37; Case C-301/12, *Cascina Tre Pini Ss*, paras. 28-31.

59 The ECJ has already held that Member States cannot derive an advantage from their failure to adhere to their obligations under the EU Nature Directives, see Case C-347/98, *Commission v France*, para. 50. See also more generally as regards the duty to remedy non-compliance with EU law, Case C-201/02, *Wells*, para. 68.

60 See questions 5 and 5a in Case C-293/17 and questions 3 and 3a in Case C-294/17.

61 See more extensively Schoukens, H. (2017) 'Proactive Habitat Restoration and the Avoidance of Adverse Effects on Protected Areas: Development Project Review in Europe After Orleans', Journal of International Wildlife Law & Policy, pp. 125-154.

62 Cases C-387/26 and C-388/15, *Orleans*, para. 50.

Be that as it may, both the Dutch government and the Dutch Council of State were of the opinion that the CJEU's rationale is to be confined to the context of habitat interventions which lead to a direct loss of protected natural habitats. The latter was not the case with the Dutch PAS given that new nitrogen emissions would not have significant effects on natural habitats in the short term.[63] However, this reasoning can easily be rebutted. Amongst others, in order to assess the significance of impacts, one needs to carefully consider the definition of 'conservation status of a habitat', which does not only take into account direct physical interventions but also obstacles to the long-term maintenance of the functions of a natural habitat. Arguably, a continued excessive input of nitrogen into a vulnerable ecosystem is to be regarded as such a threat; irrespective of the (assumed) possibility to fully offset these effects on the short term, such impacts therefore need to be regarded as 'significant effects' against the backdrop of the second sentence of Article 6(3) of the Habitats Directive.[64] Differently put, if the Dutch view were to prevail, it would no longer be unthinkable to use generic conservation measures, which are already mandatory under the EU Nature Directives, as offset for new economic developments in the vicinity of Natura 2000 sites. It is not hard to imagine how such interpretation, which might result in restoration turning into an almost exclusively development-led activity, could ultimately compromise the effectiveness of recovery strategies in the years to come.

As a preliminary conclusion, it can therefore be entertained that there exists a serious possibility that the CJEU will be found unwilling to justify the reliance on the positive effects of future conservation and protection measures in the context of the general appropriate assessment underpinning new and ongoing harmful economic activities. Even in the context of an adaptive management approach, one should thus be wary of using existing and mandatory commitments as a cover-up for new developments which might, in the long run, render the comprehensive recovery of ecosystems even less likely.

3.2. ADAPTIVE MANAGEMENT AS A MEANS TO OVERCOME INHERENT UNCERTAINTIES: GOING BEYOND DEFERENCE?

The legal soundness of the PAS is not solely contingent on its level of ambition in terms of the pace of recovery of nitrogen-affected habitats. Another potential obstacle for adaptive management applications in the EU is the precautionary principle, which is to be treated as one of the hallmarks of the EU environmental policy. This might sound counterintuitive, seeing that Member States would

63 See e.g. Stichting Werkgroep Behoud De Peel, *supra* note 46, paras. 10.18 to 10.23.

64 See in a similar vein Schoukens, *supra* note 7, pp. 488-489.

precisely be keen to use adaptive management strategies to mitigate inherent uncertainties linked to natural ecosystems. Even so, the margin to implement more flexible approaches appears rather limited in view of the relatively strict approach set out in the available jurisprudence. It is indeed settled case law that Member States need to ascertain there remains no reasonable scientific doubt as to the absence of significant effects when authorising potentially harmful projects pursuant to Article 6(3) of the Habitats Directive.[65] In the specific context of the Dutch PAS, it is of major importance to take into account the recent case law developments at the CJEU as regards the use of future restoration actions within the context of an appropriate assessment. Most tellingly, in *Briels*, a Dutch case in which future restoration actions were integrated into a planning permit for a road extension to offset the nitrogen impact on another part of the affected Natura 2000 site, the CJEU dismissed the Dutch take on mitigation. Apart from the fact that the restoration measures in *Briels* did not directly address the natural habitats to be affected, which were furthermore located elsewhere in the Natura 2000 site, the CJEU also held that taking into consideration future restoration actions in an appropriate assessment is at odds with the precautionary principle given.[66] In its subsequent ruling in *Orleans*, the CJEU moreover reasserted the latter view in the context of a harbour expansion plan which made the construction of new port facilities contingent on the prior realisation of new nature offset areas.[67] In its decision of 21 July 2016, the CJEU adamantly rejected the integral management approach because the result of the creation of these habitats was still uncertain at the time of the assessment of the significance of the effects.[68]

With this case law in mind, a scenario in which the CJEU approves the substantive underpinnings of the appropriate assessment carried out for the PAS appears to be very improbable. In spite of this, the Dutch Council of State was of the opinion that the *Briels* and *Orleans* cases need to be distinguished factually from the scenario at hands with the PAS. This was on display in the above-mentioned decisions of 2017 on the legality of the Dutch PAS. Here, it argued that the recovery strategies and reduction measures will eventually succeed in creating more resilient habitats which will be able to absorb the additional nitrogen emissions authorised by the PAS.[69] In my view, the latter reasoning no longer holds ground. As of today, even the fact that the implementation of future

65 See more extensively on the precautionary principle Opdam, P.F.M. *et al.* (2009) Identifying Uncertainties in Judging the Significance of Human Impacts on Natura 2000 Sites, Environmental Science & Policy, pp. 912-917.

66 Case C-521/12, *Briels*, para. 32. See more elaborately Schoukens, H. (2017) 'Habitat restoration measures as facilitator for economic development within the context of the EU habitats Directive: balancing no net loss with the prevention approach?', J Environ Law, pp. 47-73.

67 Schoukens, *supra* note 61, pp. 143-145.

68 Orleans, *supra* note 62, paras. 50-59.

69 See e.g. Stichting Werkgroep Behoud De Peel, *supra* note 46, paras. 10.13-10.32.

restoration measures is legally guaranteed does not automatically render it eligible under Article 6(3). In addition, it appears to be common ground that the mere fact that monitoring and adjustment provisions are provided in the PAS, which could force the competent authorities to revise recovery strategies and/or adapt room for development in view of intermitting results, will probably not be sufficient to ensure alignment with the strict precautionary approach underlying Article 6(3) of the Habitats Directive.[70] Recent decisions as regards the usage of inherently vague monitoring protocols seem to reassert this more restrictive stance, leaving even less leeway for Member States when developing adaptive management approaches.[71]

Stringent as this position might appear from a developer's perspective, it is acceptable within the rationale of Article 6 of the Habitats Directive. Whereas monitoring might indeed be a valuable tool to implement the non-regression clause laid down in Article 6(2) of the Habitats Directive, it remains doubtful at best whether it can be used as a means to overcome high (unacceptable) levels of uncertainty tied to permission for new activities in the context of vulnerable Natura 2000 sites.[72] What is more, one could also argue that the approach at issue in *Orleans*, where the harmful interventions would only take place *after* the realisation of nature core areas, was even more cautious than the rationale of the Dutch integrated approach. In other words, the liberal premises of the Dutch PAS go beyond the rather reluctant time-frame taken into account in the integral offset scheme which was at stake in *Orleans*. Admittedly, under the terms of the PAS, the implementation of restoration and reduction actions is legally guaranteed and the room for development will only be gradually allocated.[73] At the same time, though, some 60 per cent of the room for development was already allocated during the first three years of the PAS, which means before the restoration and reduction measures had taken effect. In *Orleans*, no destruction would be allowed prior to the implementation of the future restoration measures. Furthermore, whereas the monitoring and adjustment clauses in the PAS *can* be used to mitigate the impact of new developments when the projected measures would fail to produce the desired effects, there is no strict legal duty to do so. Agency deference may therefore lead to further deterioration when enforceable monitoring provisions are lacking.[74] Moreover, it remains to be seen to what extent a stringent application of monitoring protocols might not be challenged in court by the affected project-developers and farmers.

The above-voiced criticism is moreover neatly supported by recent scientific findings pertaining the limited short-term effectiveness of restoration measures

70 Schoukens, *supra* note 61, pp. 137-138.
71 Case C-142/16, *Commission v Germany*.
72 Schoukens, *supra* note 61, p. 138.
73 PAS, *supra* note 6, pp. 26-33.
74 Schoukens, *supra* note 7, p. 491.

for nitrogen-impacted ecosystems.[75] For instance, *Stevens* recently concluded that recovery from nitrogen deposition is a slow process in which a lot of substantial delays need to be taken into account, ranging from a few years to several decades.[76] There is moreover considerable scientific uncertainty about the reversibility of adverse nitrogen deposition effects.[77] These more general reservations about the limited results of restoration measures are further underpinned in some of the recovery strategies that are part of the PAS.[78] In addition, it is also noteworthy that some of the management measures to be implemented in the livestock sector are not binding and thus dependent on voluntary scheme.[79]

Even more worrisome is the fact that, as had already been put forward by some environmental NGOs during the consultations prior to the issuance of the PAS, the levels of nitrogen deposition have not dropped significantly in several Dutch Natura 2000 sites over the past ten years.[80] Hence, it is certainly not unlikely that at least a substantial part of the purported reduction strategies are not as effective as expected. This potential mismatch has been corroborated by more recent data, which indicate that after an initial dip in 2014-2015, nitrogen deposition levels have risen again in many Natura 2000 sites.[81] In other words, the entry into force of the PAS might have led to the distribution of non-existing room for development, which has rendered the much-needed recovery of the nitrogen-sensitive natural habitats even more unlikely.

The lack of a true experimental stage in the context of the Dutch PAS, during which no further development would be allowed awaiting the materialization of the beneficial effects in the field, might cost the Dutch government dearly if it loses the pending court cases. The recent figures clearly demonstrate that the authorisation of new room for development in the context of Dutch Natura 2000 sites was premature given the absence of any evidence as regards the effectiveness of the proposed reduction and restoration data. In its 2017 decisions, the Dutch Council of State therefore asked for more scientific backing from the Dutch government at this point.[82] A more sensible approach would thus have rendered the authorisation of new developments contingent on the prior evaluation of the

75 Stevens, C.J. et al. (2013) Review of the Effectiveness of On-site Habitat Management to Reduce Atmospheric Nitrogen-deposition-impacts on Terrestrial Habitats ((CCW Science Series Report No: 1037 (part A)).

76 Stevens, C.J. *et al.* (2016) 'Can semi-natural habitats recover from atmospheric nitrogen deposition?', Biological Conservation, pp. 160-167.

77 Hicks, W.K. *et al.*, Nitrogen deposition and Natura 2000: Science and practice in determining environmental impacts, COST729/Nine/ESF/CCW/JNCC/SEI, Workshop proceedings.

78 de Heer *et al.*, *supra* note 7, p. 108.

79 See e.g. Stichting Werkgroep Behoud De Peel, *supra* note 46, para. 20.

80 Vanderaa, E., De bom onder de PAS, Vakblad natuur bos landschap, December, pp. 3-7.

81 Ibid.

82 Stichting Werkgroep Behoud De Peel, *supra* note 46, para. 15.

effectiveness of the first generation of recovery strategies. Understandably, the Dutch stance might be more attractive from a developer's point of view, yet if applied on a wider scale it might ultimately compromise the aspirational objectives of the adaptive management approach on the ground.

3.3. ADAPTIVE MANAGEMENT AND COMPENSATION: BYPASSING THE PREVENTION PRINCIPLE AND THE APPLICATION OF DEROGATION CLAUSES?

A last substantive issue to be addressed when implementing adaptive management approaches relates to the usage of conservation measures as mitigation within the context of an appropriate assessment pursuant to Article 6(3) of the Habitats Directive. The usage of restoration measures as mitigation is one of the ultimate premises upon which the adaptive management strategy of the PAS is grounded. However, this stance is equally debatable. From a purely legal perspective, it seems more sensible to treat restoration measures as 'compensation' for an unavoidable damage. However, compensation measures can only be considered within the strict confines of the derogation procedure as set out by Article 6(4) of the Habitats Directive, which remains a difficult hurdle for justifying the presence of intensive agricultural activities close to impacted Natura 2000 sites. And thus governments seek to find strategies to avoid such an unwelcome outcome.

As can be inferred from above, the Dutch government championed a more flexible understanding of Article 6(3) of the Habitats Directive. Even so, it remains uncertain whether reduction and recovery strategies can effectively be considered as mitigation or protection measures within the context of an appropriate assessment. Recent case law development seem to leave little room for such a more liberal reading of the Habitats Directive. In its judgment in *Briels*, the CJEU already declared that future restoration measures could not, as a matter of principle, be considered in the context of an appropriate assessment if their purpose was to offset actual damage to protected habitats.[83] The CJEU pointedly based its judgment on two principal assumptions. First and foremost, it assumed that if the future creation of an area of equal or greater size than that adversely affected by a project occurred in a part of the site on which the project had no impact at all, then it could not sensibly be regarded as a measure taken to avoid adverse effects.[84] A similar rationale was subsequently reiterated by the CJEU in *Orleans*.[85]

83 Briels, *supra* note 66.
84 Ibid., para. 30.
85 Orleans, *supra* note 62, paras. 59-64.

According to the Dutch government, though, this case law does not stand in the way of the rationale upon which the recovery strategies of the PAS are grounded. In response to the mounting criticism, the Dutch government needed to be creative. The main counterargument relates to the simple finding that the effects of the additional deposition authorised through the PAS will only materialise in the future, preferably after the reduction efforts have taken effect and the natural habitats have become more resilient through the robust recovery strategies. However, while this position is already unpersuasive in view of the precautionary principle (see *supra*), it also appears to be contrary to the preventative approach put forward in the mentioned decisions. The reduction and restoration, measures described in the Dutch PAS, might thus not be eligible as genuine protective measures.

As underlined by the CJEU in *Waddenzee* and, more recently, in *Sweetman*, account needs to be taken of the constitutive elements of the Natura 2000 site in question in order to determine whether a project or plan can give rise to adverse effects within the meaning of the second sentence of Article 6(3) of the Habitats Directive.[86] These constitutive elements are further translated into the site-specific conservation objectives, which are the fundamental benchmark against which new developments are to be assessed. In this regard, the mere fact that the additional nitrogen emissions will not lead to the immediate 'destruction' of nitrogen-sensitive natural habitats appears to be less relevant. For one, also in the context of the Dutch PAS, it was possible to quantify the additional losses and/or impacts that would be generated by the new developments, which in turn makes it possible to align the Dutch situation with the decisions of the CJEU in *Briels* and *Orleans*. Moreover, also the loss of potential habitats might be significant in terms of Article 6(3) of the Habitats Directive, especially when the site-specific conservation objectives require the implementation of additional recovery measures.[87] Lastly, it remains unclear to what extent future restoration measures are to be categorised as 'mitigation' or 'protection' measures when their implementation, at least partly, takes place *after* additional development has been authorized in several Natura 2000 sites.

The Dutch government initially claimed that by only handing out 'merely' 60 per cent of the room for development it might avoid the creation of irreversible adverse effects on their Natura 2000 sites. However, it has been reported that in several instances, up to or even more than 100 per cent of the development space has been handed out through the issuance of new permits for dairy farming.[88] Ultimately, in February 2018 this forced the Dutch Council of State to suspend

86 See e.g. Case C-258/11, *Sweetman*, para. 39.

87 This view was recently acknowledged by Advocate General Tanchev in an Opinion of 19 April 2018. See Opinion, Case C-164/17, Edel Grace, paras. 75-76.

88 See for more information: http://mobilisation.nl/nl/index.php?id=18 (consulted 20 April 2018).

four permits which were based on the flawed version of the AERIUS calculation tool.[89]

Against the backdrop of these more recent revelations, it remains tricky at best to posit that especially the restoration measures put forward by the PAS will succeed in preventing and/or reducing the purported damage in the first place. At least from a legal perspective, such actions need to be approached as compensatory measures and can only be taken into account if the requirements of the derogation procedures of Article 6(4) of the Habitats Directive are met. It appears that the Dutch government was unwilling to carry out this balancing test for the authorisation of new developments related to dairy farming and livestock activities. In view of the strict conditions set out by Article 6(4) of the Habitats Directive, the issuance of derogations for dairy farming practices will therefore always remain exceptional. On a more general level, one could perhaps argue that sustaining some level of intensive agriculture can be related to the economic policy priorities of a state and thus still be eligible as a so-called 'imperative reason of overriding public interest'. However, in order to do so, the Dutch government would have been required to provide additional motivation, which it declined to do because it was of the opinion that it is possible to reconcile intensive agriculture with ecological recovery. And it was precisely this fundamental discussion that the Dutch PAS aimed to avoid in the first place.

4. CONCLUSION

The concrete application of adaptive management approaches often gives rise to many complexities and criticism. One of the most pervasive counterarguments against an overly wide use of adaptive management is that it might succeed in hiding the more fundamental policy choices at stake in the face of seminal environmental threats.[90] Ironically, the Dutch PAS might be cited as an unfortunate example of the latter approach. Granted, some authors have hailed the Dutch PAS as a promising example of effective sustainable development 'aiming for a balance between the societal, scientific, juridical and practical perspective'.[91] However, this paper has demonstrated that, in spite of all its merits, the concrete articulation of the reconciliatory and adaptive approach in the PAS leaves a lot to be desired. To be more precise, the sheer size of the integrated approach obscures the fact that its concrete application may in some instances even worsen the existing environmental conditions, in particular the nitrogen

89 See e.g. Decision of the Dutch Council of State, 28 February 2018 ECLI:NL:RVS:2018:795.

90 Kallis G. *et al.* (2009) Collaborative governance and adaptive management: Lessons from California's CALFED Water Program, Environmental Science & Policy, pp. 639-641.

91 See e.g.: de Heer *et al.*, *supra* note 7, pp. 109-110.

deposition levels, on the ground. Recent experiences have effectively demonstrated that the risk of the PAS turning into a 'ecological black box', with limited transparency, ineffective participation, insufficient application on the ground and relatively modest ecological gains is certainly not unreal. In that regard, the Dutch PAS fails to acknowledge the fundamental policy challenges related to the massive pollution problem related to intensive livestock farming and constitutes yet another illustration of how many protected sites, in spite of strict protection commitments, still remain under intense human pressure.[92]

Along those lines, the PAS, as applied during the past years, might be called an example of the 'too fast, too soon'-narrative, which is based upon the faulty preconception that nature can easily be fixed from past encroachments. One of the ultimate flaws of the integrated approach might be related to the fact that it assumes that the robust recovery of degraded ecosystems can be reconciled with further, some might say unfettered, economic expansion. It seems that the Dutch approach is not willing to address the real 'elephant in the room', being the large-scale impacts related to industrial farming on vulnerable ecosystems, and simply assumes that we can have both resilient ecosystems and continued expansion of livestock farming at the same time. It is precisely this illusion that might be shattered by the EU judges in their future ruling on the compatibility of the PAS with the Habitats Directive.

92 See Jones, K.R. (2018) 'One-third of global protected land is under intense human pressure', Science, pp. 788-791.

CHAPTER 11

BALANCING NATURE PROTECTION AND OTHER PUBLIC INTERESTS: THE CZECH EXAMPLE

Vojtěch VOMÁČKA*

ABSTRACT

This paper focuses on the broader scope and the implications of recent changes in the Czech nature conservation policy in which EU rules on habitat protection are perceived as a major obstacle to infrastructure development. It analyses the case law of the Czech Supreme Administrative Court to see whether it is in compliance with the requirements of the Habitats Directive (HD), as interpreted by the Court of Justice of the European Union. In particular, it focuses on interpretation of the most important conditions for derogating procedures under the Habitats Directive, the absence of an alternative solution, and the existence of imperative reasons of overriding public interest.

The author concludes that there is basically no major difference in divergent procedures between the long-established national system of nature protection and the requirements of EU law. Furthermore, the Czech courts interpret individual conditions for derogation in the same or similar way to the findings of the Court of Justice. In practice, however, the goals of EU law are undermined by incorrect transposition of the Habitats Directive and constant attempts of the Czech government to avoid its protective regime.

* The author is assistant professor at the Faculty of Law of Masaryk University and legal advisor at the Supreme Administrative Court of the Czech Republic (vomacka@mail.muni.cz).

1. INTRODUCTION

The EU has long been committed to protecting nature, namely since the adoption of the first version of the Birds Directive[1] (BD) in 1979. Even nowadays, however, EU law does not constitute a comprehensive system that encompasses all the aspects of managing natural resources. Biodiversity protection in the Member States is therefore two-fold in its structure, based on the implemented EU rules and the specific national system, which often has its legal roots far in the past. It seems, consequently, that the effectiveness of legal instruments and approaches towards biodiversity protection and the overall quality of the sustainable management of natural resources in the Member States depends on the relationship between EU law and the traditional system of nature conservation. Where these two systems of legal regulations collide, their goals are simply jeopardized.

Should the requirements of EU nature conservation law turn out to be overly strict, then the national legislator may soon face pressure to breach EU law or to weaken national rules which have not been harmonized at the EU level (other than Natura 2000 rules).[2] In this respect, we may perceive balancing the public interest in the narrow sense as a process preceding a specific interference with nature, and in a wider sense as a political consideration and further legislative adjustments of the laws towards more relaxed regulation.

The introduction to Natura 2000, in particular, caused some controversy in the Member States. Some perceived it merely as an unnecessary additional conservation tool,[3] while others, especially farmers, forest owners and hunters, were widely opposed to it.[4] It was also believed to significantly influence the development of nature-based sport and outdoor recreation.[5] Some governments, on the other hand, showed little hesitation in agreeing to early EU biodiversity

1 Directive 2009/147/EC on the conservation of wild birds.

2 See Schoukens, H. and A. Cliquet (2014) 'Mitigation and Compensation under EU Nature Conservation Law in the Flemish Region: Beyond the Deadlock for Development Projects?', Utrecht Law Review, 2, p. 195: *'Dissatisfied with the alleged rigidity of EU nature conservation law, project developers and planning authorities sought new ways to reconcile nature conservation with their more economically inspired spatial interests.'*

3 See Grodzinska-Jurczak, M., and J. Cent (2011) 'Expansion of nature conservation areas: problems with Natura 2000 implementation in Poland?' Environ. Manage. 47, p. 11.

4 See Rosa, H. D. and J. Marques da Silva (2005) 'From environmental ethics to nature conservation policy: Natura 2000 and the burden of proof', Journal of Agricultural and. Environmental Ethics, 18, pp. 107, 109.

5 See Pröbstl, U. (2003) 'Natura 2000: the influence of the European Directives on the development of nature-based sport and outdoor recreation in mountain areas', Journal for Nature Conservation, 11, p. 340.

proposals, believing that their own policy practices were well in advance of anything that the EU was likely to develop.[6]

In the Czech Republic, the EU rules on Natura 2000 were not warmly welcomed, nor did they face any strong opposition. They were simply transposed using the copy and paste method; the traditional nature conservation system was not changed.[7] Currently, however, the country is witnessing a dramatic withdrawal from its previous commitment to nature protection. Environmental non-governmental organisations (ENGOs)[8] and even nature itself[9] are constantly blamed for the slow development of infrastructure. Numerous leading politicians and lobby groups representing the building industry share the common opinion that it is simply no longer possible to build any large project in the Czech Republic because of the strict requirements of EU law.[10] But is this truly the case?

The main underlying research question of this paper is whether the current antipathy to EU regulation may be traced in the case law of the Czech courts. In particular, I am concerned whether, despite of several attempts of the Czech government and strong lobby organisations to limit the influence of EU nature protection law and ENGOs, in reality the case law of the Czech Supreme Administrative Court (SAC)[11] is generally in line with the requirements of the Habitats Directive[12] when it comes to accepting derogations for harmful projects in protected areas. To answer the question, I will start with a brief description of the traditional system of nature conservation in the Czech Republic and its recent transformation. This should provide an overall picture of the relationship between the Natura 2000 rules and the traditional Czech system of nature conservation. After that, I will focus on the findings of the Court of Justice of the

6 Fairbrass, J. and A. Jordan (2001) 'Protecting biodiversity in the European Union: national barriers and European opportunities?', Journal of European Public Policy, 8:4, p. 508.

7 See Ferranti, F., R. Beunen and M. Speranza (2010) 'Natura 2000 Network: A Comparison of the Italian and Dutch Implementation Experiences', Journal of Environmental Policy & Planning, 12:3, p. 304: *'Following the BD and HD, Member States need to adapt the existing nature conservation systems.'*

8 The ENGOs are frequently called green terrorists and eco-swindlers. President Miloš Zeman suggested to lock the activists in their own reservation without electricity. See Zeman: Zeleným aktivistům vytvořme rezervaci bez energií, 29 May 2017, available at: https://www.tyden.cz/rubriky/domaci/zeman-zelenym-aktivistum-vytvorme-rezervaci-bez-energii_432001.html (accessed on 15 February 2018).

9 Minister of Transport Dan Ťok blames bees and hamsters for incomplete highway projects. See Cafourek, T. (2018) 'Stavby silnic brzdí včely i křečci', MF DNES, 17. 1. 2018, available at: https://www.pressreader.com/czech-republic/mf-dnes/20180117/281526521464982 (accessed on 15 February 2018).

10 Minister of Transport Dan Ťok said: *'It seems to me that soon we will have to deal with all the fauna and flora we have in Czechia.'* See Ťok: Dostavba obchvatu Otrokovic by měla začít příští rok. Brzdí ji ekologové, 28 August 2017. Available at: https://byznys.lidovky.cz/tok-dostavba-obchvatu-otrokovic-by-mela-zacit-pristi-rok-pe9-/doprava.aspx?c=A170828_164449_ln-doprava_mha (accessed on 15 February 2018).

11 Complete case law of the SAC is available at www.nssoud.cz.

12 Directive 92/43/EEC on the conservation of natural habitats and of wild fauna and flora.

European Union (CJEU) regarding derogating procedures under the HD and compare them with the case law of the SAC. Finally, I will try to identify any faults in transposition of the HD which may cause problems with its interpretation in future.

2. BIODIVERSITY CONSERVATION IN THE CZECH REPUBLIC AND ITS RECENT TRANSFORMATION

Even before the Czech Republic joined the European Union, the preservation and maintenance of nature was at the forefront of environmental law in Czechoslovakia and later in the Czech Republic. The origin of territorial protection dates back beyond 1918 when the Czech lands were part of the Austrian-Hungarian Empire. The first protected nature reserve was established in 1838 and the first comprehensive list adopted in 1933 covered 142 reserves.[13] The most significant or unique areas have been proclaimed protected landscape areas since 1955 and national parks since 1963. During this period, the basic protective rules were embodied in Act No. 40/1956 on State Protection of Nature. The approach to natural resources management was rather modest: Protection was introduced for important territories, natural monuments and selected species of animals, plants, minerals and fossils. An implementing regulation was expected to provide detailed rules. Derogations from nature conservation were presumed, but no specific conditions were stipulated.[14] The huge bulk of implementing sub-legislation remained silent in this respect and the particular documents usually stated that it was possible to grant an exception from territorial protection. As a result, decision-making practice varied in the fragmented hierarchy of the responsible administrative authorities. A similar situation emerged in the protection of endangered species of plants and animals.[15] In 1992, the comprehensive Act No. 114/1992 Coll. on Nature and Landscape Protection, was adopted. It replaced and codified the previous regulation and most notably added general nature and landscape protection, which would apply to all parts of nature even without specific qualities. A complex, systematic approach to the protection

13 Hort, L. and T. Vrška (2008) 'Historie vzniku lesních rezervací v ČR do roku 1945', Ochrana přírody, 1, p. 8; Franková, M. (2014) 'Právní úprava chráněných území na ochranu přírody do roku 1956', České právo životního prostředí, 4 (36), p. 103.

14 § 11 (2): *Exceptions to the provisions of paragraph 1 may be granted by the Ministry of Education and Culture; for national parks only if this does not contradict the status of the national park.*

15 See § 5 of the Decree of the Ministry of Education and Culture April 1958, No. 54/1958, on protected plant species and the conditions for their protection. And also § 2 and § 12 of the Decree of the Ministry of Education and Culture of 13 July 1965, No. 80/1965, on the protection of wildlife.

of biodiversity was implemented and several modern legal instruments were introduced, for example, territorial systems of ecological stability or the protection of important landscape elements. Furthermore, ENGOs were granted the right to participate in all proceedings that would involve interests protected by the Act, including all the important permit procedures under the Czech Building Act.[16]

25 years later, the act still remains in force. It has been amended more than thirty times, most notably before joining the European Union in 2004. It now contains a specific part dealing with the Natura 2000 network and its protection, which simply overlaps the traditional regime. Valuable territories may therefore be designated protected national reserves and at the same time special protection areas (SPAs) under the BD or special areas of conservation (SACs) under the HD.[17] This is not only a matter of geographical overlap. There is a difference also as to how the legal requirements are formulated, the nature reserve regulations being more specific, while the Natura 2000 protection relates only to the impact assessment and other requirements stipulated in the HD.

As regards EU requirements, there is no doubt that the level of nature conservation has increased significantly due to the existence of new protected areas. There are so far 41 SPAs in the Czech Republic and the total number of SACs is currently 1112.[18] Some of the new sites overlap the traditional protected reserves as mentioned above, but many do not. Natura 2000 sites therefore do not fully correspond to the traditional protected areas. It is, however, questionable whether this fact alone may be considered a serious threat to large projects.

Unfortunately, the hardship of the transition process that hit the former Czechoslovakia in 1992 caused a shift from an enthusiastic pro-active environmental movement towards a more pragmatic approach that prioritized economic growth over environmental protection.[19] The privatization of industry, forestry, agriculture and pressure on infrastructure development led to increasing social conflict, especially over wildlife issues. The additional EU requirements in the environmental field have come to be seen as deadly for industry and infrastructure development, drawing attention away from well-known issues such

16 Act No. 183/2006 Coll. on town and country planning and building code (Building Act).

17 See Vomáčka, V. *et al.* (2017) 'Zákon o ochraně přírody a krajiny. Komentář', C. H. Beck, p. 338.

18 The list of the sites is available at: http://www.nature.cz/natura2000-design3/web_lokality.php?akce=seznam&cast=1805&quickfilter=3&show_all=0 (acceded on 15 February 2018).

19 See Tomoszková, V. (2015) 'Implementation of the EU Directive on Environmental Impact Assessment in
the Czech Republic: How Long Can the Wolf Be Tricked?', Wash. & Lee J. Energy, Climate & Env't. 451, pp. 457-458.

as the incapacity of the official authorities, corruption and the complicated multi-level decision-making process.[20]

It has become somewhat normal for the Czech government to trick the EU and avoid its membership duties in the most important fields of environmental protection such as air quality protection, environmental impact assessment and nature conservation. When at risk of losing money from EU funds, the government usually proposed amendments to the regulation that was the cause of the trouble, but intervention from Parliament members presenting various lobby groups in the legislative process often caused even more problems. This is one of the reasons why nature conservation law, including subordinate decrees, is rarely open to amendments which would update the obsolete regulation from the early nineties. There is a shared fear that the proposal would turn into something completely different from what was intended.

As regards ENGOs, analysis of judicial case law in environmental matters suggests that ENGOs are much less active than suggested. Between 2012 and 2016, they have challenged a total of 166 administrative decisions before the courts, which is equivalent to 3.02 cases annually per regional court. More importantly, ENGOs have often been successful and the courts ruled that 79 decisions were illegal. Not a single action has been rejected for abuse of participatory rights. However, in an unprecedented move, Czech Parliament members, supported by the project developers and lobbyists, recently decided to restrict environmental ENGOs from participation in a wide range of permitting procedures.[21] Since 1 January 2018, ENGOs may not participate in procedures concerning building projects other than those requiring an EIA.[22] Some decisions under the Act on Nature and Landscape Protection have been transformed into binding statements, effectively further restricting public participation. It is rather symbolic that this change occurred without proper public discussion and the amendment was adopted after being proposed by a single Parliament Member with no reasons provided.[23]

Do the Natura 2000 rules deserve such fear and criticism for being overly strict? One may argue that the EU protection is as effective as its weakest point. In this case, probably the derogation regime of the HD provides such point, similarly to the derogating procedures in the national law. In order to fully trace the influence of EU law on the traditional Czech nature conservation system, it is

20 See Humlíčková, P. and V. Vomáčka (2018) 'Public Participation and EIA in the Multi-Stage Decision Making Process: The Czech Example' in J. Jendroska and M. Bar (eds.), Procedural Environmental Rights: Principle X in Theory and Practice. Intersentia, pp. 353-372.

21 A substantive amendment (Act No. 225/2017 Coll.) to the Czech Building Act was supposed to speed up the procedures.

22 See Stejskal, V. (2017) 'Veřejný, nebo soukromý zájem na ochraně přírody a krajiny?', Acta Universitatis Carolinae Iuridica, 3 (63), p. 82.

23 Unlike government proposals, amendments drafted by the Parliament Members do not have to provide any reasons or undergo impact assessment.

therefore necessary to focus on the conditions of national and EU derogating procedures and their interpretation.

4. DEROGATIONS FROM PROHIBITIONS UNDER ARTICLE 6(4) OF THE HABITATS DIRECTIVE

Article 6 of the HD seeks to balance the advantages of a plan or project against its damaging effects on the conservation of natural habitats. Article 6(4) presents derogation to the safeguards in Article 6(3). A plan or project that will adversely affect the integrity of a protected site can only be authorized under Article 6(4) of the HD if three basic criteria are met: there must be an absence of alternative solutions; compensatory measures must be taken; and there must be imperative reasons of overriding public interest in favour of the development. The interpretation of derogations advocated by the CJEU is deliberately restrictive.[24] It seems that the Commission insists on the precise implementation of the HD and does not tolerate vague phrases that would undermine its objectives, add further potential derogations, or widen the possibility of using the derogation provided for.[25]

It is evident that Article 6(4) of the HD provides Czech authorities with certain leverage in the context of project developments prone to adversely affect EU protected nature. Only the projects which serve public interest can eventually be carried out despite their negative impacts on the protected site. Therefore interpretation of overriding public interest seem to be of a major importance. Cluten and Tafur even conclude that the purpose of the HD really is imperilled by the interpretation being accorded in practice to the phrase 'imperative reasons of overriding public interest'. In their opinion, through the derogation, the conservation interests can be overridden with ease which casts serious doubt on its effectiveness as a conservation tool.[26]

According to Article 6(4) of the HD, considerations on absence of alternative solutions must precede any considerations on existence of overriding public interest. I will therefore focus on the interpretation of both these conditions provided by the CJEU and the SAC. Before that, however, it should be stressed that the Czech Act on Nature and Landscape Protection stipulates that the

24 See for example Case C-293/17, *Commission v United Kingdom*, para. 111 or Case C-304/05, *Commission v Italy*, para. 82.

25 Action brought on 12 November 2007, Case C-494/07, *Commission v Greece*.

26 Clutten, R. and I. Tafur (2012) 'Are Imperative Reasons Imperilling the Habitats Directive? An Assessment of Article 6(4) and the IROPI Exception' in Jones, G. The Habitats Directive: A Developer's Obstacle Course? Bloomsbury Publishing, p. 180.

derogations apply only if there is a *significant* negative assessment of the plan or the project.[27] Such threshold is clearly not in compliance with Article 6(4) of the HD which requires the conditions to be met for all plans or projects with merely negative implications for the site.[28]

5. INTERPRETATION OF THE ABSENCE OF ALTERNATIVE SOLUTIONS BY THE CJEU AND THE CZECH COURTS

As regards absence of alternative solutions, the Commission guidance on Article 6(4) of the HD underlines the importance of examining all feasible alternatives, including the zero option. After the competent authorities analyse and demonstrate that there is a need for the plan or project in the first place, the authorities must examine solutions other than the one proposed, which may better respect the integrity of the site.[29] The CJEU confirms that the assessment of alternative solutions is the responsibility of the competent authority.[30] It does not require an assessment of all the possible alternatives, but states that the alternatives cannot be immediately ruled out as incapable of constituting alternative solutions, even where they might present certain difficulties.[31] If an option entails risks of potentially significant deterioration or disturbance, it cannot be regarded as an alternative solution under Article 6(4) of the HD.[32] It is not clear, which criteria can or should be used when comparing alternatives. According to the EU Commission guide, '*the reference parameters for such comparisons deal with aspects concerning the conservation and the maintenance of the integrity of the site and of its ecological functions. In this phase, therefore, other assessment criteria, such as economic criteria, cannot be seen as overruling ecological criteria.*'[33]

The condition of the non-existence of another satisfactory solution appears in the Czech Act on Nature and Landscape Protection exclusively in relation to

27 § 45i of the Nature and Landscape Act.

28 The SAC seems to be aware of this problem and refuses to distinguish between negative assessment and significant negative assessment. However, this applies only to the cases which reach the SAC. See judgment of the SAC of 20 May 2010, No. 8 Ao 2/2010-644.

29 European Commission (2007) 'Guidance document on Article 6(4) of the 'Habitats Directive' 92/43/EEC', p. 6.

30 See Case C-241/08, *Commission v France*, paras. 72-73; Opinion of Advocate General Kokott of 25 June 2009, Case C-241/08 *Commission v France*, para. 98.

31 See Case C-239/04, *Commission v Portugal*, paras. 36-39, and Opinion of Advocate General Kokott of 27 April 2006, Case C-293/04, *Beemsterboer*, paras. 44-46.

32 See Case C-399/14, *Grüne Liga Sachsen and Others*, para. 77.

33 European Commission (2007) 'Guidance document on Article 6(4) of the 'Habitats Directive' 92/43/EEC', p. 7.

the protection of species and habitats protected by EU law. This is probably the most important difference between the traditional system of biodiversity protection and the new rules that had to be implemented before the Czech Republic joined the EU.

Within the traditional system of nature conservation, the requirement of absence of alternative solution is derived from case law. In their interpretation of the concept of overriding public interest, Czech courts concluded that consideration of an optimal solution must be part of the balancing of concurring public interest, even within the traditional system of biodiversity protection. The SAC, for example, stated that in order to grant an exception for the construction of a highway, an '*assessment of whether the proposed highway route is an optimal solution for the protection of endangered plant and animal species*'[34] must be undertaken. Similarly, the Municipal Court in Prague came to the conclusion that a significant overriding public interest can only be present where it cannot be satisfied by another solution, without adversely affecting protected species, or with minimal effects. And that it is the duty of the nature conservation authority to assess the consequences of the construction.[35] Recently, the SAC confirmed this approach in two judgments, but drew a line between the condition of the existence of another public interest and the non-existence of a satisfactory solution. According to its findings, the latter condition is a solid aspect of balancing public interest. This means that any better alternative to the plan or project concerned should work as the decisive factor for assessing whether the other public interest is overriding or not.[36] It cannot, however, be conceived extensively. Nature conservation authorities are neither expected, nor allowed, to come up with completely new alternatives and compile an extensive assessment similar to the SEA or EIA statements.[37]

As regards Natura 2000 protection, the step by step approach prescribed by Article 6.4 of the HD is followed. The assessment of alternative solutions is part of the EIA or SEA procedure in the Czech Republic. Hence the question whether there are imperative reasons of overriding public interest is raised after the conclusion that there is an absence of alternative solutions. It seems rather confusing that a different logic is applied to the traditional nature conservation system and Natura 2000 protection. In its case law, the SAC asks for a comprehensive assessment of alternatives at the regional level of the land use planning because '*there is still room for finding alternative solutions which, later on, will no longer be available.*'[38] At the same time, the SAC approved a common

34 Judgment of the SAC of 23 June 2011, No. 6 As 8/2010-323.
35 Judgment of the Municipal Court in Prague of 31 August 2006, No. 11 Ca 41/2006-61.
36 Judgment of the SAC of 23 September 2014, No. 1 As 100/2014-36.
37 Judgment of the SAC of 20 February 2015, No. 5 As 54/2013-78. See also judgments of the SAC of 20 May 2009, No. 1 As 111/2008–363, and of 10 October 2014, No. 5 As 6/2013-97.
38 Judgment of the SAC of 20 May 2010, No. 8 Ao 2/2010-644.

practice that usually only two similar alternatives of the large projects such as highway corridors are considered, because otherwise the particular regional spatial plan would not respect the national spatial development policy.[39] This approach does not seem to be fully compatible with the requirements of the HD because no alternatives of the large projects with possible negative impact on Natura 2000 sites were assessed during preparations of the current spatial development policy of 2008.[40] It is even questionable whether it provides a sufficient level of detail which is necessary for assessment of all feasible alternatives of the projects. Even though it is subject to the SEA procedure, according to the settled case law of the SAC, the spatial development policy cannot be challenged at the court because it has no effects on individuals and cannot violate their subjective public rights.[41] The regional spatial plans are subject to judicial review but so far, the courts have put more emphasis on their compliance with the spatial development policy than with the requirements of the HD.

There are more examples of non-compliance with the HD regarding assessment of alternative solutions. In January 2018, for example, the government adopted a strategic material concerning plans to develop inland waterways including constructions on the Elbe River.[42] The material requests the Minister for Transport to prepare a comprehensive plan for 2016–2023 with a list of compensatory measures for projects with estimated negative impact on Natura 2000 sites. The assessment of alternative solutions is not expected, which is not surprising. The said project to construct low head dams (weirs) on the River Elbe, which is part of the plans to develop inland waterways, was the only reason why for many years the Czech government refused to list the valleys of the Elbe River near Hřensko, north Bohemia (*Porta Bohemica*), and Přelouč, east Bohemia (*Slavíkovy ostrovy*) as protected sites. The Czech Republic even has to face an infringement procedure,[43] but despite the recent amendment to the list of protected sites it is still determined to construct a lock and a weir on this section of the river, ignoring recent CJEU findings in similar matters.[44]

39 Judgment of the SAC of 21 June 2012, No. 1 Ao 7/2011-526.
40 The Policy was adopted despite negative statement of the Ministry of Environment.
41 Order of the SAC of 18 November 2009, No. 9 Ao 3/2009-69.
42 The decree of the Government of the Czech Republic of 17 January 2018, No. 46.
43 Infringement No. 20164003.
44 Case C-141/14, *Commission v Bulgaria* and Case C-399/14, *Commission v. Germany*.

6. INTERPRETATION OF THE OVERRIDING PUBLIC INTEREST BY THE CJEU AND THE CZECH COURTS

The Czech administrative courts have had to deal with balancing public interests in nature and landscape conservation several times. They have never expressly referred to the case law of the CJEU, but their conclusions seem to be in line with it.

The CJEU shared its opinion on the interpretation of the concept of overriding public interests in particular in judgments in the cases *Commission v. Germany* (C-57/89),[45] *Solvay and Others* (C-182/10)[46] and *Nomarchiaki Aftodioikisi Aitoloakarnanias and Others* (C-43/10).[47] As regards specific activities that may fall under the category of overriding public interest, the CJEU stressed in *Commission v Germany*, in its assessment of the construction work carried out to reinforce the coastal dam at Leybucht, that the reasons justifying the reduction of the specially protected area must be in the general interest, which overrides the general interest represented by the environmental objective of the Directive. The danger of flooding and the protection of the coast, according to the Court, constitute sufficiently serious reasons to justify the dyke works and the reinforcement of coastal structures as long as those measures are confined to a strict minimum and involve only the smallest possible reduction of the special protection area.[48] It should be noted, however, that the court also took into account the beneficial consequences of the plan's implementation for the habitat of birds.[49]

In *Solvay and Others*, the CJEU considered a project for an infrastructure designed to accommodate the administrative centre of a private company and stated that an overriding public interest must be '*both "public" and "overriding", which means that it must be of such an importance that it can be weighed up against that directive's objective of the conservation of natural habitats and wild fauna and flora. (…) the CJEU, the mere construction of infrastructure designed to accommodate a management centre cannot constitute an imperative reason of overriding public interest.*'[50] In *Nomarchiaki Aftodioikisi Aitoloakarnanias*, the CJEU stated that '*Irrigation and the supply of drinking water meet, in principle, those conditions and are therefore capable of justifying the implementation of a project for the diversion of water in the absence of alternative solutions. (…) As*

45 Case C-57/89, *Commission v Germany*.
46 Case C-182/10, *Solvay and Others*.
47 Case C-43/10, *Nomarchiaki Aftodioikisi Aitoloakarnanias and Others*.
48 Case C-57/89, *Commission v Germany*, para. 23.
49 Ibid., para. 25.
50 Case C-182/10, *Solvay and Others*, paras. 75-78.

regards irrigation, it is evident that it cannot in principle qualify as a consideration relating to human health or public safety. On the other hand, it appears more plausible that irrigation may, in some circumstances, have beneficial consequences of primary importance for the environment. In contrast, the supply of drinking water is, in principle, to be included within considerations relating to human health.'[51]

According to the SAC, the existence of other public interest cannot be simply anticipated; the facts of the case have to be taken into consideration.[52] This does not mean that the authorities have to formulate these public interests themselves as this is, in principle, the task of the legislator (not necessarily at the national level).[53] Certainly, there is some kind of discretion involved in law-making and therefore public interests promoted by the legislation can stir up controversy. The SAC addressed this aspect in relation to support for the production of energy from renewable sources: '*In the context of environmental protection, it is considered desirable in the current state of political and professional discourse, although it can be considered extremely controversial from a number of professional (especially economic and environmental) aspects, to promote the production of electricity from so-called renewable sources. At present, there is a broad majority of political consensus, as expressed by various political and legislative acts at international, European and national levels, that renewable energy production is geared towards a higher level of environmental protection. It is therefore in the interest of the whole of society that the projects of renewable energy production are under reasonable conditions carried out.*'[54]

The decisive moment for such an assessment lies prior to the granting of the exemption and is essential in terms of providing the relevant evidence, or evaluating the evidence submitted by the applicant.[55] In order to comply with the principles of process economics and speed, it is necessary to first assess whether the plan or project conforms to the category of public interest and, only if the answer is positive, consider whether such public interest outweighs nature conservation.[56] In the end, maximum of the concurring public interests should be preserved.[57]

The SAC further concluded that reasons of overriding public interest may vary in nature, including various social or economic interests, but they must still be public interests, regardless of whether they are supported by public or private

51 Case C-43-10, *Nomarchiaki Aftodioikisi Aitoloakarnanias and Others*, paras. 122-128.
52 Judgment of the SAC of 23 August 2012, No. 9 As 30/2012-88.
53 Judgment of the SAC of 10 May 2013, No. 6 As 65/2012-161.
54 Judgment of the SAC of 13 January 2017, No. 2 As 207/2016-46.
55 Judgment of the SAC of 23 September 2014, No. 1 As 100/2014-36.
56 Judgments of the SAC of 23 August 2012, No. 9 As 30/2012-88, and of 12 November 2015, No. 10 As 2/2015-251.
57 Judgment of the SAC of 10 May 2013, No. 6 As 65/2012-161.

bodies. The public interest competing with biodiversity protection must be always considered *ad hoc* and cannot be justified by the type of plan or project: '*The conservation authorities must identify, in the context of each individual case, whether a public interest other than biodiversity conservation exists, and afterwards, in the case of species protected under the Habitats Directive, to describe such interest in line with § 56 of the Act.*'[58]

Based on the findings of the SAC, it is possible to compile a group of plans and projects which are more likely to be considered to represent public interest. It comprises highway construction,[59] projects promoting renewable energy[60] or measures preventing floods.[61] Even in these cases, however, the existence of overriding public interest cannot automatically be presumed and will always depend on the specific situation and the ratio of 'costs' and 'benefits' of the particular project.[62] The correct administrative assessment of public interests in relation to the construction of wind turbines was approved by the SAC, which stated that '*a suitable compromise between the conflicting interests can be seen in the location of one higher wind farm of ECOENERGY, Ltd. and the three lower wind power plants of the same investor.*'[63]

Local private projects are less likely to obtain the status of overriding public interest, although this is not completely out of the question. The SAC did not find any public interest in the permanent placement of a caravan on the edge of a protected site[64] or terrain works for access to a private house.[65] In both cases, the Court emphasized that its conclusions do not completely preclude the whole group of similar projects from derogative regimes.

There seems to be a wide grey area between the two categories comprising projects which in particular demand a very precise and rigorous assessment of the purpose and circumstances of their implementation. This includes, for example, the renewal of mining projects,[66] the discharge of mine water into groundwater,[67] the construction of a residential complex of buildings which would disturb wild animals and damage their habitats,[68] the development of industrial zones which should promote employment, or the development of waterways to improve river navigation.[69]

58 Judgment of the SAC of 10 May 2013, No. 6 As 65/2012-161.
59 Judgment of the SAC of 23 June 2011, No. 6 As 8/2010-323.
60 Judgment of the SAC of 13 January 2017, No. 2 As 207/2016-46.
61 Judgment of the SAC of 25 May 2009, No. 8 As 5/2008-93.
62 Judgment of the SAC of 13 January 2017, No. 2 As 207/2016-46.
63 Judgment of the SAC of 17 September 2009, No. 5 As 63/2008-78.
64 Judgment of the SAC of 30 March 2017, No. 10 As 252/2015-77.
65 Judgment of the SAC of 23 September 2014, No. 1 As 100/2014-36.
66 Judgment of the SAC of 12 November 2015, No. 10 As 2/2015-251.
67 Judgment of the Regional Court in Pilsen of 30 October 2015, No. 57 A 10/2014-57.
68 Judgment of the SAC of 10 May 2013, No. 6 As 65/2012-161.
69 Judgment of the SAC of 23 August 2012, No. 9 As 30/2012-88.

Czech courts seem to struggle with some questions, for example whether the assessment of public interest in one permit procedure is binding for some or any subsequent procedure which also requires the same condition of overriding public interest to be fulfilled.[70] This problem is caused by the complex decision-making process which is comprised of more procedures, each with its individual subject and scope. In my opinion, the binding character of the assessment of public interest may not be in compliance with the requirements of the HD.

There have been constant efforts to explicitly establish a specific overriding public interest in the law and avoid any doubts on this matter in the decision-making phase. Most notably, Act No. 114/1995 Coll. on inland navigation was amended in 2004 to determine that development and modernization of the largest watercourses of the River Elbe and Vltava are in the public interest. The adoption of the amendment was clearly driven by intentions to avoid EU requirements. The amendment was quashed by the Constitutional Court, because it would protect the nature conservation authority from identification and the balancing of specific public interests.[71]

7. CONCLUSION

The current development in the Czech Republic suggests that balancing of nature protection and other public interests takes place even at a much earlier stage than within the derogating procedures under the Habitats Directive. Public interests are balanced at a higher level of policy making and law-making, which seems completely natural in principle.[72] In the Czech Republic, unfortunately, any sense of self-satisfaction regarding nature conservation that might have existed among national policy-makers in the early nineties was largely misplaced by short-term economic interests. The political considerations seem to be biased towards industry and infrastructure development, and unable to conceive nature conservation as an opportunity for human activities,[73] which was illustrated by the project to construct the weirs on the River Elbe.

---

70 See judgments of the SAC of 19 January 2010, No. 1 As 91/2009-83, and of 23 June 2011, No. 6 As 8/2010-323.

71 Ruling of the constitutional Court of the Czech Republic of 28 June 2005, No. Pl. ÚS 24/04.

72 See Vikolainen, V., H. Bressers and K. Lulofs (2013) 'The role of Natura 2000 and project design in implementing flood defence projects in the Scheldt estuary', Journal of Environmental Planning and Management, 56:9, 1377: *'At the national level, projects implemented predominantly for economic benefit (Deurganck dock) are faced with the environmental requirements of Natura 2000, while local flood defence projects (Kruibeke flood control area) are accorded low political priority.'*

73 Palerm, J. (2006) 'The Habitats Directive as an Instrument to Achieve Sustainability? An Analysis Through the Case of the Rotterdam Mainport Development Project', European Environment 16: p. 127: *'This integration of ecological and socio-economic criteria in Natura 2000*

The traditional Czech nature conservation system has not been consumed or displaced by the requirements of EU rules. Both systems employ a slightly different approach to territorial protection, but the derogations in general rely on the same set of conditions. The interpretation of the most important conditions for derogating procedures under the Habitats Directive provided by the SAC seems to be in line with case law of the CJEU. However, the SAC should pay more attention to the requirement of assessment of alternative solutions as stipulated by Article 6(4) of the HD. Moreover, the SAC only rarely refers to the conclusions of the CJEU. Further explanation of the differences between the traditional system of nature conservation and the EU rules on habitat protection would certainly help the administrative bodies and the national judiciary, because some important documents such as the Commission guidance on Article 6(4) of the HD and some judgments of the CJEU have not been translated into Czech.

---

allows conceiving of nature conservation as an opportunity for, rather than an obstacle to, human activities.'

PART VI

SUSTAINABLE RESOURCE MANAGEMENT: SPECIFIC ISSUES

CHAPTER 12

SIGNIFICANCE OF AIR QUALITY PLANS: THE CZECH EXPERIENCE

Ilona JANČÁŘOVÁ*

ABSTRACT

Air quality plans (AQPs) have become a significant part of the legal regulation in the field of air protection at the EU as well as at national law levels. This contribution focuses on problems concerning the interpretation and implementation of Article 23(1) of the EU Air Quality Directive (AQD). With respect to this, a non-compliance with the directive may arise from the failure to establish AQPs for areas with excessive air pollution, from the failure to implement established AQPs or from the adoption of AQPs containing measures, which fail to be sufficiently effective to reduce air pollution. The question is, if the mere non-compliance with air quality standards should be automatically conceived as the failure to adopt adequate AQPs as required by Article 23(1), namely without proper analysis and assessment of proposed measures. The author attempts to show this approach is incorrect since measures proposed in AQPs must be supported by other legal instruments and properly enforced at the national level to create effective regulation capable of complying with the basic requirement, that is to achieve a good quality of ambient air. The author analyses the role of AQPs in the Czech national legislation and concludes that AQPs are just programme documents which the national law must interconnect with other legal tools. The role of AQPs is no more important than the role of other regulatory instruments, which must work efficiently as a coherent system.

* The author is Associate Professor of law at Masaryk University in Brno, Czech Republic. Since 2013, she has been the head of the Environmental Law Department (Ilona.Jancarova@law.muni.cz).

1. INTRODUCTION

Since the 1970s, EU environmental law and policy is directed at combatting air pollution. The adoption of the Thematic Strategy on Air Pollution in 2005 under the Sixth Environmental Action Programme further intensified the EU´s effort to improve air quality. Various regulatory approaches and legal measures were employed to meet the objectives.[1] Programme documents, e.g. plans and programmes, have become a significant regulatory tool of EU environmental law.[2] EU Member States are obligated to introduce different kinds of programmes and plans to national laws by various sources of EU law. In the field of air protection, there are three different kinds of programme documents: emission reduction programmes, air quality plans and short-term action plans. Emission reduction programmes pursuant to Directive 2001/81/ EC on national emission ceilings for certain atmospheric pollutants (NECD) which was repealed by Directive 2016/2284/EU on the reduction of national emissions of certain atmospheric pollutants[3] aim to reduce emissions of polluting substances, in particular of nitrogen oxides and fine particulate matter. Former emission reduction programmes are to be transformed to national air pollution control programmes pursuant to the new directive. Even though they are part of source-related regulation, national emission reduction programmes/air pollution control programmes are contributing effectively to the achievement of the air quality objectives and should, to that end, contribute to the successful implementation of air quality plans established under Article 23 of Directive 2008/50/EC of the European Parliament and of the Council.[4]

In order to reduce air pollution effects, particularly in cities where the majority of the European population lives, it is important to define effective planning strategies for air quality improvement. For this purpose, air quality plans (AQP) establishing emission abatement measures, previously known as plans and programmes, had to be designed and implemented by the Member States (MS) of the European Union (EU) in accordance with Framework

1 Čavoški, A. (2017) 'The unintended consequences of EU law and policy on air pollution', RECIEL, 26, p. 259.

2 Tadei, U. (2016) 'A Right to clean air in EU law? Using litigation to progress from procedural to substantive environmental rights', Environmental Law Review, 18(1), pp. 3-7.

3 The new Directive 2016/2284/EU repeals and replaces Directive 2001/81/EC on national emission ceilings from the date of its transposition (30 June 2018) ensuring that the emission ceilings for 2010 set in that directive shall apply until 2020. Directive 2016/2284/EU also transposes the reduction commitments for 2020 made by the EU and its Member States under the revised Gothenburg Protocol and sets more ambitious reduction commitments for 2030 so as to cut the health impacts of air pollution by half compared with 2005.

4 Preamble (18), Directive 2016/2284/EU of the European Parliament and of the Council of 14 December 2016 on the reduction of national emissions of certain atmospheric pollutants, amending Directive 2003/35/EC and repealing Directive 2001/81/EC.

Directive 96/62/EC on ambient air quality assessment and management. In 2008, the new Directive 2008/50/EC of the European Parliament and of the Council of 21 May 2008 on ambient air quality and cleaner air for Europe (the Air Quality Directive – AQD) was published, introducing new concepts, and simplified and reorganized guidelines.[5] Besides the air quality plans, the Air Quality Directive regulates short-term action plans designed to manage the situations of high concentration of pollutants in ambient air which pose a risk to human health from a brief exposure of the population.[6]

The programmes and plans in the field of air protection are closely interrelated in spite of specific goals and different contents. The above-mentioned directives establish air quality standards and emission limitations to air polluting activities with the aim to achieve the required quality of ambient air that would be safe for human health and the environment. An air-quality-regulation approach is thus complemented by a source-related approach which is necessary to achieve a sustainable management of natural resources.

The EU Member States are required to reduce concentrations of polluting substances in the zones and agglomerations affected by excessive air pollution and to attain the quality of the air where it is good. On the other hand, the objective is not to seal the area and/or to ban further development. Thus, the primary aim of the legal regulation in this field is to enable economic development while setting boundaries for the sake of environmental protection. In this way, programmes and plans contribute to the implementation of the sustainable development principle. Nevertheless, the biggest problems refer to areas with a long lasting, excessive air pollution. In this regard, programme documents are an ideal instrument for a gradual pollution reduction.

This contribution is focused especially on air quality plans, since there are many questions regarding their implementation by individual Member States, such as which measures are 'appropriate', which time period is 'as short as possible', and which measures are sufficiently effective to satisfy the EU requirement that the exceedance period can be kept as short as possible? Therefore, attention will be given to the interpretation and implementation of Article 23(1) of the EU Air Quality Directive. With respect to this, a non-compliance with the Directive may arise either from the failure to establish AQPs for areas with excessive air pollution or from the adoption of AQPs containing

5 Miranda, A. (2015) 'Current air quality plans in Europe designed to support air quality management policies', Atmospheric Pollution Research, 6(3), pp. 434-443.

6 For the complete notion, it is necessary to mention that pollutants such as arsenic, cadmium, nickel and benzo(a)pyrene are covered by Directive 2004/07/EC that established a target value for concentrations of these substances in ambient air so as to avoid, prevent or reduce harmful effects of arsenic, cadmium, nickel and polycyclic aromatic hydrocarbons on human health and on the environment as a whole. No AQPs are envisaged by this directive. It remains an independent directive, however, in the future, it will probably be incorporated into Directive 2008/50/EC.

measures which fail to be sufficiently effective to reduce air pollution. There are numerous cases at national level where the national courts ruled that the air quality plans were flawed by errors of law.[7]

Pursuant to Article 23(1) Member States must ensure that air quality plans are established for zones or agglomerations where the levels of pollutants in ambient air exceed any limit value or target value, plus any relevant margin of tolerance in each case. Nevertheless, the primary duty is to ensure good quality of ambient air throughout all regions and agglomerations in all EU Member States. The question is, if the mere non-compliance with air quality standards should be automatically conceived as a failure to adopt adequate AQP as required by this Article, e.g. without proper analysis and assessment of proposed measures. This approach seems to be incorrect since measures proposed in AQPs must be supported by other legal instruments and properly enforced at national level to create effective regulation capable of complying with the basic requirement to achieve a good quality of ambient air throughout the European Union, which is comprised of various policy-making levels, where policy and legal measures are defined at EU and national level, but mostly enforced at regional or local level.[8]

EU law does not expressly require that AQPs must have binding character. Therefore, Member States may establish AQPs containing non-binding measures; however, these AQPs must be supported by other legal instruments enabling proper implementation of the AQD in order to achieve compliance with both Article 23(1) and Article 13(1). The aim of this contribution is to demonstrate the role and legal character of AQPs in the Czech national legislation; what rules shape their content and what legal character and position do they have in the national legal system with respect to other regulatory instruments. The author intends to show that AQPs are just programme documents, which would be ineffective, if national law would not interconnect them with other legal tools. Their effectiveness thus depends, beside the quality of proposed measures, on relations to other regulatory instruments and, especially, on whether decision-making authorities are directly bound by the respective AQP while executing their powers or if they are under the obligation just to base their decisions on measures proposed in the AQP and to weigh other public interests at the same time. It is argued that the role of AQPs should not be considered more important than the role of other regulatory instruments, which must work efficiently as a coherent system.

This contribution is divided into several parts. At first, attention will be given to air quality plans from the point of view of general EU law requirements. The analysis and interpretation of relevant rules will be supported by findings of the

7 Čavoški, A. (2017) 'The unintended consequences of EU law and policy on air pollution', RECIEL, 26, pp. 255-256.

8 Ibid., p. 264.

Court of Justice of the European Union (CJEU). Then Czech national law will be analysed in order to find out the consistency/inconsistency with EU law requirements and to show the possible aftermath. The ultimate objective is to find out whether air quality plans are an effective legal instrument or whether their significance is exaggerated.

2. AIR QUALITY PLANS IN EU LEGISLATION

2.1. DIRECTIVE 2008/50/EC ON AMBIENT AIR QUALITY

At EU level, air quality plans were introduced by Council Directive 96/62/EC of 27 September 1996 on ambient air quality assessment and management. In order to incorporate the latest health and scientific developments and the experience of the Member States, it was substantially revised and repealed by Directive 2008/50/EC on ambient air quality. At the same time, the new directive replaced three other directives[9] in the interests of clarity, simplification and administrative efficiency.[10]

The main objective of Directive 2008/50/EC is expressed in its preamble: 'Air quality status should be maintained where it is already good, or improved. Where the objectives for ambient air quality laid down in this Directive are not met, Member States should take action in order to comply with the limit values and critical levels, and where possible, to attain the target values and long-term objectives.' The Directive covers the main pollutants, such as sulphur dioxide, nitrogen dioxide, particulate matter (PM_{10} and $PM_{2,5}$), lead, benzene carbon monoxide and ozone. For these substances, thresholds, limit values and target values are set to assess the quality of ambient air. The limit values for human health are specified for sulphur dioxide, nitrogen dioxide, benzene, carbon monoxide, lead and PM_{10} in Annex XI, while the target and limit values for $PM_{2,5}$ are set in Annex XIV. As far as $PM_{2,5}$ is concerned, the limit value applies from 1 January 2015 (Article 16(2) in connection with Annex XIV, part E). Until that date, there was only a target value which involved an obligation to take all

9 Directive 2008/50/EC replaced Council Directive 96/62/EC of 27 September 1996 on ambient air quality assessment and management; Council Directive 1999/30/EC of 22 April 1999 relating to limit values for sulphur dioxide, nitrogen dioxide and oxides of nitrogen, particulate matter and lead in ambient air; Directive 2000/69/EC of the European Parliament and of the Council of 16 November 2000 relating to limit values for benzene and carbon monoxide in ambient air; Directive 2002/3/EC of the European Parliament and of the Council of 12 February 2002 relating to ozone in ambient air; and Council Decision 97/101/EC of 27 January 1997 establishing a reciprocal exchange of information and data from networks and individual stations measuring ambient air pollution within the Member States.

10 Directive 2008/50/EC, Preamble (3).

necessary measures not entailing disproportionate costs.[11] Since the limit values are set differently for 1 day average and 1 year average, it is also necessary to differentiate the averaging period.

Air quality plans relate to SO_2, NO_2, benzene, carbon monoxide, lead, PM_{10} and $PM_{2,5}$. Pursuant to Article 4 of the directive, the Member States have a duty to establish zones and agglomerations in their territory. Throughout all these zones and agglomerations, the Member States are obligated to ensure that the levels of pollutants in ambient air do not exceed the limit values laid down in Annex XI. Where it is apparent that the conformity with the limit values for pollutants established in Annex XI cannot be achieved in a given zone or agglomeration and the levels of pollutants in ambient air exceed the limit value plus a relevant margin of tolerance in each case, air quality plans must be introduced to correct the situation. Article 22 of the directive provides for postponement of attainment deadlines as well as for exemption from the obligation to apply certain limit values, but these provisions were only relevant during the first years after the directive entered into force.[12]

Information to be included in air quality plans is delimited in section A of Annex XV of the Directive. Apart from others, AQPs must encompass data on the origin of pollution and details of those measures or projects for improvement which existed prior to 11 June 2008, together with the observed effects of these measures, details of those measures or projects adopted with a view to reducing the pollution following the directive's entry into force along with a timetable for the implementation and an estimate of the improvement of air quality planned and of the expected time required to attain these objectives. Details of the measures or projects planned or being researched for the long term should be included as well.[13] AQPs may include specific measures to protect sensitive groups, such as children. A consistency with other plans required under other directives (2001/81/EC) must be ensured to a feasible extent.[14] From the previously stated, one can conclude that Directive 2008/50/EC has a character of a 'mixed act' since it establishes not only the aim in the form of limits and threshold values for ambient air quality to be achieved and attained, but it sets the way how this objective is to be achieved by setting the requirements on measures that should ensure good quality of air. These are included in programme documents. By setting the rules for which plans the Member States must adopt

---

11 Jans, J.H. and H.H.B. Vedder (2012) European Environmental Law, 4th edition, Europa Law Publishing, p. 421.

12 Langlet, D. and S. Mahmoudi (2016) EU Environmental Law and Policy, Oxford University Press, p. 214.

13 Section B of the Annex XV concerns the status of implementation of a number of directives and of all pollution abatement measures that have been considered at appropriate local, regional or national levels.

14 Directive 2008/50/EC, Article 23.

and which measures are to be included in these plans, EU legislation substantially limits the freedom of Member States to choose forms and ways of implementing the directive in national legislation. Nevertheless, it is for the Member State to identify specific measures.[15, 16]

For legal interpretation, the trickiest requirement regarding the content of AQP is laid down in Article 23(1): 'The air quality plans shall set out appropriate measures, so that the exceedance period can be kept as short as possible.' To meet this requirement, the exceedance must be brought to an end within a certain period. However, no certain period is either expressly laid down in the air quality directive nor can it be inferred from the directive. While the Member States have a certain degree of discretion in deciding which measures to adopt, those measures must, in any event, ensure that the period during which the limit values are exceeded is as short as possible. Nevertheless, which period of time is 'as short as possible' can only be determined on the basis of assessing each individual case.

In the past, the Commission successfully took some Member States to Court (CJEU) for failing to ensure good quality of air. However, these rulings failed to have any practical effect because the Court simply declared that the Member State had breached limit values in certain years in the past. Inasmuch as these Court rulings only covered the failure to comply with the air quality limit values in the past, providing little incentive for Member States to act on future exceedances, the Commission decided to take a fresh approach to infringement cases and enlarged the scope of the legal action since 2013.[17] Therefore, Member States are taken to Court for non-compliance with the obligation established by both Article 13(1) and Article 23(1) to ensure that the exceedance period can be kept as short as possible.[18] This approach seems to be questionable, should the Commission rely just on monitoring data and not on a proper analysis of measures proposed in the AQPs and/or actual causes of limit values exceedances. Only after such an analysis can a conclusion be drawn regarding which measures are sufficiently effective to satisfy the EU requirement that the exceedance period can be kept as short as possible. This was confirmed by findings of the CJEU. In case C-488/15, the Court concluded: '*the fact that a Member State exceeds the limit values for PM_{10} concentrations in ambient air is not in itself sufficient to find that that Member State has failed to fulfil its obligations under the second*

15 See Directive 2008/50/EC of the European Parliament and of the Council of 21 May 2008 on ambient air quality and cleaner air for Europe.

16 Jančářová, I. (2017) 'Conception Documents as a Pollution Reduction Tool – the Czech Experience', Ecology & Safety, 11(1), pp. 24-32.

17 European Commission – Press Releases: Environment: a fresh legal approach to improving air quality in Member States. http://europa.eu/rapid/press-release (accessed on 4 March 2016).

18 The Commission´s fresh approach to infringement cases, https://legal.cleanair-europe.org/legal/eu/infringement-procedure/ (accessed on 10 May 2018).

subparagraph of Article 23(1) of Directive 2008/50'[19] and the same was held in case C-336/16.[20]

One may argue that establishing AQPs with effective measures is not the only thing that matters. It is true that Member States may adopt perfect AQPs with progressive measures and still such plans would not work – their effectiveness would be low because the projected measures are not carried out properly at national level. On the other hand, the quality of ambient air can improve even though the planned measures are ineffective (because of the economic crisis, a change of weather patterns etc.). Therefore, the abovementioned obligations should not be mixed or confused, and the inefficiency of AQPs should not lean on compliance/non-compliance with Article 13(1),[21] but on a proper analysis of measures proposed in individual AQPs if they are eligible to satisfy the requirements set out in Article 23 of the directive, as the CJEU stated in case C-488/15 that it should be ascertained, on the basis of a case-by-case analysis, whether the plans drawn up by the Member State concerned comply with the second subparagraph of Article 23(1) of Directive 2008/50.[22]

Since the air quality directive requires EU Member States to establish AQPs with effective measures, implementation of these measures is a matter of complying with Article 13(1). A non-compliance with EU law may thus arise from the failure to implement adequate AQPs or from the failure to establish AQPs for areas with excessive air pollution or from the adoption of AQPs containing measures which fail to be sufficiently effective to reduce air pollution, since '*the fact that a plan is merely established cannot satisfy the obligation under the second paragraph of Article 13(1) of Directive 2008/50/EC*' (Case C-404/13).[23] It implies that the establishment of whatever AQP would not suffice for meeting the directive´s formal and substantive requirements on AQPs. There is nothing ambiguous about this. It can be derived from the wording of Article 23(1) that the measures proposed in AQPs should be efficient, nevertheless, the assessment of such efficiency or non-efficiency will depend on specific circumstances, causes of excessive pollution in specific areas and real possibilities to reduce the pollution including economic and social ones. As the Court ruled in Dieter Janecek case (C-237/07) regarding action plans on measures to be taken in the short term where there is a risk of the limit values being exceeded under Article 7(3) of Directive 96/62, '*it is for the Member States to take measures capable of*

---

19 Case C-488/15, *Commission v Bulgaria*, para. 107.

20 Case C-336/16, *Commission v Republic of Poland*, para. 94.

21 Article 13(1): 'Member States shall ensure that, throughout their zones and agglomerations, levels of sulphur dioxide, PM_{10}, lead, and carbon monoxide in ambient air do not exceed the limit values laid down in Annex XI.
In respect of nitrogen dioxide and benzene, the limit values specified in Annex XI may not be exceeded from the dates specified therein.'

22 Case C-488/15, Commission v Bulgaria, para. 108.

23 Case C-404/13, *ClientEarth v The Secretary of State for the Environment, Food and Rural Affairs*.

reducing, to a minimum, the risk of the limit values and/or alert thresholds being exceeded and the duration of such an occurrence, taking into account all the material circumstances and opposing interests'.[24] In this connection, the Court also recognized that in exercising their discretion, the Member States should, in addition to the aim of minimizing the exceedance, also take into account the balance which must be maintained between that objective and various opposing public and private interests. Lately, this point of view was supported by Juliane Kokott in relation to case C-488/15[25]: '*The air quality plans under Article 23(1) of Directive 2008/50 can also be adopted only on the basis of such a balance of interests. The high importance of ambient air quality for the protection of life and health leaves only very little room for consideration of other interests. It therefore also requires a strict review of the assessment made. However, there are undeniably overriding interests which may preclude certain appropriate measures*'.[26] It is obvious that a non-compliance with the limit values does not form the basis for infringement of the second subparagraph of Article 23(1) of Directive 2008/50, but is '*merely an indication that air quality plans do not satisfy the requirements. Whilst this cannot be inferred from the first exceedance, the longer the exceedances persist, the more they show how effective — or ineffective — the measures already taken to improve air quality were*'.[27]

The AQD does not require that measures proposed in AQPs should be binding upon the national authorities of EU Member States. Thus the crucial point is what the national system of other legislative instruments is and how these instruments are interrelated with programme documents to create an effective regulation. It has to be stressed that a wide range of legal tools is available to governments in their effort to meet the duty of Article 13(1) and to implement the objectives set by Directive 2008/50/ES. The AQP is one of these tools. Therefore, one thing is to propose adequate measures in the AQP, another is to establish other regulatory tools ensuring that these measures will be properly carried out so that the primary duty laid down in Article 13(1) of the AQD will be achieved. Based on this opinion, it can be concluded that AQPs are part of the whole set of regulatory instruments by means of which the Member States are obligated to ensure that the levels of pollutants in ambient air do not exceed the limit values laid down in Annex XI throughout all zones and agglomerations.

---

24 Case C-237/07, *Dieter Janecek v Freistaat Bayern.*

25 Case C-488/2015, *Commission v.Bulgaria.*

26 Opinion of Advocate General Kokott delivered on 10 November 2016.

27 Ibid.

2.2. DIRECTIVE 2004/107/EC RELATING TO ARSENIC, CADMIUM, MERCURY, NICKEL AND POLYCYCLIC AROMATIC HYDROCARBONS IN AMBIENT AIR

Some EU Member States including Czechia have problems with higher concentrations of other air pollutants emitted mainly by heavy industry. Arsenic, cadmium, nickel and some polycyclic aromatic hydrocarbons are human genotoxic carcinogens. There is no identifiable threshold below which these substances do not pose a risk to human health. Directive 2004/107/EC established a target value for the concentration of arsenic, cadmium, nickel and benzo(a)pyrene in ambient air so as to avoid, prevent or reduce harmful effects of arsenic, cadmium, nickel and polycyclic aromatic hydrocarbons on human health and the environment as a whole. With a view to cost-effective measures, the Directive limited itself to setting the target values, which are defined as '*a concentration in the ambient air fixed with the aim of avoiding, preventing or reducing harmful effects on human health and the environment as a whole, to be attained where possible over a given period*'.[28]

Similarly to Directive 2008/50, the objective of Directive 2004/107/EC is to ensure, with respect to arsenic, cadmium, nickel and polycyclic aromatic hydrocarbons, that the ambient air quality is maintained where it is good and that it is improved in other cases. Both directives react to similar problems, laid down similar objectives; however, no AQPs are envisaged in the latter. In order to achieve the objective, Directive 2004/107/EC established the duty for the Member States to take all necessary measures not entailing disproportionate costs to ensure that, as from 31 December 2012, the concentrations of arsenic, cadmium, nickel and benzo(a)pyrene in ambient air do not exceed the target values laid down in Annex I. For areas where these target values are exceeded, the Member States are required to demonstrate that they have applied all necessary measures not entailing disproportionate costs, directed in particular at the predominant emission sources, in order to attain the target values.[29] Since the Member States are obligated to bring laws, regulations and administrative provisions necessary to comply with this Directive into force, they may enlarge the scope of AQPs to substances regulated by Directive 2004/107/EC, even though there is no such direct requirement.

---

28 Krämer, L. (2011) EU Environmental Law, 7th edition, Sweet and Maxwell, p. 284.

29 In the case of industrial installations covered by Directive 96/61/EC, this means the application of BAT as defined by Article 2(11) of that Directive.

3. AIR QUALITY PLANS IN CZECH NATIONAL LEGISLATION

Despite the obligation for governments to ensure the good air quality and to establish AQPs, the situation is not good. In Czechia the AQPs became an integral part of the air protection legislation in January 2003, when the previous Air Protection Act No. 86/2002 Coll. came into force; still in some zones/agglomerations the daily limit values mainly for PM_{10} particles, NOx and penzo(a)pyren are exceeded. This implies for these zones/agglomerations that AQPs must be established by the Czech government pursuant to Article 23(1) of the AQD, which is currently transposed by Air Protection Act No. 201/2012 Coll., as amended (APA).

Pursuant to the new APA, section 9, the Ministry of the Environment (MoE) in cooperation with the competent regional authority is in charge of preparing an air quality plan (which in Czech is called an 'Air Quality Improvement Programme') for those zones and agglomerations where the limit values established according to Directive 2008/50/EC are exceeded.[30]

At the national law level, the content of air quality plans is delimited in Annex V of the Air Protection Act.[31] The prescribed form of these plans in Czech national law is a 'general measure' (Allgemeinverfügung) providing the public concerned with the access to administrative courts to repeal the air quality plans. AQPs provide a frame for deciding on future projects and activities since the MoE is not entitled to establish duties and directly regulate the process of emission reduction. Measures included in AQPs are not binding on private persons; they become the basis for decision-making by administrative authorities. Pursuant to section 12(1) APA, these authorities have to 'base their decisions on AQPs', which can be interpreted to mean that they are not directly bound by reduction measures established in these plans. AQPs thus serve as instructions on how to achieve the objectives. They may include some duties, nevertheless, it is a planning document setting out aims that are to be achieved and that must be taken into account in decision-making and in applying other regulatory tools.[32]

On the other hand, the Czech Air Protection Act established the rule that the air protection authorities are directly bound by limit values for the concentration of the main pollutants[33] in ambient air in their decision-making.[34] This means

---

30 Jančářová, I. (2017) Conception Documents as a Pollution Reduction Tool – the Czech Experience. Ecology & Safety, 11(1), pp. 24-32.

31 The data that must be part of AQPs include regional emission ceilings. The Czech Air Protection Act established the duty for competent authorities to respect emission ceilings set by the law in their decision-making procedures related to the sources of air pollution (§ 9(3)).

32 See also the Administrative Court in Prague, case No. 3A 139/2016-85.

33 SO_2, NO_2, CO, benzene, particles PM_{10} and $PM_{2,5}$.

34 APA, section 3(1).

that they should not approve of any new development projects that may have an impact on the air quality in those zones/agglomerations where the limit values have already been exceeded. The air protection authorities are entitled to depart from this rule only if adequate compensatory measures are proposed in regard to the projected activity. These compensatory measures should ensure that the level of pollution in the given area would not increase with the establishment of a new source of pollution. This legislative provision seems to be much stricter than the rules related to AQPs.

To sum this up, the Czech APA distinguishes between different approaches to achieving limit values in decision-making regarding activities with possible impact on air quality, expressing this in three different terms. With respect to the limit values for the main pollutants listed in Annex I to the APA,[35] the competent authorities are 'bound' by these limit values in their decision-making, while they just have to 'consider' the level of pollution compared to the limit values for other polluting substances (arsenic, nickel, cadmium, benzo(a)pyren and tropospheric ozone). With respect to air quality plans, the authorities are obligated 'to base' their decisions on these plans. This seems not to preclude the carrying out of a projected activity in an excessively polluted area in consistence with Kokott´s opinion mentioned above, since people in these areas can hardly be prevented from any future economic and social development.

Nevertheless, the abovementioned holds just for the decision-making on new installations and does not influence already existing sources of pollution in Czechia where problems with air quality persist on 13.5 per cent of the territory. The figure below[36] shows the map of the Czech Republic with those areas where the limit values are exceeded (mainly in the capital and in the industrial North Moravian Region). Because of problems with excessive air pollution, the Commission launched an infringement procedure against the Czech Republic. In February 2013 an additional formal notice, and in 2015 a reasoned opinion, were delivered to the government despite the fact that the situation improved slightly in 2014. The Commission concluded that the limit values for PM_{10} were exceeded and despite AQPs being elaborated, the Czech Republic failed to adopt appropriate measures in the areas with bad air quality to comply with Articles 13(1) and 23(1) of the Directive.[37] It has to be stressed that AQPs provide a framework for decision-making on new projected activities and, at the same time, they provide for measures aimed at reducing the existing excessive pollution. The question still remains to be answered: which role is played by AQPs and what is their significance and position in the Czech national legislation?

---

35 SO_2, NO_2, CO, benzene, particles PM_{10} and $PM_{2,5}$.

36 Available at http://portal.chmi.cz/files/portal/docs/uoco/isko/grafroc/14groc/gr14cz/png/oVII1.png (accessed on 27 June 2018).

37 European Commission – Fact Sheet, MEMO/15/4666.

OBLASTI SE ZHORŠENOU KVALITOU OVZDUŠÍ 2014

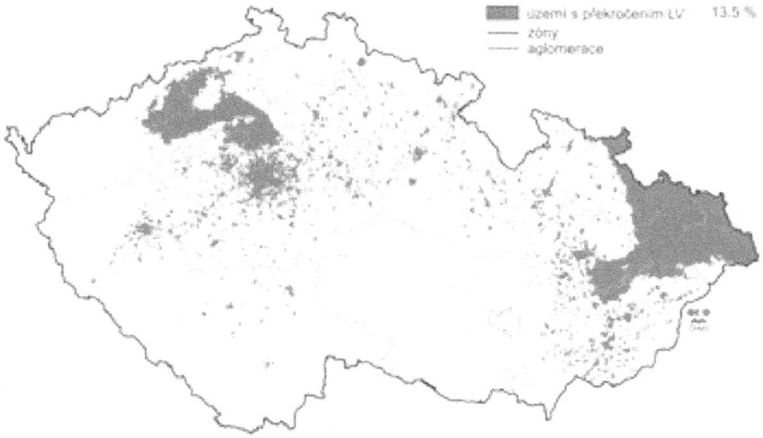

Obr. VII.1 Vyznačení oblastí s překročenými imisními limity pro ochranu zdraví bez zahrnutí přízemního ozonu, 2014

Zdroj: MŽP

Let us demonstrate the situation that has occurred in Prague (the capital) recently. The air quality plan for the Prague agglomeration contains measures to reduce the negative impact of traffic on the air quality. These measures include a parking policy with the limitation of parking in the city, the preference of public mass transportation, a restriction of transportation in specific zones, the limitation of dust by means of planting trees and others. Let us presume that a developer applied for a construction permit regarding a new building for an established bank with a large parking lot in the inner city. It is obvious that the projected activity (the parking lot) is in discrepancy with the measures to reduce the impact of traffic on air quality pursuant to the AQP. Does the Czech national legislation enable the developer to carry out such a project?

While analysing national laws and EU laws, the author has to emphasize once more that the limit values for the concentration of main pollutants (SO_2, NO_x, CO, benzene, PM_{10} and lead) in ambient air are binding for the air protection authorities in their decision-making. Thus, the new project that will contribute to the existing pollution may be permitted on condition that compensatory measures are taken. Pursuant to the Air Protection Act, air protection authorities must not permit the operation of a source of pollution prior to the realization of projected compensatory measures; moreover, they are entitled to set conditions in the permission to carry out activities that are directed towards keeping possible contribution to the existing air pollution at a minimum.

Regarding air quality plans, the competent air protection authorities are obligated to base their decisions on these plans. To 'base the decision on the AQP' is to be interpreted as to take the planned measures into account. This provides for consideration of other interests inasmuch as the wording 'to base decisions on AQP' must not be interpreted that AQP measures are absolutely binding per se. Measures laid down in an AQP are not strictly mandatory for deciding on the project, on the other hand authorities must not disregard them. It is necessary to emphasize that this rule is subject to national law and the Air Quality Directive does not pay attention to this problem, since it relates to the responsibility of EU Member States to implement the primary duty laid down by Article 13(1).

Therefore, the building with the parking lot may be permitted in Prague on conditions that compensatory measures will be carried out to minimize the pollution and no other preferable solution (consistent with the AQP) can be found to meet the needs for the development. With respect to the national legislation applicable to areas with excessive air pollution, the following conclusion may be drawn:

1) No increments to existing pollution are allowed.
2) A reduction of existing pollution should be gradual and consistent with AQPs; however, other interests must be taken into account and the AQPs should be adopted on the basis of a balance of interests.

Both ambient air quality in Prague and the construction of the new building with a large parking lot for a bank can be considered as contradictory public interests that are weighted in a decision-making procedure. If the project does not meet the requirements and criteria mentioned above, the decision may be appealed and a final decision may be reviewed by the Administrative Court. Similarly, in case 52 A 45/2015-593[38] the claimant (Frank Bold) succeeded when the Czech Administrative Court quashed the decision permitting to enlarge the capacity of the electric power plant in Chvaletice because of the existing excessive PM_{10} pollution in that region. This court decision supports the view that, in Czechia, it is possible to challenge a permission which is inconsistent with the measures outlined in AQPs.

Moreover, in compliance with the Czech legal order, persons who claim an infringement of their rights including the public are entitled to challenge the content or quality of the AQP, if the AQP does not comply with the requirements set by national law and the requirements laid down in Article 23(1) of the Air Quality Directive, and may require its abolishment pursuant to the Czech Administrative Judicial Procedure Act No. 150/2002 Coll., as amended (§ 101a). In Czechia, NGOs submitted several actions challenging the effectiveness of measures included in AQPs. Claimants claimed an infringement of their right to

38 Regional Court Hradec Králové, Case No. 52 A 45/2015-593.

a healthy environment, the right to health and property rights because the MoE failed to meet its duty to adopt an AQP containing appropriate measures. In case 11A 84/2016[39] two NGOs and Mr. B. took the Ministry of the Environment of the Czech Republic to the Administrative Court. They claimed that the AQP for the Ostrava-Karviná agglomeration did not include air pollution reduction measures capable of achieving the air quality limit values so that the exceedance period could be kept as short as possible. A Municipal Court declared that the AQP was a programme document which was subject to a strategic environmental impact assessment. Based on it, the Court denied to review expert findings and dismissed the case. However, the case was submitted to the Supreme Administrative Court for a review. The claimants were partially successful this time, even though the Court held that the AQP is a programme document determining steps and measures which should lead to the objective within an indeterminate time period. Since AQPs are adopted in the form of a general measure, courts are called upon to their review. Nevertheless, the Court concluded that is not empowered to substitute an expert opinion of the state governmental authority, nor is it gifted as an augur to say if the realization of proposed measures will suffice to achieve the objective. Still, the decision of the Municipal Court was abolished because the Supreme Administrative Court had to admit that the AQP lacked any timetable and review mechanisms and that the proposed measures were not prioritized. On the other hand, the Court held that AQPs are not directly binding on persons or municipalities to carry out the proposed measures and were inclined towards the previous court's opinions considering AQPs – that they are just programme documents without a binding effect.[40]

4. CONCLUSION

If other interests should be taken into account, it is very difficult to assess the effectiveness of AQPs, namely if the measures they include are appropriate. How can one deduce what time period is 'as short as possible' and what measures are appropriate? Based on the findings above it may be concluded that:

1) The duty not to exceed the limit values is based on Article 13(1).
2) AQPs must demonstrate how the conformity with the limit values will be reasonably achieved.

39 The Municipal Court in Prague, Case 11A 84/2016.

40 Žídek, D. (2015) Stát jako subjekt zodpovědný za znečištění ovzduší – aktuální vývoj judikatury, in T. Kyselovská, V. Kadlubiec; J. Provazník, N. Springinsfeldová, A. Virdzeková, (eds.) Cofola conference proceedings, Masaryk University, p. 1006.

3) AQPs are part of the whole system of legal tools; their significance should not be exaggerated.
4) A non-compliance with Article 23(1) should not be derived just from the bad air quality in individual zones and agglomerations, but from the proper assessment of measures proposed in AQPs.

Even though the interpretation of Article 23(1) is difficult, the analysis supports the view that AQP is a planning document, one part of which contains the obligations and the other part measures to co-ordinate the common effort to comply with established air quality limit values. The CJEU has repeatedly held that the mere exceedance of the limit values infringes Article 13 and Annex XI of Directive 2008/50,[41] unless force majeure is proven.[42] It thus constitutes an obligation of result and not a duty merely to make efforts to comply with the limit values,[43] which, on the other hand, is the role of AQPs. This is crucial for the relation of Article 13(1) and Article 23(1). The obligation to comply with the limit values (Article 13(1)) is almost absolute and independent of any other obligation laid down by the directive. Vice versa a non-compliance with Article 23(1) should not be derived just from the bad air quality in individual zones and agglomerations, but from a proper analysis and assessment of reduction measures proposed in the AQP.

The conclusion may be drawn that the AQPs are just programme documents and they do not have to have binding character. In this case, the implementation of measures laid down in AQPs must be supported by other regulatory tools which must work together as a system aimed at achieving the emission limit values. Pertaining exceedance of limit values in certain zones and agglomerations, or a slow progress in a pollution reduction, does not permit the view that AQP in itself is ineffective. It is not sufficient for the Member States to establish AQPs without ensuring their proper implementation and enforcement in decision-making processes together with other regulatory instruments. Therefore, the role of AQP should not be considered more important than the role of other regulatory instruments which must work efficiently together as a coherent system.

41 Case C-365/10, *Commission v Slovenia*, para. 24; Case C-79/10, *Commission v Sweden*, paras. 13 to 16; and Case C-34/11, *Commission v Portugal*, para. 52.

42 Case C-68/11, *Commission v Italy*, paras. 41 and 59 to 66.

43 Opinion of Advocate General Kokott delivered on 10 November 2016. Case C-488/12, *European Commission v Republic of Bulgaria*, para. 70.

CHAPTER 13

BEING REASONABLE: HOW DOES RATIONALITY AFFECT PARTICIPATORY ENVIRONMENTAL GOVERNANCE?

Caer SMYTH*

ABSTRACT

The precarious state of our natural environment is an urgent issue that demands a close examination of our legal systems and the ways of thinking underpinning these systems. In this chapter I contend that the decisions produced in participatory environmental decision-making processes are shaped by rationalist assumptions, and that this can undermine arguments for the environment. This chapter will explore the rationalist assumptions that shape spaces for public participation in environmental decision-making, firstly by introducing some initial findings from ongoing empirical research taking place at a public inquiry into a major infrastructure project with significant environmental implications. From there, the chapter will consider how these initial findings might be accounted for by exploring key assumptions in Enlightenment rationality and in *Habermas*' theory of communicative rationality. This chapter will additionally explore how these assumptions inform participation in environmental decision-making, and how these assumptions are challenged by environmental justice theorists.

* The author is a PhD candidate at Cardiff University School of Law and Politics (smythc@cardiff.ac.uk). The author is grateful to supervisors Ben Pontin (Cardiff University) and Karen Morrow (Swansea University) for their invaluable advice and support with this chapter.

1. INTRODUCTION

Participatory governance is an established principle in environmental legislation; it is considered to be an effective approach to environmental governance, one that instills concern for the environment in our communities, engages the public in environmental decision-making, and better protects the planet's natural resources for future generations.[1] However, this understanding of participatory governance seems to suppose that public participatory procedures are inherently adept at considering arguments concerning environmental issues. What if this is not the case? What if the embedded assumptions that shape our understanding of nature and shape the way we argue are reproduced in our processes for public participation in decision-making? What then for the sustainable management of these natural resources?

This chapter outlines my ongoing research project, which explores the effect that embedded rationalist assumptions have on processes of participatory governance. Specifically, my research examines the possible ways in which rationalist assumptions might shape the consideration of environmental issues in a public local inquiry into a major infrastructure project in the UK.[2] This chapter firstly introduces the fieldwork[3] element of the research, and some initial reflections are discussed. As this inquiry remains open, and as research into this site is ongoing, the site will remain anonymous. This chapter explores how emotion is expressed at the inquiry (2.2), how the physical space of the inquiry might inform the decision-making process (2.3), and how local and expert knowledge is treated (2.4). From there, this chapter explores theoretical concepts that might account for these initial findings. It outlines some key assumptions of Enlightenment rationalist philosophy (3.1.1), *Habermas*' theory of communicative rationality (3.1.2), relevant aspects of theories of participatory governance (3.2) and of environmental justice (3.3), and considers how insights in these fields illuminate some of the assumptions that shape processes of participatory governance, and shape environmental arguments (3.4). It is the intention of this chapter, and the rationale for taking a socio-legal approach in this research project, to take these sometimes abstract theoretical considerations and ground them, through ethnographic research methods, in the typical

1 Lee, M. and C. Abbot (2003) 'The Usual Suspects? Public Participation under the Aarhus Convention' Modern Law Review, 66(1) p. 8.

2 This chapter focuses on the perspective of participants directly advocating for the environment at the inquiry; e.g. environmental objectors. The indirect benefits provided by public participation in environmental issues is a rich area for research; however it lies outside of the focus of this chapter.

3 This research takes a qualitative, ethnographic approach to empirical research. Consequently, this chapter refers to fieldwork, and not case study, the term for this method more typical in socio-legal research.

arguments, discussions and activities of a UK public inquiry. The preliminary findings presented in this chapter employing this methodology raise the question as to whether rationalist assumptions limit people's ability to advocate for the environment in these processes. Additional research is thus necessary to further interrogate this proposition.

2. FIELDWORK

As highlighted above, this chapter will firstly lay out the empirical element of this research project, exploring three key issues prominent in the initial fieldwork; how emotion is expressed at the inquiry, how the physical space of the inquiry might inform the decision-making process, and how local and expert knowledge is treated. Before examining these themes however, the field-site and the methods chosen for empirical research will be introduced.

2.1. INTRODUCTION TO FIELDWORK

For this fieldwork element, I am using a mixture of methods; I am conducting participant observation, and I am also interviewing key participants at the inquiry, including members of staff at the inquiry, environmental objectors, expert witnesses for the developers and the objectors and legal counsel for developers and the objectors. I will additionally analyse inquiry documents that are centrally concerned with the environment. The field-site for this research is a public inquiry into a proposed large infrastructure project that affects residents, local businesses and the environment. It affects four SSSI[4] areas, which are habitats for multiple rare species of flora and fauna. For the purposes of this chapter, this field-site will remain anonymous. There are many forms of participatory environmental decision-making process (public inquiries, residents' meetings, local hearings, consultation by environmental organizations to name a few); why have I chosen to research a public inquiry? Moreover, why have I chosen to research a UK public inquiry? Public inquiries in the UK are quite formal in their approach.[5] I contend that the rationalist assumptions I am investigating in this research project are more clearly illuminated in this formal setting. Moreover, due to the high scale and cost of the proposed project at the

---

4 A site of special scientific interest (Wildlife and Countryside Act 1981, section 28). This is a common conservation designation and a building block of environmental legislation in the UK.

5 Moore, V. (2010) A Practical Approach to Planning Law 11th Edition, OUP, p. 349.

heart of this inquiry, the unique features of the UK public inquiry are intensified. Its rules are particularly rigid; it is particularly adversarial.[6]

The public inquiry[7] considered in this project was in session for 83 days. Its key actors included: the inspector and the assistant inspector, who will ultimately make recommendations to the relevant Minister in this case; the developer and their legal team; the objectors and their legal team (at this inquiry, the most prominent environmental objectors presented their objections to the proposal as a single unit); the expert witnesses for the developers and for the objectors, and the residents objecting to the scheme. The inquiry is formal in style; its physical setting resembles a courtroom.

It is worth highlighting that this is not wholly a group decision-making process, as it is the inspectors who ultimately make the decision. The inquiry is a tool for gathering information in which voice of the public[8] is included. I attended the inquiry from April 2017 to March 2018, and have initially begun document analysis and interviewing. The findings explored in this chapter are initial reflections on the data collected in participant observation. The three themes to be explored in this chapter are as follows:

- Emotion as a counter to reason
- Set and stage direction at the inquiry, and
- The treatment of local and expert knowledge

These are themes that came across strongly in the fieldwork; I suggest that they might affect the effectiveness of environmental arguments in participatory decision-making processes.

6 McGillivray, D. and J. Holder (2007) 'Locality, environment and the law: the case of town and village greens', International Journal of Law in Context, 3(1), p. 10; Aitken, M. (2009) 'Wind power planning controversies and the construction of 'expert' and 'lay' knowledges', Science as Culture, 13(1), p. 58; Cowell, R. and M. Lennon (2014) 'The utilization of environmental knowledge in land-use planning: drawing lessons for an ecosystems services approach' Environment and Planning C: Government and Policy, 32, p. 266.

7 UK planning law requires the relevant authority to hold a public inquiry where applications require compulsory purchase orders be made and objections are raised in respect of them.

8 The type of 'public' included at this particular inquiry is an interesting topic, however one I do not have the space to address in any detail. Members of the public were welcome to sit in the public gallery, but they would have to sign the register. Those wishing to present evidence at the inquiry needed to inform the Inspector and/or the programme officer, and there was a deadline for submissions. As the inquiry continued, the Inspector began to ask if any members of the public in the public gallery wished to speak, or wanted him to ask a question of a particular witness.

2.2. EMOTION AS A COUNTER TO REASON

The first theme to be considered is reason and emotion, or more specifically, the ways in which emotion is employed or avoided. Rational argument is typically understood in relation to emotion as an emotionally neutral and objective form of argument. It is interesting to consider in which circumstances, and by which actors, emotion is used and avoided. Two examples from the inquiry are described below, the first concerning a resident and the second concerning the lead advocate for the proposing side. These examples illustrate two distinct ways of managing emotion in decision-making processes.

The Resident

> During the inquiry, a resident became emotional as she gave her testimony, as she considered the importance of the potentially affected natural environment to the community and particularly for the children in the area. The atmosphere was a little awkward in the inquiry as this happened. The inspectors smiled at her and gave her time to collect herself. The counsel for the proposing side did not really examine this witness.

The impact of this kind of testimony is difficult to quantify. The inspectors didn't seem to take many notes during the testimony. This leads one to wonder about the impact of this testimony; and, if it had an impact, how would this be recorded or remembered? This example frames emotion as a disturbance, an obstacle to a person making their case, and to the inspectors hearing their case. This follows quite a typical, perhaps unsurprising presentation of emotion at a public inquiry. The second example offers an alternative interpretation of the role of emotion.

The Counsel

> The legal team of the proposing side is led by a senior, experienced counsel. If one was to rank the actors in this inquiry in terms of their power and influence, this counsel would be close to the top. At points in their cross-examination, the counsel seemed almost angry. They used somewhat emotive language, for example,
> Don't look to Mr B to answer for you...
> Have you actually read...
> You haven't done us this courtesy
> You know that, don't you Mr B...

At points, the counsel seemed irritated; irritated by evasive answers, by what they seemed to imply was the lack of professionalism or preparedness of some of the objectors' witnesses. There was a sense that this approach made the objectors' witnesses panic, and encouraged a feeling of not having done one's homework. As this happened repeatedly, it would lead one to suppose that this was a deliberate approach. I would argue that the counsel had a freedom to use emotion in a way that was unavailable to other actors whose legitimacy was not so assured. Their position as a rational actor was not under any doubt, and so they had a freedom to use emotion tactically. Other actors would be more likely to be seen as irrational, and therefore would not be able to use emotion in the same way.

2.3. SET AND STAGE DIRECTION

The second theme to be discussed in this chapter can be grouped as physical set and unseen stage direction; this refers to the influence of the physical space in which the actors operate, and the influence of the implicit and explicit codes to which actors in the inquiry adhere.

The Physical Set

The room in which the inquiry takes place is quite formal. It is set up like a courtroom, with the inspectors up on a dais facing the public gallery, and with the developers on the left of the inspectors and facing the witnesses. People attending the inquiry sign a register before entering the room. People are quiet and discreet; there is rarely any talking in the public section, and people tend not to move around while the inquiry is in session. Taken together, this creates a space that does not feel public. On my first day at the inquiry, I found it quite intimidating, and hard to enter. It is worth noting that while it is intimidating to some, it is everyday and comfortable to others. Every day I have attended the inquiry, the significant majority of people in the room are men in suits. The inspectors try to make the inquiry friendlier by chatting with the 'regulars' in the public gallery. However, the strictly limited times where they feel able to do this serves to underline the formal nature of the space. When I initially assessed the inquiry as a potential field-site, I thought that it would not be a good site for this research, as I could not really see much public participation. On later reflection, I realised that it was this seeming absence that made the inquiry a valuable research site.

The Unseen Stage Directions

The inquiry is shaped by rules that govern who talks to whom, and when, and what can be said. This includes explicit rules and also codes of behaviour, typical patterns of speech that are more nuanced, phrases that subtly assert the confidence and assuredness of the actor employing them. As with the physical set, these rules are known by some and are not known by others, again reproducing a hierarchy of position and power among the various participants. Observing any given day at the inquiry will provide multiple examples of these unseen stage directions. It occurred one day at the inquiry when the actors were stood around a table, examining a map; a county councillor asked a question at the table that should have been included in formal cross-examination and was told to by the inspector that she couldn't ask that question then. This is a minor event; however, it unsettles the actor who is corrected, and can serve to reinforce inequalities in knowledge and comfort at the inquiry.

2.4. LOCAL KNOWLEDGE AND EXPERTISE

The final theme to be explored here is the treatment of local knowledge and expertise at the inquiry. It is interesting to consider the different kinds of knowledge gathered at the inquiry. The inquiry is an opportunity for public participation in decision-making processes. However, it is also a mechanism through which the two inspectors must listen to a huge amount of information, and make judgments on a number of complex issues. This second role tends to rely more on the testimony of expert witnesses; people with extensive professional experience who typically hold postgraduate qualifications. These two roles can be at odds with each other, and throughout the inquiry it seemed as though local knowledge was not treated as equivalent to expert knowledge. What follows stood out as an unusual moment at the inquiry and illustrates the different treatment of, and I would contend, value attached to, local and expert knowledge at the inquiry.

The Shift Change

> A local councillor and four residents were being heard at the inquiry. Members of the inquiry were stood around a table; expert witnesses, councillor, residents, inspectors and the legal teams. The councillor and residents were discussing the tranquillity of the area and the potential adverse impact of the proposed infrastructure project. The proposing side's witnesses contended that the area highlighted by the residents was not particularly tranquil, and the inspectors noted that they had conducted a site visit to that area and agreed it was not particularly tranquil. This led to the following exchange between one of the residents and the inspector.
>
> Resident (hesitantly): Can I ask what time you visited?
> Inspector: Approximately 2.30pm
> Resident: So, close to the shift change then.
> Attention heightened around the table as it was evident that neither the inspectors nor the expert witnesses had taken this piece of local knowledge into consideration, that local factory workers finished and began their shifts at this time and so the roads would be busier.

This is an example of local, experience-based knowledge playing an important role in the inquiry. The sense of surprise among the actors suggests that this treatment of local knowledge as equivalent to expert knowledge was an exception and not the rule, revealing a tiered distinction between local and expert knowledge.

The treatment of emotion as a counter to reason, the physical setting and unseen codes of behaviour and the distinct treatment of local and expert knowledge, are some of the themes that were most prominent whilst undertaking participant observation at the public inquiry. What might the impacts of these themes be? Might these themes have particular impact on the effectiveness of arguments pertaining to the environment at the inquiry? What might account for the prominence of these themes? The following section turns to developments in rationalist philosophy and in theories surrounding participatory governance and environmental justice, and explores whether they provide any insights for this research.

3. THEORETICAL FRAMEWORK

The points for analysis illuminated by the fieldwork and considered above touch on multiple schools of thought. However, it is the contention of this chapter that Enlightenment rationality and communicative rationality, participatory governance and environmental justice, are especially pertinent. These three fields of thought will be discussed in turn, keeping a focus on how they might add to our understanding of these themes. Firstly, rationalist philosophy will be considered; more specifically, this chapter will explore the central assumptions of Enlightenment rationality, and from there, it will consider *Habermas*' theory of communicative rationality, which is particularly relevant to processes of participatory governance. From there, critical concepts in theories of participatory governance and in environmental justice will be explored.

3.1. RATIONALIST PHILOSOPHY

3.1.1. Key tenets of Enlightenment rationality

A belief in the innate nature of reason is a defining characteristic in rationalist thought. For rationalist philosophers, the finite beings that make up the observable world are fragments, copies of the infinite.[9] We catch a glimpse of these perfect concepts with the infinite part of our own being, our mind. The mind is integral to the pursuit of knowledge; knowledge, and the parts of humans that deal with knowledge, are "non-sensory, general and unchanging or eternal".[10]

9 Nelson, A. (2005) in A. Nelson (ed.), A Companion to Rationalism, Blackwell, p. 6.
10 Ibid., p. 4.

Rationalist philosophers, notably *Descartes*, contend that ideas are innate or invented; they have an intellectual, innate source, or a sensory, adventitious source.[11] *Descartes* argues that our minds are perfectly designed to comprehend concepts that seemingly have no corporeal existence.[12] The part of human beings attuned to these innate concepts is the human capacity for reason. Our capacity for reason is not applicable to all forms of knowledge. What we can understand with our capacity for reason, without any sensory involvement, are innate truths.[13] This includes mathematical concepts, metaphysics and logic. These are considered ideas of pure intellect, as the senses play no role in their reasoning. For *Descartes*, sensory involvement in intellectual ideas is only possible as an inspiration,[14] as when the use of an analogy enables a deeper insight into an intellectual concept. This understanding of ideas underlines Descartes' position that not only is there a distinction between intellectual/rational and sensory/empirical knowledge, but that rational knowledge is superior to empirical knowledge. *Descartes* contends that our senses are unreliable; "[were the mind] released from the prison of the body, it would find them [innate truths] within itself".[15] It is the mind, and not the body, that has the capacity to capture these innate, rational truths. Rationalists contend that sensory knowledge does not illuminate deeper truth; it 'accidentally' inspires the mind to perceive the primary qualities of the body being experienced.[16]

The next section considers the theory of communicative rationality developed by Jürgen *Habermas*. The relevance of communicative rationality to the processes of a public inquiry is perhaps more readily evident; however, Enlightenment rationality also provides valuable insight, in particular with this notion of mind-body dualism. This foundational concept of rationalist philosophy positions the mind as not only separate to, but also superior to the body. It is through the logical deductions of the mind and not the sensory information of the body that humans can access reason. From this it follows that, according to rationalist assumptions, logic-based arguments would be superior to experience-based arguments. This chapter suggests that this prioritising of logic-based arguments over experience-based arguments in rationalist thought might in part account for the prioritising of expert knowledge over local knowledge evident at the inquiry.

11 Newman, L. (2005) in A. Nelson (ed.), A Companion to Rationalism, Blackwell, p. 181.
12 Ibid., p. 192.
13 Ibid., p. 179.
14 Ibid., p. 182.
15 Cottingham, J., R. Stoothoff, D. Murdoch, and A. Kenny (1991:190) in Newman, L. (2005) in Nelson A. (ed.), A Companion to Rationalism, Blackwell, p. 181.
16 Newman, L. (2005) in Nelson, A. (ed.), A Companion to Rationalism, Blackwell, p. 183.

3.1.2. Habermas' theory of communicative rationality

Twentieth century thinkers linked to the rationalist school of thought tend to distance their work from the stricter elements of Enlightenment rationalist philosophy; this runs parallel with attempts to expand the narrow framing of rationality evident in Enlightenment philosophy.[17] *Habermas* seeks to advance the rationalist project, not only by approaching rationality through the frame of intersubjectivity, but also by restoring to rationalist thought its emancipatory potential.[18] In advocating for rationalism to be understood as a positive force, *Habermas* is aided by the linguistic turn in twentieth century philosophy. The world of the Enlightenment, peopled by individual subjects, is transformed into an intersubjective world.[19] This key development had a profound impact on *Habermas'* thinking, evident particularly in his theory of communicative rationality.

Habermas argues that it is a naïve realism to think that we live in a world "immediately and identically accessible to all without intersubjective checking or collaborative interpretation". Knowledge and moral beliefs are not arrived at in solitary contemplation; rather, *Habermas* proposes that social conventions are established through discussion,[20] through people reflecting on and defending their beliefs. Further, *Habermas* argues that norms must be defended by justifiable, reasonable argument.[21] When we agree with one another, we recognise the validity-claims inherent in our respective positions, acknowledging the comprehensibility and/or 'rightness' of the corresponding argument.[22] *Habermas* argues that this is a rational process;

> "...If the acceptability of speech act offers rests on the possibility of redeeming the validity claims they contain, then the acceptability of speech act offers is also tied to reason."[23]

When people communicate, they mutually understand one another, facilitating consensual, co-operative action.[24] Discourse underpins legal and moral norms, shaping not only the structure of political bodies, but also the culture within which these bodies develop and operate. This culture is influenced by the

---

17 Outhwaite, W. (1996) Habermas Reader, Polity Press, p. 16.
18 Crossley, N. and J.M. Roberts (eds.) (2004), After Habermas: New Perspectives on the Public Sphere, Wiley, p. 7.
19 Ibid., xv.
20 Outhwaite, W. (1996) Habermas Reader, Polity Press, p. 13.
21 Habermas, J. (1973, 1988) The Legitimation Crisis, Polity Press, p. 105.
22 Ibid., p. 119.
23 Warnke, G. (1995) Communicative Rationality and cultural values, in S.K. White (ed.), The Cambridge Companion to Habermas, Cambridge University Press, p. 123.
24 Ibid., p. 120.

availability of public information, of education, the ability to debate issues that challenge social norms, and by the character of public debate.[25] The normative aspects of the theory of communicative rationality inform *Habermas'* political philosophy. *Habermas* contends that innate reason is attainable through communication, and consequently, that discussion brings about better understanding, and through this, better political decisions. *Habermas* states that truth is found in rational discourse, when the *kommunikationsgemeinschaft*, the group of people talking together affected by the norm in question, tests the 'validity claims' of these norms, is persuaded of them with reasonable argument, and concludes that they are 'right'.[26] This presupposes a form of 'best-practice' discourse, where "no force except that of the better argument is exercised"... "and that, as a result, all motives except that of the cooperative search for truth are excluded".[27] The assumption that reasonable argument is the most decisive factor in group decision-making processes is fundamental to processes of participatory governance. Moreover, it is an assumption that is somewhat contradicted by the themes reflected at the inquiry, such as the importance of physical space and codes of behaviour. It is helpful to recognise that the 'rational actors' making 'reasonable, justifiable arguments' in this room are actors situated in specific bodies, in specific positions of power, in a specific space.

3.2. PARTICIPATORY GOVERNANCE

Having highlighted some central rationalist assumptions, this chapter will now explore theories informing participatory governance, taking particular note of areas where rationalist assumptions might influence these forms of governance. Participatory governance is embedded in environmental law, among other fields of law. It has been present from the start of international environmental governance with the Stockholm Conference in 1972, in the 1992 Rio Declaration and in the 1998 Aarhus Convention, and was inspired by, and subsequently empowered by, new kinds of international environmental actors i.e. international organizations, NGOs and individuals.[28] This emphasis on public participation in environmental law can partly be explained by the unique nature of the value-issues raised in environmental law. Environmental impacts are long-term and diffuse; they do not fit neatly into the short-term legal and political structure,

25 Outhwaite, W. (1996) Habermas Reader, Polity Press, p. 13.
26 Habermas, J. (1973, 1988) The Legitimation Crisis, Polity Press, p. 105.
27 Ibid., p. 108.
28 Beyerlin, U. (2015) 'Aligning international environmental governance with the 'Aarhus' principles and participatory human rights' in A. Grear and L. Kotze, Research Handbook on Human Rights and the Environment, Elgar, p. 334.

thus raising questions of ethics and legitimacy in environmental decision-making.[29]

Participatory governance is shaped by the assumption that increased public participation in governance will result in 'better' decision-making, decision-making that better reflects and accounts for the diverse needs of its constituent community and enhances the democratic legitimacy of the decision-making process. This view of public participation procedures is intrinsically informed by Sagoff's concept of the dual role of the individual in society; that an individual can act as a self-interested consumer and as a citizen, "capable of embracing and advancing values which do not reflect their own selfish interests, but define the kind of society in which they wish to live".[30] Linking with the work of *Habermas*, theories of deliberation are foregrounded in participatory governance due to its focus on reasonable, purposeful decision-making.[31] Public participation grounds governance by empowering citizens to bring their situated knowledge into the decision-making process.[32] Participatory governance bodies are considered to be solutions-focused; they are generally linked to specific actions, and are geared towards achieving a genuine consensus.[33] These positive attributes of participatory governance are particularly evident on environmental issues. Returning to *Sagoff's* notion of the individual as consumer/citizen, environmental issues benefit from a forum where the long-term, complex challenges associated with environmental policy can be addressed.[34] It moves environmental governance on from individual preference-counting; while an individual might not always act in an environmentally sustainable manner, they might nevertheless view environmental protection as an essential aspect of the world in which they want to live.[35]

However, participatory governance does not receive blanket praise. While increased public participation often results in an increase in citizens' rights,[36] some theorists argue that an emphasis on rational argument limits the inclusivity of these forums, privileging some voices and drawing the outsider perspective

29 Steele, J. (2001) 'Participation and Deliberation in Environmental Law: Exploring a problem-solving approach' Oxford Journal of Legal Studies, 21(3), p. 423.

30 Ibid., p. 424.

31 Crossley, N. (2004) and J.M. Roberts (eds.), After Habermas: New Perspectives on the Public Sphere, Wiley, p. 7.

32 Steele, J. (2001) 'Participation and Deliberation in Environmental Law: Exploring a problem-solving approach' Oxford Journal of Legal Studies, 21(3), p. 437.

33 Crossley, N. (2004) and J.M. Roberts (eds.), After Habermas: New Perspectives on the Public Sphere, Wiley, p. 17.

34 Beyerlin, U. (2015) 'Aligning international environmental governance with the 'Aarhus' principles and participatory human rights' in A. Grear and L. Kotze, Research Handbook on Human Rights and the Environment, Elgar, p. 336.

35 Steele, J. (2001) 'Participation and Deliberation in Environmental Law: Exploring a problem-solving approach' Oxford Journal of Legal Studies, 21(3), p. 424.

36 Ibid., p. 416.

into the centre.[37] Others further contend that inequalities in education are reproduced in public participation procedures.[38] The conflict between 'rule by the people' and 'rule by experts' is intensified in processes of participatory governance,[39] particularly in processes of participatory governance in environmental regulation. UK environmental regulation has historically been closed to the public, a discussion limited to the regulators and the regulated body existing within the strict parameters of scientific expertise.[40] Both the voices of the expert and the citizen appeal to different kinds of legitimacy in law-making; namely, is the law effective, or is it democratic? Effective regulation ought to reflect not only the relevant data but also public concerns on the issue under consideration. Public participation is useful when weighing different perspectives on risk, and when taking into account the diverse values upon which any particular issue might touch.[41]

What do these concepts in participatory governance illustrate regarding the themes highlighted in the fieldwork? Some of these considerations reflect rationalist assumptions explored in preceding sections, and similarly are queried by fieldwork findings. Participatory governance, in its focus on reasonable, purposeful decision-making, echoes *Habermas* and his concept of 'reasonable, justifiable argument'. The elements of the public inquiry that would not be considered reasonable argument, such as physical space and codes of behaviour, and indeed the use of emotion at the inquiry, serve to question this assumption. Likewise, advocates of participatory governance would contend that decision-making is improved by citizens bringing their situated knowledge into the decision-making process. This assumption is at odds with the hierarchical distinction between logic and experience-based arguments presented by rationalist philosophy, and further at odds with the initial findings of this fieldwork.

3.3. ENVIRONMENTAL JUSTICE

The final field of thought to be discussed in this chapter will be environmental justice, in particular those environmental justice theories that criticize the dominance of rationalism. Environmental justice came to prominence in the

37 Ibid., p. 436.

38 Squintani, L. (2017) 'The Aarhus Paradox: Time to Speak about Equal Opportunities in Environmental Governance', Journal for European Environmental Planning and Law, 14(1), p. 4.

39 Fisher, E. (2016) 'Review Essay – The Enigma of Expertise – of S Owens (2015) Knowledge, Policy and Expertise: The UKRC on Environmental Pollution 1970-2011' Journal of Environmental Law, 28(3), p. 552.

40 Steele, J. (2001) 'Participation and Deliberation in Environmental Law: Exploring a problem-solving approach' Oxford Journal of Legal Studies, 21(3), p. 418.

41 Ibid., p. 424.

latter half of the twentieth century.[42] The environmental justice movement highlights the connections between social and environmental injustices and brings a more explicitly political perspective to the environmental movement. A divide developed between environmental justice activists and 'mainstream' environmental organizations, in terms of background, tactics and focus;[43] environmental justice actors remain suspicious of environmental sustainability discourses that omit any reference to social issues.[44] Critics of the sustainability discourse contend that it perpetuates the inherent inequalities of the neo-liberal system by failing to challenge these structural issues.[45] The notion of progress has long faced opposition from social and environmental justice actors, who argue that the rationalist idea of progress, "whose simple, abstract rules of equivalence and replaceability do not fit the real, infinitely complex world of flesh and blood, root and web on which they are so ruthlessly imposed", is implicated in the precarious state of the environment.[46]

The distinction between mind and body, foundational to rationalist thought, is reflected in other rationalist dualisms, most relevantly, in the nature/culture dualism. It is important to note that this dualism, while thoroughly embedded in Western thought, is absent from conceptions of nature found in many indigenous communities.[47] Non-Western concepts of nature are distinct from Western concepts of nature; these perspectives are typically marginalized in international environmental law contexts, as is highlighted below. *Buen Vivir*, a worldview popular in Latin America, is particularly relevant here. It positions itself as an alternative to the rationalist paradigm. Translated as Good Living, *Buen Vivir* promotes the achievement of a good quality of life, which is only possible when living in harmony in a community, nature being part of that community.[48] *Buen Vivir*,

> "Prioritises harmony, co-operation and humility over possessive individualism, Eurocentric rationality, turbo-charged capitalist consumption, and technological fetishism that leads to hubristic illusions over domination over nature."[49]

---

42 Bullard, R.D. *et al.* (2008) 'Toxic Wastes and Race at Twenty: Why Race Still Matters After All of these Years' 38(1), Environmental Law, p. 371.

43 Agyeman, J. et al. (2016) 'Trends and Directions in Environmental Justice', Annual Review of Environmental Resources, 41(1), p. 328.

44 Ibid., p. 326.

45 Shaw, C. (2016) 'The role of rights, risks and responsibilities in the CJ debate', International Journal of Climate Change strategies and management, 8(4), p. 508.

46 Plumwood, V. (2002) Environmental Culture: the ecological crisis of reason, Routledge, p. 14.

47 Gudynas, E. (2011) 'Buen Vivir: Today's Tomorrow', Development, 54(4), p. 442.

48 Ibid., p. 441.

49 Adelman, S. (2015) 'Epistemologies of Mastery', in A. Grear and L. Kotze (eds.), Research Handbook on Human Rights and the Environment, Edward Elgar, p. 19.

The above description foregrounds *Buen Vivir* as a counter-narrative to dominant discourses around nature, culture and progress. *Buen Vivir* is treated with ambivalence in international environmental law. It is followed by some of the communities most affected by environmental degradation and is enshrined in the constitutions of Bolivia and Ecuador;[50] it is also included in *The Future We Want*, the outcome document of the Rio+20 talks.[51] However, this recognition of alternative conceptions of the human-nature relationship is given while re-affirming signatories' commitment to economic development, demonstrated here; "we note that some countries recognise the rights of nature in the context of the promotion of sustainable development".[52] In negotiations, *Buen Vivir* is not always treated with respect; this was evident in the 2013 UN Climate Change Conference where Bolivia's appeal to defend the rights of nature was treated as irrational.[53] The uncertain position of *Buen Vivir* might also be a result of its overtly critical stance. Advocates of *Buen Vivir* criticize capitalism for its "logic of competition, progress and limitless growth".[54]

Ecofeminism, like *Buen Vivir*, questions rationalist assumptions. Ecofeminist scholars highlight the parallels between women and nature in the rationalist paradigm, including the notion that 'being woman' and 'being nature' are inherently irrational and consequently lack value.[55] These inequalities lie, according to some ecofeminist scholars, in the "transcendent dualism" embedded in Western philosophy.[56] Ecofeminism demands a deeper investigation of the relationship between humans and nature and of the impacts of these entrenched dualisms.[57] Ecofeminist scholars frame the environmental crisis as a crisis of reason, generated by, as *Grosz* terms it,

> "The historical privileging of the purely conceptual... over the corporeal; ... a consequence of the inability of western knowledges to conceive their own processes of (material) production, processes that simultaneously rely on and disavow the role of the body."[58]

---

50 Gudynas, E. (2011) 'Buen Vivir: Today's tomorrow', Development, 54(4), p. 441.
51 'The Future We Want', UNGA Res 66/288 (27 July 2012), II, B, 39.
52 Ibid.
53 Kortetmaki, T. (2016) 'Reframing CJ: a 3D view on just climate negotiations', Ethics, Politics & the Environment, 19(3), p. 328.
54 Adelman, S. (2015) 'Tropical Forest and Climate Change: a critique of green governmentality', International Journal of Law in Context, 11(2), p. 204.
55 Plumwood, V. (1986) 'Ecofeminism: an overview and discussion of positions and arguments' Australasian Journal of Philosophy, 64(1), p. 120.
56 Ibid., p. 121.
57 Ibid., p. 133.
58 Grosz, E. (1993) 'Bodies and Knowledges: Feminism and the Crisis of Reason', in L. Alcoff and E. Potter (eds.), Feminist Epistemologies, Routledge, p. 187.

Rationalist thought positions the material world as inferior to world of ideas.[59] Part of this process is the polarization of humans and nature, establishing reason as the defining characteristic of humans, and framing nature as inferior to human life; it is not unique, but rather is passive and tradeable.[60] Not only are mind/body, human/nature, reason/emotion and culture/nature distinct from one another, they are defined by their opposite pair and one is better than the other; this leaves no room for complexity or overlap. These dualisms can be seen as expressions of a 'patriarchal logic' informing the structures through which Western society oppresses nature and women.[61] Ecofeminist scholarship has encountered considerable criticism. Certain theorists criticize elements within ecofeminism for employing a form of biological essentialism in their celebration of woman's innate relationship with nature.[62] *Hunt* responds to this criticism, arguing that while recognising the 'special relationship' between women and nature might be challenging for Western feminists, it is congruent with an understanding of nature in non-Western cultures where women's reproductive roles transcend the family and are reflected in other parts of the community, including nature.[63]

Strands of environmental justice are therefore critical of rationalist philosophy. They highlight the existence of embedded rationalist assumptions and contend that they have a particularly damaging impact on nature, by privileging economic progress, according to advocates of *Buen Vivir*, and by maintaining the nature-culture dualism, according to eco-feminist theorists. This research endeavours to add to this analysis of the impact of rationalist assumptions in the processes of environmental law, by exploring the possible impacts of these assumptions on the everyday activities of a public inquiry.

3.4. HOW DOES THIS AFFECT PARTICIPATORY ENVIRONMENTAL DECISION-MAKING?

This chapter has outlined some of the central assumptions asserted in Enlightenment and communicative rationality, and in theories of participatory governance. It has also explored critiques of rationalist thought developed by environmental justice theorists, namely ecofeminists and advocates of *Buen Vivir*. Throughout, it has considered how these fields of thought might enhance the

59 Ibid.
60 Plumwood, V. (2002) Environmental Culture: the ecological crisis of reason, Routledge, p. 4.
61 Phillips, M. (2016) 'Embodied care and Planet Earth: Ecofeminism, maternalism and postmaternalism' Australian Feminist Studies, 31(90), p. 471.
62 Griffin, S. (2001) 'Ecofeminism revisited: Rejecting Essentialism and Re-Placing Species in a Materialist Feminist Environmentalism', Feminist Formations, 23(2), p. 31.
63 Hunt, K.P. (2014) '"It's more than planting trees, it's planting ideas": ecofeminist praxis in the Green Belt Movement' Southern Communication Journal, 79(3), p. 243.

analysis of the initial fieldwork findings; the treatment of emotion and reason, the importance of physical space and codes of behaviour, and the treatment of local and expert knowledge at the inquiry. Briefly, this section highlights the key insights that these fields of thought bring to this research. This also serves as a summary of the principal points covered thus far.

Firstly, considering rationality and its role in decision-making, this chapter identifies that rationalist philosophy assumes the existence of an objective truth. Rationalist philosophy maintains that the mind is the superior part of the human and that good decisions are made from the mind alone. Stemming from this contention, and of particular relevance to processes of participatory governance, is the assumption that logic-based arguments are privileged over experience-based arguments. This chapter suggests that this prioritising of logic-based arguments over experience-based arguments in rationalist thought might in part account for the prioritising of expert knowledge over local knowledge evident at the inquiry. Further, it is evident that *Habermas*' theory of communicative rationality makes some normative assumptions of participatory decision-making. *Habermas* argues that reason is attainable through reasonable, justifiable argument, and therefore that debate between rational actors leads to better understanding, and with it, better political decisions. An examination of theories around participatory governance reveals similar normative assumptions. This assumption that reasonable argument is the most decisive factor in group decision-making processes is questioned in initial fieldwork findings. The actors in the public inquiry operate at different levels of power and of comfort with the procedure; these disparities are reflected in the physical setting of the inquiry and in the codes governing behaviour at the inquiry. The presence of these disparities suggests that the participants at the inquiry are not actors engaged in reasoned discussion on an equal level, unencumbered by any other consideration. Moreover, the presence, and indeed the strategic use, of emotion at the inquiry further points to the existence of factors beyond reasonable justifiable argument that influence debate at the inquiry. When participatory decision-making processes debate issues of environmental justice, the picture becomes more complex. Environmental justice theorists, such as eco-feminist theorists and advocates of *Buen Vivir*, are critical of rationalist assumptions that subordinate considerations of the environment, by promoting a rationalist idea of progress, and by reproducing a hierarchical and polarising distinction between nature and culture. Arguments countering the rationalist idea of progress, or arguments highlighting the destructive capacity of rationalist dualisms, can be made through public decision-making processes, and so the rationalist assumptions shaping these processes can then also be contested through these processes.

4. CONCLUSION

By investigating one specific participatory environmental decision-making process, a public inquiry into a major infrastructure project in the UK, and by considering this field-site from the perspective of embedded rationalist assumptions in participatory environmental decision-making processes, this research highlights several areas for further exploration. The treatment of emotion, physical space and expertise at the inquiry indicate some of the ways in which rationalist assumptions shape public participation in environmental decision-making. The data gathered at the public inquiry suggests that rationalist assumptions influenced the everyday activities and arguments of the inquiry. It further suggests that these impacts typically remain hidden from view, and that they might have a disproportionate impact on the treatment of the environment in these processes. Accordingly, the question is raised as to whether rationalist assumptions shape the actions and arguments of the participants of the inquiry in ways that potentially impede arguments affecting the environment, and arguments seeking to protect the environment.

Rationalist philosophy presupposes the existence of an objective truth that can be found through argument and deliberation. It further reinforces a tendency towards logic-based argument over experience-based argument, a tendency that could conceivably undermine the capacity of participatory governance to bring specific knowledge into decision-making. It is therefore suggested that rationalist assumptions might have a particularly detrimental impact on the effectiveness of environmental arguments in these decision-making processes. Ecofeminists and *Buen Vivir* theorists contend that rationalist assumptions, in particular the rationalist tendency towards dualisms, underpin human disregard for the environment; these tendencies are played out repeatedly in participatory decision-making processes. It is worth reiterating that this chapter does not contend that rationalist assumptions are wholly negative or positive. Rather it underlines the importance in conducting further analysis to develop our understanding of rationalist assumptions and their roles in participatory environmental governance.

CHAPTER 14

INDIGENOUS PEOPLES' RIGHT TO NATURAL RESOURCES: REFLECTIONS FROM THE ARCTIC

Tanja JOONA*

ABSTRACT

Arctic energy development has considerable effects on the area's future, but also globally the growing need for new resources is forcing us to explore new territories. At the same time, the Arctic is largely inhabited by indigenous peoples and has special environmental vulnerabilities that can contribute to impacts on Arctic indigenous peoples. Norms of consultation with indigenous peoples thus have a particular importance in Arctic contexts. Arctic countries like Norway and Denmark have ratified the only legally binding international convention dedicated to indigenous peoples, the International Labour Convention No. 169 (hereafter *ILO 169*) concerning the rights of indigenous peoples. Finland is considering the ratification, while its neighbouring country Sweden seems to have dropped the idea, for now at least. The main challenge is related to land rights, especially the ownership and possession of traditionally occupied lands (Article 14). However, a more contemporary issue seems to be the exploration and exploitation of natural and mineral resources for the growing needs of global markets. This is often made in areas where ownership questions are unresolved or areas that are used for the purposes of traditional livelihoods. ILO 169 states that exploitation of natural resources should not take place in indigenous territories without the peoples' prior, free and informed consent. They have the right to a fair share of the benefits from such activities in their lands, and the right to just

* The author is a senior researcher at the Arctic Centre of the University of Lapland, Finland (Tanja.Joona@ulapland.fi).

and fair compensation. According to ILO 169, these rights should be settled through appropriate negotiations and proper agreements with the indigenous peoples concerned. This article will explore the participatory mechanisms and gives an example from Finland.

1. INTRODUCTION

The issue of ethnic minorities and indigenous peoples' right to land and other natural resources is an important and controversial issue in international politics and law. However, the issue is very contemporary in the Arctic context, where energy development has been very fast recently and will have considerable effects on the areas in future, but also globally the growing need for new resources is forcing us to explore new territories. At the same time, the Arctic is largely inhabited by indigenous peoples and other local people and has special environmental vulnerabilities that can contribute to impacts on Arctic indigenous peoples and other communities.

Norms of consultation with indigenous peoples and local peoples thus have a particular importance in Arctic contexts. This chapter elaborates what is meant by participatory rights within international law, although indigenous peoples' right to natural and mineral resources can be approached from several legal points of view. Often, domestic laws and international law become mixed and it is rather difficult to estimate the right angle for an approach. Also, non-legally binding instruments, like the UN Declaration on the Rights of Indigenous Peoples,[1] are often referred to simultaneously with different domestic and local voluntary procedures and guidelines for participation and consultations. This might be confusing to officials but for indigenous peoples themselves.

This chapter focuses on ILO 169 concerning the rights of indigenous peoples.[2] Even though Finland has not ratified ILO 169, it has tried to meet many of the provisions of the convention, for example in the Sámi Act of 1995. Finland also likes to follow quite carefully what is happening in the neighbouring countries, especially in Norway that has ratified ILO 169 and tried to find solutions for the Sàmi land right questions. So, in many countries, the convention is used as a guiding tool when policies or projects affecting indigenous and tribal peoples are applied and implemented.

Indigenous peoples possess diverse languages, cultures, livelihood practices and knowledge systems. However, in many countries, they face discrimination

1 61/295. United Nations Declaration on the Rights of Indigenous Peoples. Resolution adopted by the General Assembly on 13 September 2007.

2 Convention concerning Indigenous and Tribal Peoples in Independent Countries (Entry into force: 05 Sep 1991) Adoption: Geneva, 76th ILO session, (27 June 1989).

and exploitative labour conditions, which are interconnected with their generalized marginalization and poverty situation. The ILO's concern for indigenous peoples dates back to the 1920s in Latin America and originated in the quest to overcome the discriminatory working conditions they live under. In recognition of the complexities and specificities of indigenous peoples' situations, ILO 169 takes a holistic approach covering a wide range of issues that affect the lives and wellbeing of these peoples. The convention has become a global reference point with impact on governance and development policies that spans far beyond the countries that have ratified it. Further, it is an instrument for governments to foster a favourable environment for the creation of sustainable enterprises.[3]

ILO 169 represents a consensus reached by ILO tripartite constituents on the rights of indigenous and tribal peoples within the nation-states where they live and the responsibilities of governments to protect these rights. It is based on respect for the cultures and ways of life of indigenous peoples and recognizes their right to land and natural resources and to define their own priorities for development. The convention aims at overcoming discriminatory practices affecting these peoples and enabling them to participate in decision-making that affects their lives. Therefore, the fundamental principles of *consultation* and *participation* constitute the cornerstone of the convention. Further, the convention covers a wide range of issues pertaining to indigenous peoples, including employment and vocational training, education, health and social security, customary law, traditional institutions, languages, religious beliefs and cross-border cooperation.[4] This chapter, however, focuses on Articles 13-19, dealing with indigenous peoples' ownership right to lands and the right to natural resources.

So far, the convention has been ratified by 22 countries,[5] which is a fairly low number, since indigenous and tribal peoples constitute at least 5000 distinct peoples with a population of more than 370 million, living in 70 different countries. This diversity cannot easily be captured in a universal definition of term 'indigenous peoples' and it is neither necessary nor desirable. Similarly, there is no international agreement on the definition of the term 'minorities' or the term 'indigenous peoples'.[6] It is considered that the fundamental difference between indigenous peoples and minorities lies in indigenous peoples' ties to

3 Handbook for ILO Tripartite Constituents. Understanding the Indigenous and Tribal Peoples Convention, 1989, (No. 169). International Labour Office, Switzerland, 2013, p. 11.

4 *Ibid.*, p. 1.

5 Argentina, Bolivia, Brazil, Central African Republic, Chile, Colombia, Costa Rica, Denmark, Dominica, Ecuador, Fiji, Guatemala, Honduras, Mexico, Nepal, Netherlands, Nicaragua, Norway, Paraguay, Peru, Spain, Venezuela.

6 The United Nations Minorities Declaration (adopted by consensus in 1992) in its Article 1 refers to minorities as based on national or ethnic, cultural, religious and linguistic identity, and provides that states should protect their existence. There is no internationally agreed definition

their territory of origin or specific livelihoods when nomadic. In many indigenous belief systems, land has a symbolic and spiritual value, as well as a social and economic function within the group, even for those who live outside of the homeland. Some minorities have territories they traditionally occupy, but indigenous peoples are also considered the first inhabitants of their territories.[7]

ILO 169 does not strictly define who are indigenous and tribal peoples, but rather describes the peoples it aims to protect. According to Article 1 of the convention, it applies to:

> '(a) tribal peoples in independent countries whose social, cultural and economic conditions distinguish them from other sections of the national community, and whose status is regulated wholly or partially by their own customs or traditions or by special laws or regulations;
> (b) peoples in independent countries who are regarded as indigenous on account of their descent from the populations which inhabited the country, or a geographical region to which the country belongs, at the time of conquest or colonisation or the establishment of present state boundaries and who, irrespective of their legal status, retain some or all of their own social, economic, cultural and political institutions.
> 2. Self-identification as indigenous or tribal shall be regarded as a fundamental criterion for determining the groups to which the provisions of this Convention apply.
> 3. The use of the term peoples in this Convention shall not be construed as having any implications as regards the rights which may attach to the term under international law.'

The convention's coverage is based on a combination of the objective and subjective criteria. Thus, self-identification complements the objective criteria, and vice versa. The convention also takes an inclusive approach and is equally applicable to both indigenous and tribal peoples. It thereby focuses on the present situation of indigenous and tribal peoples, although the historical continuity and territorial connection are important elements in the identification of indigenous peoples.[8]

The criteria elaborated in Article 1.1(b) of ILO 169 have been applied widely for the purpose of identifying indigenous peoples in international and national

---

as to which groups constitute minorities. It is often stressed that the existence of a minority is a question of fact and that any definition must include both objective factors (such as the existence of a shared ethnicity, language or religion) and subjective factors (including that individuals must identify themselves as members of a minority), available at: http://www.ohchr.org/EN/Issues/Minorities/Pages/internationallaw.aspx (acceded on 20 March 2018).

7 How do minorities differ from indigenous peoples? Minority Rights group international, available at: https://www.minorityrightscourse.org/mod/page/view.php?id=1591 (accessed on 20 March 2018).

8 Indigenous & Tribal Peoples' Rights in Practice. A Guide to ILO Convention No. 169. Programme to Promote ILO Convention No. 169 (PRO 169). International Labour Standards Department, 2009, p.10.

political and legal processes, far beyond the group of states that have ratified the convention. It is used as an international working definition for the purpose of identifying indigenous peoples, including the application of the UN Declaration on the Rights of Indigenous Peoples, and has also been the basis on which various UN specialized agencies have developed their own operational definitions of the term indigenous peoples, including the World Bank and the United Nations Development Programme.[9]

In the context of land rights, the right to natural and mineral resources, and the right to participate in the use and management of these resources the question of a rights holder is a relevant question. And when there is no universal definition on what is meant by indigenous peoples, there is also a large variety of ownership models with different combinations of rights holder positions. Some indigenous lands can be owned collectively by a community; they can be individual property, family owned, shared or a mixed model with several different ownership models. This is, of course, an issue that needs to be taken into account, when participatory rights are implemented. In its view concerning oil exploitation in Ecuador, the supervisory body of the ILO (CEACR, Committee of Experts on the Application of Conventions and Recommendations) underlined that 'that the principle of representativity is a vital component of the obligation of consultation'. It noted that 'it could be difficult in many circumstances to determine who represents any given community. However, if an appropriate consultation process is not developed with the indigenous and tribal institutions or organizations that are truly representative of the communities affected, the resulting consultations will not comply with the requirements of the Convention.'[10]

2. WHAT DOES ILO 169 AIM TO PROTECT?

The ILO was originally concerned with indigenous and tribal peoples, primarily in their role as workers. Following the creation of the United Nations in 1945, the ILO widened its examination of indigenous workers to address issues pertaining to indigenous and tribal peoples generally. In 1957, the ILO adopted the Indigenous and Tribal Populations Convention, C107 (hereafter *Convention 107*),[11] which was the first international treaty ever to be adopted on this subject.

9 *Ibid.*

10 Indigenous & Tribal Peoples' Rights in Practice. A Guide to ILO Convention No. 169. Programme to Promote ILO Convention No. 169 (PRO 169). International Labour Standards Department, 2009, p. 111.

11 Convention concerning the Protection and Integration of Indigenous and Other Tribal and Semi-Tribal Populations in Independent Countries (Entry into force: 2 June 1959). Adoption Geneva, 40th ILC session (26 June 1957).

It was ratified by 37 countries, and remains in force still for countries that have not ratified ILO 169 (27 countries). As years went by and public opinion evolved, certain weaknesses in Convention 107 began to attract attention, in particular its assumptions that integration into larger society was the only possible future for indigenous and tribal peoples and that all decisions regarding development were a concern of the state rather of the people most affected. The Governing body of the ILO responded by putting the revision of Convention 107 on the agenda of the International Labour Conference (ILOC) in 1988 and 1989. In June 1989 ILO 169 was adopted to include the fundamental concept that the ways of life of indigenous and tribal peoples should and will survive. Another fundamental change is the premise that these peoples and their traditional organizations should be closely involved in the planning and implementation of development projects that affect them, and indeed in all the measures taken to apply the convention.[12]

Arctic countries like Norway and Denmark have ratified the convention, while Finland is considering the ratification and Sweden has taken another approach. It has developed Sámi rights through national legislation and there has recently also been several legal cases concerning the rights to reindeer herding, fishing and hunting.[13] The main challenge in countries that have ratified the convention or are considering it, is related to land rights; especially the question related to indigenous peoples' ownership and possession of traditionally occupied lands is very controversial and has been interpreted in different ways. According to Article 14:

> '1. The rights of ownership and possession of the peoples concerned over the lands which they traditionally occupy shall be recognised. In addition, measures shall be taken in appropriate cases to safeguard the right of the peoples concerned to use lands not exclusively occupied by them, but to which they have traditionally had access for their subsistence and traditional activities. Particular attention shall be paid to the situation of nomadic peoples and shifting cultivators in this respect.
> 2. Governments shall take steps as necessary to identify the lands which the peoples concerned traditionally occupy, and to guarantee effective protection of their rights of ownership and possession.
> 3. Adequate procedures shall be established within the national legal system to resolve land claims by the peoples concerned.'

12 International Labour Standards Department, Programme to Promote ILO Convention No. 169 (PRO 169) and International Labour Standards Department, 19 February 2013.

13 In Sweden for example the courts have shown a more favourable attitude to the issue of Sámi rights than legislature has. Three decisions by the Supreme Court are preeminent: the *Taxed Mountain Case* (1981), the *Nordmaling Case* (2011) and a very recent one, the *Girjas Case* (2016).

According to the ILO handbook, the convention recognizes indigenous peoples' rights to the land and resources they traditionally occupy and use in a broad sense. It gives importance to the concept of territories, covering the total environment of the areas they occupy. The recognition of land rights is based on the traditional occupation, meaning the land where indigenous peoples have lived over time and want to pass on to future generations. It is thus the traditional occupation and use which is the basis for establishing indigenous peoples' land rights, and not the eventual official recognition or registration of that ownership. As mentioned earlier, these land rights comprise both individual and collective aspects of ownership. Further, governments are required to establish procedures to identify indigenous peoples' lands and protect their rights of ownership and possession, including through demarcation and titling, and to establish mechanisms to resolve land claims.[14] For example in Norway, the land identification process is going on at the moment. It is estimated that this carefully planned and conducted work will take several years, even decades.

However, a more contemporary issue seems to be the exploration and exploitation of natural and mineral resources for the growing needs of global markets. This is often made in areas where ownership questions are unresolved or areas that are used for the purposes of traditional livelihoods. These questions are examined more thoroughly in the following chapters.

3. INDIGENOUS PEOPLES' RIGHT TO NATURAL AND MINERAL RESOURCES

The recognition of indigenous peoples' rights to natural resources is inextricably tied to the rights to lands and territories. Therefore, ILO 169 establishes as a basic principle that indigenous peoples have the rights to natural resources pertaining to their lands and to participate in the use, management and conservation of these resources. According to Article 15.1:

> 'The rights of the peoples concerned to the natural resources pertaining to their lands shall be specially safeguarded. These rights include the right of these peoples to participate in the use, management and conservation of these resources.'

The convention thus specifies that indigenous peoples have rights to the natural resources of their territories, including the right to participate in the use, management, protection and conservation of these resources. As a basic

14 Handbook for ILO Tripartite Constituents. Understanding the Indigenous and Tribal Peoples Convention, 1989, (No. 169). International Labour Office, Switzerland, 2013, p. 21.

principle, these resources comprise both renewable and non-renewable resources such as timber, fish, water, sand and minerals.

However, there are many cases in which the state constitution provides that the state alone owns mineral and other resources. Article 15.2 recognizes this situation while also stipulating that indigenous peoples have rights regarding consultation, participation in the benefits of resource exploitation as well as compensation for damages resulting from this exploitation. There are numerous examples where the exploration or exploitation of mineral or sub-surface resources on indigenous peoples' lands has led to conflicts. In these situations, Article 15.2 of the convention seeks to reconcile interests by recognizing the rights of indigenous peoples. It must also be specifically noted that the responsibility for ensuring that these rights are respected lies with the concerned governments and not with the private companies or entities that are licensed to undertake the exploration or exploitation.[15] Article 15.2 stipulates: 'In cases in which the State retains the ownership of mineral or sub-surface resources or rights to other resources pertaining to lands, governments shall establish or maintain procedures through which they shall consult these peoples, with a view to ascertaining whether and to what degree their interests would be prejudiced, before undertaking or permitting any programmes for the exploration or exploitation of such resources pertaining to their lands. The peoples concerned shall wherever possible participate in the benefits of such activities, and shall receive fair compensation for any damages which they may sustain as a result of such activities.'

ILO 169 states that exploitation of natural resources should not take place in indigenous territories without *prior, free and informed* consent by the peoples concerned. They have the right to a fair share of the benefits from such activities in their lands, and the right to just and fair compensation. According to ILO 169, these rights should be settled through appropriate negotiations and proper agreements with the indigenous peoples concerned.

Inadequate implementation of the provisions regarding consultation, participation and impact assessment in the context of natural resource exploration and exploitation is quite common and is the subject of the most frequent complaints brought to the attention of the ILO's supervisory bodies. Often, conflicts occur between indigenous peoples and private sector actors, who have obtained concessions or licenses from the state. In this context, it is important to underline that the responsibility for ensuring the correct application of the right to consultation and participation lies with the state. Failure to comply with this responsibility will pose a risk to the investments of the private sector, as indigenous peoples may rightfully invoke their rights under the convention.

---

15 *Ibid.*

4. WHOSE CONSULTATION AND PARTICIPATION? AN EXAMPLE FROM FINLAND

It is considered that consultation and participation are fundamental principles of democratic governance and of inclusive development. The rights to be consulted and to participate in decision-making constitute the cornerstone of ILO 169 and the basis for applying the broader set of rights enshrined in the convention. Yet, the implementation of these rights remains one of the main challenges in a number of countries.[16]

The concept of participation is closely linked to that of consultation. In a general manner, the convention states in Article 6.1 that governments shall 'establish means by which these peoples can freely participate, to at least the same extent as other sectors of the population, at all levels of decision-making in elective institutions and administrative and other bodies responsible for policies and programmes which concern them'.[17]

The convention requires that indigenous peoples are able to effectively participate in decision-making processes which may affect their rights or interests. The establishment of processes of consultation is an essential means of ensuring effective indigenous peoples' participation in decision-making. Thus, Articles 6 and 7 on consultation and participation are key provisions of the convention and the 'basis for applying all the others', though a number of other articles also make reference to consultation and participation.[18]

According to Article 6.1 and 6.2:

> 'In applying the provisions of this Convention, governments shall: (a) consult the peoples concerned, through appropriate procedures and in particular through their representative institutions, whenever consideration is being given to legislative or administrative measures which may affect them directly; (b) establish means by which these peoples can freely participate, to at least the same extent as other sectors of the population, at all levels of decision-making in elective institutions and administrative and other bodies responsible for policies and programmes which concern them; (c) establish means for the full development of these peoples' own institutions and initiatives, and in appropriate cases provide the resources necessary for this purpose.

---

16 Committee of Experts, General Observation on Convention No. 169, 79th Session, 2008, published 2009.

17 Handbook for ILO Tripartite Constituents. Understanding the Indigenous and Tribal Peoples Convention, 1989, (No. 169). International Labour Office, Switzerland, 2013, p. 18.

18 See, for example, Committee of Experts, 76th Session, 2005, Observation, Guatemala, published 2006, para. 6

> The consultations carried out in application of this Convention shall be undertaken, in good faith and in a form appropriate to the circumstances, with the objective of achieving agreement or consent to the proposed measures.'

Also Article 7 stipulates on participation:

> 'The peoples concerned shall have the right to decide their own priorities for the process of development as it affects their lives, beliefs, institutions and spiritual well-being and the lands they occupy or otherwise use, and to exercise control, to the extent possible, over their own economic, social and cultural development. In addition, they shall participate in the formulation, implementation and evaluation of plans and programmes for national and regional development which may affect them directly.'

The general requirement to consult with indigenous peoples is reflected in Article 6.1 of ILO 169. Consultation with indigenous peoples thus arises as a general obligation under the convention, whenever legislative or administrative measures affect them directly. The main objective of these provisions is to ensure that indigenous peoples can effectively participate at all levels of decision-making in political, legislative and administrative bodies and processes which may affect them directly. Under the convention, consultation is viewed as a crucial means of dialogue to reconcile conflicting interests and prevent as well as settle disputes. Through the interrelatedness of the principles of consultation and participation, consultation is not merely the right to react but indeed also a right to propose; indigenous peoples have the right to decide their own priorities for the process of development and thus exercise control over their own economic, social and cultural development.[19] One has to bear in mind that the core area of application for the concepts of consultation and participation is in the context of relationships between indigenous peoples and states.

Measures that could require consultation are, for example, the elaboration of national legislation regarding consultations or the construction of road infrastructure on the lands of a specific indigenous community. In addition, the convention particularly emphasizes the need to consult under certain circumstances, including prior to exploration or exploitation of sub-surface resources and prior to relocation and land alienation.

The convention particularly emphasizes the need to consult in the following circumstances:

- Prior to exploration or exploitation of mineral and sub-surface resources (Article 15.2);

19 Indigenous & Tribal Peoples' Rights in Practice. A Guide to ILO Convention No. 169. Programme to Promote ILO Convention No. 169 (PRO 169). International Labour Standards Department, 2009, p. 60.

- Prior to relocation, which should take place only with a free and informed consent (Article 16);
- When considering alienation or transmission of indigenous peoples' lands outside their own communities (Article 17);
- On the organization and operation of special vocational training programmes (Article 22);
- On literacy and educational programmes and measures (Articles 27 and 28).

As an example of the practical implementation of consultation procedures, in 2005 the Government of Norway and the Sámi Parliament agreed on procedures for what is regarded as 'normative guidelines'. The obligation to consult the Sámi Parliament includes all material and immaterial forms of Sámi culture, including music, theatre, literature, art, media, language, religion, cultural heritage, immaterial property rights and traditional knowledge, place names, health and social welfare, day care facilities for children, education, research, land ownership rights and rights to use lands, matters concerning land administration and competing land utilization, business development, reindeer husbandry, fisheries, agriculture, wind power, hydroelectric power, sustainable development, preservation of cultural heritage, biodiversity and nature conservation. The most important requirement is that necessary consultation processes and procedures are established in order to enable the Sámi Parliament to exert real influence on the process and the final result, where consent to the proposed measures does not necessarily need to be reached.[20]

The UN Declaration on the Rights of Indigenous Peoples[21] also focuses on consultation and participation and establishes that the purpose of the consultation is to achieve *free, prior and informed consent*. Moreover, the declaration recognizes that indigenous peoples, in exercising their right to self-determination, have the right to autonomy or self-government in matters relating to their internal and local affairs (Article 4). An interesting point of view is that the expression 'free, prior and informed consent' is mentioned six times in UNDRIP and once in ILO 169. In UNDRIP, the principle of free, prior and informed consent is related to context of relocation, dispossession of lands, resources and cultural/spiritual property, storage of hazardous waste, legislation that may affect indigenous peoples and, maybe most importantly, the approval of any project affecting their land and territories. On the other hand, in ILO 169, free, prior and informed consent is only considered in situations for relocation.

---

20 See more: Henriksen, J. (2008) Key Principles in Implementing ILO Convention No. 169, ILO.

21 Adopted by the General Assembly on Thursday, 13 September 2007.

Overall, this is clearly a more limited scope of the application of the principle of free, prior and informed consent.[22]

There are representative advisory bodies established in Norway, Sweden and Finland in 1987, 1992 and 1995 by the so-called Sámi Act with a view to allowing the consultation of Sámi people on matters affecting them. The mandate and regulation of this body may change considerably from one country to another. In particular, it is worth noting the 'obligation to negotiate' contemplated in section 9 of the Finnish Sámi Parliament Act, since it marks a significant difference between this act and the correspondent acts enacted in Norway and Sweden.[23] Finnish authorities are, in fact, obliged to negotiate with the Sámi Parliament 'in all far-reaching and important measures which may directly and in a specific way affect the status of the Sámi as an indigenous people'.[24]Also, according to the Reindeer Husbandry Act 53.1. (848/1990, in Finnish), 'when planning measures concerning State land that will have a substantial effect on the practice of reindeer herding, the State authorities must consult the representatives of the reindeer herding co-operative in question.'

In Finland, discussion on indigenous Sámi rights to land and waters have been going on for a long time. Different stakeholders, international, national and local politics are involved when issues concerning indigenous Sámi rights to use northern lands for their traditional activities are discussed.[25] In the northern part of Finland, in Lapland, the special Sámi homeland area is about the size of 35,000 km^2. This is an area where indigenous Sámi have been granted *cultural autonomy*, as legislated by the Sámi Act (1995) and governed by the special organ established for this purpose, called the Sámi Parliament. The official number of Sámi is based on the number of people with the right to vote in the elections of the Sámi Parliament. This means that about 6,000 persons are registered and also their children are accounted as Sámi. In total, this makes about 10,000 Sámi in Finland.

In terms of consultation, the current situation is somewhat paradoxical; only 1/10 of the Finnish Sámi are reindeer herders, while much emphasis is laid down especially on consultations with the Sámi Parliament, not for example with the reindeer herding cooperatives responsible for reindeer herding locally. This

22 See more García, A.P. and A.H. Morales (2017) Greenland compliance with the ILO 169 and UNDRIP, Master's thesis, Aalborg University; see also Ward and Tara (2011) The Right to Free Prior and Informed Consent: Indigenous Peoples' Participation Rights within International Law. Northwestern Journal of International Human Rights. Vol. 10, Issue 2.

23 See more Bengtson, B. (2015) Reforming Swedish Sami Legislation: A Survey of the Arguments, in Christina Allard, Susann Skogvang (eds.) Indigenous Rights in Scandinavia, Autonomous Sámi Law, Ashgate Publishing,

24 Act on Sámi Parliament, (Laki Saamelaiskäräjistä) 17.7.1995/974.

25 See more Joona, T. (2015) The Finnish Sámi Definition and its application,. in C. Alard, S. Skogvang (eds.), Indigenous Rights in Scandinavia, Autonomous Sami Law, Juris Diversitas, Ashgate.

means that persons who represent the Sámi Parliament can live outside the Sámi homeland area, in southern cities of Finland, and may not have any cultural connection with the homeland area. Therefore, it is reasonable to question the representativity in the land use questions and situations where consultation is needed. At the local level this causes disagreements and the feeling of inequality.

The current debate in Finland is heavily connected with participatory rights and the membership selection of the Sámi Parliament and how the definition of Sáminess is applied in practice. In comparison to neighbouring countries, the estimated total Sámi population of Norway varies between 75,000 and 100,000. Similarly, in Sweden estimations vary from 27,000 to 35,000, while only 8,322 persons were registered in the Swedish Sámi Parliament electoral roll in 2013. According to research by *Torunn Pettersen*, 'we are unable to know how large this population in Norway could have been if all persons with known or unknown Sami background considered themselves to be Sami and decided to join the electoral register.'[26]

There are many open and difficult questions still related to the Sámi land right question, but also the definition of a Sámi in Finland. These have caused disagreements especially at local level. Since the definition of a Sámi is the most contemporary topic, other issues get less attention. Culture and language revitalization, the situation of the urban Sámi, future of youth and children, and those who still practice traditional livelihoods would certainly need concrete and rapid actions in preserving their traditions and identity.

5. CONCLUSION

This chapter has introduced some of the most relevant provisions of ILO 169 concerning the rights of indigenous peoples, especially those related to land rights. It has also been acknowledged that the convention does not define indigenous peoples, but describes the peoples it aims to protect. Within this context one can say that it is the indigenous peoples' special relationship with land and territories that distinguishes them from (other) minorities. This relationship is a central point of the convention and forms the basis for the realization of other indigenous rights where effective participatory rights play a key role.

However, while the majority of indigenous peoples worldwide still live in rural areas, they are increasingly migrating to urban areas, both voluntarily and involuntarily. This is a reflection of the growing trend of global urbanization,

26 Pettersen, T. (2011) 'The electoral register of the Sámediggi in Norway 1989-2009: Basis, growth and geographical shifts' (Paper prepared for presentation at European Consortium for Political Research (ECPR), Joint Sessions of Workshops, University of St Gallen, Switzerland) p. 23.

whereby the majority of the world's population will soon live in cities. Factors that contribute to indigenous peoples' urban migration include land dispossession, poverty, militarization, natural disasters, lack of employment opportunities, the deterioration of traditional livelihoods combined with the lack of viable economic alternatives, and the prospect of better opportunities in cities.

Indigenous urbanization is a fact also in the Nordic countries. In Finland out of about 10,000 Sámi almost 70 per cent are living outside the Sámi homeland area, in big southern cities like Helsinki, Oulu and Rovaniemi. Nowadays, 85 per cent of Sámi children are born outside the Sámi homeland area. This could be described as the biggest challenges of the modern Sámi community. The trend is similar in Norway and Sweden and exemplifies a more global phenomenon among the indigenous populations. In Finland, nowadays only roughly every tenth Sámi practices traditional reindeer herding, which corresponds to between 800-900 Sámi reindeer herders. The situation of the Sámi languages is also weak. Only about 1,900 people consider one of the three Sámi languages (North-Sámi, Skolt Sámi and Inari Sámi) to be their mother tongue.

The contemporary Finnish Sámi community can be described as going through considerable and rapid changes, where most of the people are living in urban surroundings and have severe challenges in preserving their indigenous culture. Traditional livelihoods no longer play a significant role in the indigenous lifestyle, but integration into the main population is apparent. In regard to the definition of indigenous peoples, the situation starts to be paradoxical; there's no longer connection with the traditional livelihoods or the territories. This causes challenges relating to the representativity and legitimacy of the Sámi Parliament. Who has to say, when northern lands are explored or exploited? Who should be consulted?

What makes the situation even more controversial is the fact that at the same time there are people who still have the strength and will to continue traditional livelihoods, living in remote northern areas of Finland with limited services, where they face different types of challenges, when seeking official recognition of their indigenous identity. Even though not officially represented at the Sámi Parliament, they are the ones who are affected by the exploitation of natural resources. The current legislative processes in Finland must address these questions – keeping in mind the survival of a unique people of the North.

CHAPTER 15

FOSTERING ENVIRONMENTAL PROTECTION THROUGH THE RIGHT TO RELIGIOUS FREEDOM

Jerônimo Basilio São Mateus*

ABSTRACT

The role of religion in conservation issues has been recognized at international level since the 1990s. Nowadays, there is little doubt about the importance of specifically addressing religious communities in conservation institutions and practices. This relationship between religion and environmentalism could be analysed from at least two different perspectives: first, from the policy and management level; and second, from the legal level. In the first case, the main concern is raised by the role of faith-based organizations in planning and implementing conservation policies. From the second perspective, the fundamental question addressed by legal scholars is the relationship between religious freedom rights and environmental protection, or environmental rights. This paper deals with the latter perspective and argues in favour of the possibility of considering the protection of sacred natural sites (SNS) through the right of worship as a common expression of the right to religious freedom. In this sense, I argue that the protection of this kind of place should be enhanced, given that religious freedom is a subjective right, which cannot be easily overridden as other land-based rights that are usually used as instruments for protecting sacred natural sites.

* PhD Candidate in Law at the Rovira i Virgili University – Tarragona, Spain (jeronimo.basilio@urv.cat), and research fellow at the Center for the Study of the Environmental Law of Tarragona (CEDAT). This research was conducted under the CONCLIMA – Global Climate Constitution: Governance and law in a complex context (DER2016-80011-P) project with grant a scholarship from the Spanish Ministry of Economy, Industry and Competitiveness.

1. INTRODUCTION

The engagement with environmental movements can be motivated by several different reasons, which can be assessed by an analysis of the different environmental discourses.[1] Despite the fact that main environmental activism and policy at international level today is motivated or inspired by what could be considered as a materialistic world view[2] – and in this sense, the object of environmental policy and law is nature, considered as a material foreground where the whole of humanity dwells, and where we all go looking for natural resources – this is obviously not the only motivation for engaging in environmental issues, and in some contexts not the best way to draw attention to environmental concerns.

For instance, in the beginning of the environmental movement, by the end of the 19th century and in the first decades of the 20th century in the United States, immaterial values, like beauty, contemplation, sublimity and spirituality were important motives of those considered as environmentalists, like Henry Thoreau, John Muir, Ralph Waldo Emerson, George Perkin Marsh.[3] At that time, nature was not yet reduced to its quantitative and measurable aspects, at least in the conservation imaginary.

Nowadays, most environmental debates, policies and law, are anchored in a well-established, and in a certain way categorical, vision of what is nature: objective, measurable, material, indisputable, object of natural sciences. Any aspect of the world that doesn´t match those features is considered as culture, that is to say something immaterial, socially constructed, subjective, and disputable.[4] In this sense, things like nature spirits, gods dwelling in forests, animals with agency,[5] shamans being able to travel between spiritual and material worlds, are considered, from a legal perspective, as beliefs of some cultures of the world, with no reality in a meaningful sense.[6]

---

1 Dryzek, J.S. (2013) The politics of the earth: environmental discourses, Oxford University Press, p. 85.

2 van Egmond, N.D. and H.J.M. de Vries (2011) Sustainability: The search for the integral worldview, Futures, Vol. 43, No. 8.

3 For historical analysis of the role of religion in the beginning of the American environmentalism, see Stoll, M. (2015) Inherit the holy mountain: religion and the rise of American environmentalism, Oxford University Press.

4 For a critique of the nature-culture division in modernity, see Latour, B. (2017) Facing Gaia: Eight Lectures on the New Climatic Regime, Polity Press, p. 41; Latour, B. (2002) We have never been modern, Harvard University Press.

5 The word 'agency"' has been used in contemporary anthropology, originally borrowed from semiotics studies, to describe various forms of action in the natural world, without linking it to intentionality or conscience. See Latour, B. (2014) How Better to Register the Agency of Things, Tanner Lectures.

6 Latour, B. (2002) We have never been modern, Harvard University Press, p. 64.

From a legal perspective, or more precisely from a legal environmental one, the problem is that the division between nature and culture is not universal, and if conservation issues or environmental problems are addressed considering only this particular ontology,[7] different kinds of difficulties and injustices would be unavoidable. A proper comprehension of particular religious cosmologies and ontologies is fundamental in any case where different views of what is considered as 'nature' are at stake. Environmental conflicts that involve religious communities or indigenous people may occur at a deeper level, precisely because there is no previous agreement on what reality and nature are. In this sense they are considered as ontological conflicts, that is to say, conflicts about the structure of reality and the beings that are part of it.[8]

These new concerns on the set-up of better methodological tools to deal with ontological differences, developed as part of the contemporary anthropological theory,[9] should also be considered within the conservation theory and in the management of natural resources. Understanding the profound differences that might be at stake in an environmental conflict associated with religious or indigenous world views, could be useful to find more just solutions within local communities' world views.

In this chapter, I focus on one concrete example of how the 'relativization' of the nature-culture division is important in environmental issues, analysing the case of sacred natural sites. I argue that sacred natural sites must be considered under the legal category of 'places of worship' and, as a consequence, be object of the subjective right to religious freedom. For that matter, my argument is structured in three phases: First, I show the importance of taking into account religions within conservation policies; then, I show how the right to religious freedom may be applied to sacred natural sites; and finally, I comment briefly on some recent court decisions, and legal innovations, to lay out possible directions for the future.

---

7 The division of the world into nature and culture is only one of the possible forms of distributing the different beings that inhabit the planet. As Phillippe Descola has shown, besides naturalism, there are at least other three ontologies that could be identified within world cultures: analogism, totemism, and animism. See Descola, P. (2014) Beyond nature and culture, University of Chicago Press, p. 129.

8 Blaser, M. (2013) Notes towards a Political Ontology of 'Environmental' Conflicts, in L. Green (ed.), Contested Ecologies: Dialoges in the South on Nature and Konwlodege, HSRC Press; Basilio Sao Mateus, J. (2017) Notas sobre el desarrollo del concepto de conflicto ambiental ontológico, Revista Catalana de Dret Ambiental, Vol. 8, No. 1.

9 For a brief summary of what is called ontological turn in anthropology, see Kohn, E. (2015) Anthropology of Ontologies, Annual Review of Anthropology, Vol. 44, No. 1. For an analysis about the application of ontological turn to environmental law theory, see Vermeylen, (2017) Materiality and the Ontological Turn in the Anthropocene: Establishing a Dialogue between Law, Anthropology and Eco-Philosophy, in L. Kotzé (ed.) Enviromental Law and Governacne for the Anthropocene, Hart Publishing, pp. 151-155.

2. THE ROLE OF RELIGION IN CONSERVATION ISSUES

Considering the contemporary environmental crisis that we are facing and that religious communities have existed for thousands of years in a consistent and sustainable way, it would be very reasonable to look at those communities, or at least to try to understand how and why they are the longest and more resilient institutions that have ever existed in the world. Nevertheless, world religions were not a matter of environmental policy up until a few years ago.[10]

Until the 1980s, the role of religions and faith-based organizations[11] in the mitigation of the contemporary environmental crisis was considered of less importance or not considered at all by scholars and international conservation institutions. In the specific case of the United Nations (UN), this fact[12] could be attributed to two reasons. The first one, because the UN is an assembly composed by very disparate states (theocracies, confessional and non-confessional states, some of them very reluctant to consider the issue), which makes dealing with religion a very delicate issue for diplomacy. The second reason, because UN institutions, particularly the UNEP, are science-based instances, which makes their incorporation into the religious discourse difficult.[13]

From the eighties this scenario began to change, and some international institutions started to address the issue, in part reflecting the academic idea that had been in development since 1960 with respect to the relationship between religion and ecology.[14] Some of the pioneer events at the international level included: In 1986, the Interfaith Partnership for the Environment (IPE) was created as a part of the UNEP;[15] in 1995, the Alliance of Religions and Conservation[16] was created on the initiative of Prince Philip from England with

10 Palmer, M. (2003) Faith in conservation: new approaches to religions and the environment, The World Bank.

11 Faith-based organizations could be defined as: 'non-state actors motivated by faith-linked concerns' Haynes, J. (2014) Faith-based organizations at the United Nations, Palgrave Macmillian, p. 9.

12 Ibid., p. 47.

13 Dahl, A.L. (2017) Why should the UN and in particular UN environment engage more with faith-based organizations?, UN Environment Perspectives, No. 23.

14 Nash, R. (1989) The rights of nature: a history of environmental ethics, University of Wisconsin Press.

15 The first publication addressing the moral and religious issues of the environmental crisis by the UNEP was Brown, N.J. and P. Quiblier (eds.) (1994) Ethics & Agenda 21: moral implications of a global consensus, UNEP.

16 This institution was created from the 'WWF Religion and Conservation Network', that was founded in 1986 as a special group functioning inside the WWF. In this event that took place in Assis five leaders of world religions (Buddhism, Christianity, Hinduism, Islam and Judaism) approved declarations on environmental issues. Palmer, M. (2003) Faith in conservation: new approaches to religions and the environment, The World Bank.

the technical support of Martin Palmer; in 1997, the UNESCO, under the Man and the Biosphere Programme (MAB), promoted a one-year study called: 'Role of sacred groves in conservation and management of biological diversity in India';[17] in 1998, the Task force on Non Material Values of Protected Areas was created under the World Commission on Protected Areas of the IUCN;[18] in 1999, the UNEP published the document 'Cultural and Spiritual Values of Biodiversity',[19] the first publication of the UNEP addressing the relation between religion and conservation; in 2004, the Secretariat of the Convention on Biological Diversity (CBD) approved the Akwé: Kon Guidelines, a series of voluntary recommendations on impact assessment of activities that may affect sacred natural sites; in 2008 the IUCN published its influential guideline: 'Sacred Natural Sites – Guidelines for Protected Area Managers'. These are only a few of the main publications and events that have occurred in the last 30 years on the issue.

The need to consider religions in environmental policies that is being recognized by those legal instruments and institutions is based on two main groups of arguments: the first group consists of those arguments that could be considered as quantitative or instrumental, meaning that they are related to the numeric importance of religious populations in the world, along with their well-established organizational structures and engagement. In this sense, it is argued, for instance, that faith-based organizations could be integrated into environmental policies in different ways and constitute a social force to support institutional decisions related with environmental problems.[20]

The second group of arguments goes further into the analysis of the importance of religions in development issues and advocates for substantive participation, considering that religions have historically been an important source of practices and values,[21] which within the current environmental thinking vocabulary could be considered as resilient or environmentally friendly. Values like frugality, fraternity, contemplation, brotherhood, respect for nature, present to some degree in all world's religions, could be important factors to drive

17 Khan, M.L. *et al.* (2008) The Sacred Groves and Their Significance in Conserving Biodiversity An Overview, International Journal of Ecology and Environmental Sciences, Vol. 34, No. 3.

18 Harmon, D. and A.D. Putney (2003) Intangible Values and protected areas: toward a more holistic approach to management, Rowman & Littlefield, p. 311.

19 The proceedings of two world conferences at the University of Reading, UK, 2-3 October 1996 and Leiden University, The Netherlands, 22-23 September 1997, about cultural and spiritual values of biodiversity, as a complementary contribution to the Global Biodiversity Assessment.

20 Also in in the broad spectrum of the development policies, the attention for the role of religions begins to be considered by the creation of the 'World Faiths and Development dialogue' by the Work Bank in 1998.

21 Gottlieb, R.S. (2006) Introduction. Religion and Ecology—What Is the Connection and Why Does It Matter?, in Gottlieb R.S. (ed.) The Oxford Handbook of Religion and Ecology, Oxford University Press, p. 8.

social change.[22] This kind of argument starts from the assumption that the environmental crisis also needs to be addressed by ethical approaches, and not only through technological solutions.[23]

This new awareness has produced important changes in conservation policies towards a more inclusive approach of religious communities and values. The most important principles that are being recognized are: first, the need of integrating local religious leaders and communities in all the steps of the management process of any protected area; and second, the need to reconfigure the environmental discourse to include the language and values that are important for local communities who are directly affected by the creation or establishment of a protected area.[24]

2.1. IMMATERIAL VALUES ASSOCIATED WITH THE NATURAL WORLD

The relationships that people establish with the environment are very complex, and culturally marked. The ways in which communities and people value what in western terms is the natural world are conditioned by its particular world view, or particular ways of understanding the human being and his/her relationship with nature.[25] Despite the differences between cultures, all the different human belief systems seem to nourish from relationships with nature that are deeper than mere subsistence ones. The value of a particular natural environment is not only given by its material benefits, like food, water, shelter, energy, and so on. Humanity has usually also considered the existence of other kinds of values, intangible ones, but equally fundamental to life. Aesthetic contemplation, spirituality or religious practices, healing and recreational activities are common experiences of different cultures associated with nature.[26]

This kind of relationship with the environment was not considered by the different international institutions dedicated to environmental issues, like the

22 Tucker, M.E. (2017) Introduction, in W. Jenkins *et al.* (eds.) Routledge handbook of religion og ecology, Routledge, p. 33.

23 Grim, J. and M.E. Tucker (2014) Ecology and religion, Island Press, p. 63.

24 For a brief assessment of the principles considered important in the management of sacred natural sites, see 'Article XVI. Indigenous spirituality' of the 'American Declaration on the rights of Indigenous Peoples'. OAS (2016), American Declaration on the Rights of Indigenous Peoples. AG/RES. 2888 (XLVI-O/16); and point 4 'Possible impacts on sacred sites and associated ritual or ceremonial activities', of the Akwe: Kon Guidelines CBD (2004), Akwé: Kon – Voluntary guidelines for the conduct of cultural, environmental, and social impact assessments regarding developments proposed to take place on, or which are likely to impact on, sacred sites and on lands and waters traditionally occupied or used by indigenous and local communities, p. 15.

25 Ramakrishnan, P.S. *et al.* (1998) Conserving the sacred: for biodiversity management, Science Publishers.

26 Cooper, N. *et al.* (2016) Aesthetic and spiritual values of ecosystems: Recognising the ontological and axiological plurality of cultural ecosystem 'services', Ecosystem Services, Vol. 21.

UNEP, or by the different conferences of the parties of the different international conventions on the topic, up until a few years ago. First, because the awareness of their importance was not raised, or they were not considered so important; and also because these experiences are not directly measurable, and its incorporation into public policies is difficult. As of 1990, those institutions began to focus attention on the importance of incorporating this kind of immaterial aspect of the relationship between humanity and nature.

For instance, the Millennium Ecosystems Assessment developed a methodology to incorporate these aspects into the assessment of the impacts of ecosystems on human life in order to facilitate public decisions. Within this initiative, the immaterial aspects of the relationship between humanity and nature are considered as 'cultural values',[27] or as a non-material function of ecosystems. Tadaki *et. al.* have identified four different conceptual approaches[28] to the use of word values within the ecosystems services literature, each one with its particular functions, and dedicated to analysing a different phenomenon. Something particularly interesting for this work is the consideration of value as relations. From this perspective, the relationship between a particular culture and its environment must be understood as contextual and must not be reduced to a general classification, common in other approaches to the concept of value. In this sense, what may be valued in a particular environment might be impossible to frame, or to translate into the vocabulary of common economic valuation and pricing.

In the same sense, the CBD referred to in the previous section established a mechanism to evaluate the impacts of activities on sacred natural sites,[29] which incorporates different principles to include the immaterial values associated with the sacredness of particular places.

In another area, the World Heritage Convention began to address the sacred element of places considered as world natural or cultural heritage in a more direct

27 Cultural values usually include spiritual and aesthetic values. There is a lot of literature related to this subject. Regarding this paper, it is particularly interesting to highlight the critique made by Nigel *et. al. Ibid.*, p. 225. in relation to the inadequacy of the economic approach to evaluate spiritual and aesthetic values, since they are non-use values. This kind of inadequacy derives from the fact that the kind of ethics that emerge from these different ontologies are deontological ethics, rather than consequentialist ethics specific to the economic evaluation of ecosystem services. (Cooper, N. *et al.* (2016) 'Aesthetic and Spiritual Values of Ecosystems: Recognising the Ontological and Axiological Plurality of Cultural Ecosystem "services"' *Ecosystem Services* 21, (225, https://doi.org/10.1016/J.ECOSER.2016.07.014).

28 They are: value as magnitude of preference; value as contribution to a goal; values as individual priorities; and values as relations. See Tadaki, M. *et al.* (2017) Making sense of environmental values: a typology of concepts, Ecology and Society, Vol. 22, No. 1.

29 Akwé: Kon – Voluntary guidelines for the conduct of cultural, environmental and social impact assessments regarding developments proposed to take place on, or which are likely to impact on, sacred sites and on lands and waters traditionally occupied or used by indigenous and local communities.

way, through the creation of the UNESCO Initiative on Heritage of Religious Interest in 2010, following the IUCN guidelines published in 2008 about the management of sacred natural sites.[30] All those instruments are innovative approaches to conservation that are still being developed and are moving the international conservation movement towards a more inclusive and effective perspective. These institutions consider that scientific language is not capable of providing a full commitment towards a behavioural change related to environmental matters; a deep emotional link is also considered necessary.[31]

2.2. SACRED NATURAL SITES

A particularly important aspect in this new influx of religious, or spiritual, element into the conservation agenda is the progressive development and institutionalization of the concept of sacred natural sites in international law.

From a geographical perspective, sacred places are 'portions of the earth´s surface which are recognized by individuals or groups as worthy of devotion, loyalty or esteem'.[32] These places are considered sacred for different reasons, which could be divided into two big groups: first, because the place itself has some sacred features; or second, because the place held a special event of religious significance. The first kind of sacred place is common to immanent religions, which consider the presence of gods in the natural world; and the second kind is more common to transcendent religions, which consider that god or the gods are a reality apart from the natural world. Most sacred places associated with chthonic traditions[33] around the globe are of the first kind, and most sacred places of the monotheistic traditions are of the second kind.

Sacred natural sites are a subcategory of sacred places that occur in natural landscapes. They can occur in different scales, from a tree to an entire forest or a mountain, and they are present in all religions.[34]

At international level, the first time that direct attention was given to the relationship between SNS and conservation was in two events organized by the UNEP and held in 1996 and 1997,[35] and also through two initiatives of the MAB – the first of them a project in Ghana's Northern Region, the 'Cooperative Integrated Project on Savanna Ecosystems in Ghana', which took place from 1993 to 1997; and the second a one-year study on the 'Role of Sacred Groves in

30 UNESCO (2010), Initiative on Heritage of Religious Interest.

31 Verschuuren, B. (ed.) (2010) Sacred natural sites: conserving nature and culture, Earthscan, p. 9.

32 Park, C.C. (1994) Sacred worlds: an introduction to geography and religion, Routledge.

33 Glenn, H.P. (2007) Legal traditions of the world: sustainable diversity in law, Oxford University Press.

34 Verschuuren, B. (ed.) (2010) Sacred natural sites: conserving nature and culture, Earthscan, p. 3.

35 The first study related to biodiversity conservation and sacred sites was published in 1976. Gadgil, M. and V. D. Vartak (1976) The sacred groves of Western Ghats in India, Economic Botany, Vol. 30, No. 2.

Conservation and Management of Biological Diversity in India' from 1996 to 1997.[36]

After that, a series of international conferences and documents of international institutions began to address the subject. To cite some of them: the International Workshop on the Importance of Sacred Natural Sites for Biodiversity Conservation, held at the Kunming and Xishuangbanna Biosphere Reserve in 2003;[37] the World Parks Congress in Durban[38] in 2003; and the International Symposium on 'Conserving Cultural and Biological Diversity: The Role of Sacred Natural Sites and Cultural Landscapes', in Tokyo, Japan in 2005.[39]

SNS are now recognized as an additional pillar for biodiversity conservation, besides the institutional protected areas system.[40] Both systems of ecosystem protection have their own ways of functioning, and they can also overlap within the same area, when a historic sacred natural site is located inside of a protected area.

Despite the similarities between SNS and conservation areas, the concepts do not always go hand-in-hand. In the SNS governance regime, the objectives are primarily religious. The place is conserved not for the preservation of some species or some ecosystem, but to fulfil a religious duty. This means that sometimes conflicts between conservation goals and religious uses of sacred sites that are also protected areas may exist.[41]

These international documents, all of them soft law documents, however, produce an increasing awareness of the importance of addressing this kind of phenomenon directly in the context of a growing number of environmental regulations at international level that affect territories of indigenous populations around the world.

---

36 Ramakrishnan, P.S. *et al.* (1998) Conserving the sacred: for biodiversity management, Science Publishers p. 5.

37 Lee, C. and T. Schaaf (eds.) (2003) The Importance of Sacred Natural Sites for Biodiversity Conservation: Proceedings of the International Workshop held in in Kunming and Xishuangbanna Biosphere Reserve, People's Republic of China.

38 IUCN (2003), Durban Agreement.

39 Before that, in 2001, the issue had already been discussed at the 'Symposium on the Importance of the Protection of Sacred Natural Sites (SNS) for the Conservation of Biodiversity', Mexico City.

40 Verschuuren, B. and N. Furuta (eds.) (2016) Asian Sacred Natural Sites: Philosophy and practice in protected areas and conservation.

41 Rutte, C. (2011) The sacred commons: Conflicts and solutions of resource management in sacred natural sites, Biological Conversation, Vol. 144, No. 10.

3. RELIGIOUS FREEDOM RIGHTS AND SACRED NATURAL SITES

In the first section of this chapter, I have argued that international institutions concerned with conservation issues are progressively incorporating religious matters within their concerns at the policy level, in other words, within the planning and management of protected areas. In this last section, I will address the same topic from a different perspective. I argue that even in the case of some environmental conflicts it is important to address directly some particular relations that exist between religious phenomena and nature. In this sense, I first argue that (3.1) the right to worship, one of the main rights associated with the right to religious freedom, includes the protection of sacred places; and then, that (3.2) the protection of sacred places, in some cases, could also be an instrument of environmental protection, as in the case of the SNS.

3.1. RIGHT TO WORSHIP AND PROTECTION OF SACRED PLACES

A fundamental part of the right to religious freedom is the protection of the places where religious activities are held. Guaranteeing freedom of religion, without assuring that people have some special places to engage in their religious activities, would compromise the exercise of this subjective right. When freedom of religion has been declared, but only in the private sphere, there is a considerable damage to religious communities, because a considerable part of religious practices is conducted in collective ways.

That is why the protection of places of worship at international level is considered as part of the right to worship. For example, in articles 2(1), 18, and 27 of the UN International Covenant on Civil and Political Rights, or in article 18 of the Universal Declaration of Human Rights. The relationship between the right to worship and the protection of religious places has been clarified in Article 6(a) of the Declaration on the Elimination of All Forms of Intolerance and of Discrimination Based on Religion or Belief (Resolution 36/55 of 25 November 1981). Resolution No. 6/37 of 14 December 2007, adopted by the UN Human Rights Council, explicitly affirms (paragraph 9 (e) and (g)) that the protection of religious places and sites should be considered as a manifestation of the right to worship.

Furthermore, all international human rights instruments concerned with indigenous peoples rights have norms that deal specifically with the protection of sacred sites, or religious places, for example Article 13 of ILO Convention No. 169 of 1989; Article 12 of the UN Declaration on the Rights of Indigenous Peoples of 2007; Article XVI (3) of the American Declaration on the Rights of Indigenous Peoples, of 2016.

If the protection provided by the right to freedom of religion includes the protection of the physical space, that means that any offense to the place is also a violation of the subjective right and in consequence could be submitted to courts.[42] The legal category of 'place of worship' is, therefore, an important element for the delimitation of the right to freedom of religion.

This could be seen as a relatively unimportant matter, given that for the main monotheistic traditions the place of worship is, in most cases, a building, like a church, or a synagogue, or a mosque, but this is a superficial approach, since the idea of place of worship can be, and in some cases must be, interpreted in a broader sense. As I will try to argue in the next section, this legal category could also include natural elements, not only in chthonic traditions,[43] but even also in the three monotheistic faiths previously referred to.

3.2. THE PROTECTION OF NATURE THROUGH THE RIGHT TO RELIGIOUS FREEDOM

The definition of place of worship must be related with the particular religion under analysis. Different religions have different religious practices and different places to conduct religious ceremonies. As we saw in the last section, SNS are places with religious importance that could be related with religious practices of worship, prayer, purification, initiation, etc., or could also be related with historical events.

SNS are much more common in chthonic traditions, but are also present in monotheistic religions. The number of existing SNS around the world is unknown, but there are some estimates that indicate that there are 250 million places around the globe that have this feature.[44] From a conservation perspective, the phenomenon of SNS is an important element that needs to be considered, mainly in cases where conflicts between conservation policies' goals and religious goals could exist. SNS are frequently common-pool resources and, in this sense, they are better addressed through institutional measures in order to avoid an overuse.[45]

If SNS are also protected by fundamental subjective rights like the right to religious freedom, there is an additional argument to be used in litigation cases, because the case could be addressed as a human rights demand, with all its

42 Bakht, N. and L.M. Collins (2016) The Earth is Our Mother: Freedom of Religion and the Preservation of Aboriginal Sacred Sites in Canada, SSRN Electronic Journal, p. 797.

43 Glenn, H.P. (2007) Legal traditions of the world: sustainable diversity in law, Oxford Universitet Press, p. 61.

44 Rutte, C. (2011) The sacred commons: Conflicts and solutions of resource management in sacred natural sites, Biological Convervation, Vol. 144, No. 10, p. 2390.

45 Ibid., p. 2392.

system and normative apparatus.[46] Using the rights approach to solve environmental conflicts related with SNS could be much more beneficial, mainly in cases where there are no already declared human rights related to the environment.

In the last decades, cases of environmental conflicts related with SNS are gaining more visibility. In a broader sense, most of the environmental conflicts related to indigenous territory have a high possibility of affecting a sacred natural site, because of their special relationship with land. In the Vedanta mining case in India, the Supreme Court of the country ruled in favour of the community, considering that the right to religious freedom, as declared in the Indian constitution, meant the protection of the religious beliefs related to the Niyamgiri hills, where a mining project was being conducted.[47] In *Ktunaxa Nation v British Columbia (Forests, Lands and Natural Resource Operations)*, the Supreme Court of Canada analysed an appeal of Ktunaxa Nation against the construction of a ski resort in land considered to be sacred, based on subsection 2(a) of the Canadian Charter of Rights and Freedoms.[48] The appeal was dismissed, because the court considered that there was no violation of the right to belief or to manifest their religious beliefs.[49]

The jurisprudence of the Inter-American Court of Justice is moving forward in this sense. Despite not recognizing the violation of any other human right, the court recognized the special relationship with land, including the spiritual aspects (paragraph 149) in the *Mayagna (Sumo) Awas Tingni Community v Nicaragua*[50] case in 2001. In its judgment the Court recognized a violation of the right to freedom of religion as a consequence of the impossibility of burying the dead, which is an important element of the Mayan culture.[51]

46 Bakht, N. and L.M. Collins (2016) The Earth is Our Mother: Freedom of Religion and the Preservation of Aboriginal Sacred Sites in Canada, SSRN Electronic Journal, p. 812.

47 Cirone, M. (2015) The Vedanta Case in India, EJOLT Factsheet No. 46.

48 An overview of the case can be consulted at Bakht, N. and L. M. Collins (2016), The Earth is Our Mother: Freedom of Religion and the Preservation of Aboriginal Sacred Sites in Canada, SSRN Electronic Journal.

49 Supreme Court of Canada (2017), *Ktunaxa Nation v British Columbia (Forests, Lands and Natural Resource Operations).*

50 Inter American Court of Human Rights (2001), *Case of the Mayagna (Sumo) Awas Tingni Community.* Judgment of August 31, 2001 (Merits, Reparations and Costs) (Ser. C) No. 79 (2001).

51 For an analysis of the most important case law about the sacred natural sites in the human rights system, see Newman, D. *et al.* (2017) Legal Protection of Sacred Natural Sites Within Human Rights Jurisprudence: Sápmi and Beyond in L. Heinämaki and T.M. Herrmann (eds.), Experiencing and protecting sacred natural sites of Sámi and other and indigenous peoples, Springer.

4. SOME NEW DIRECTIONS: LEGAL PLURALISM, RIGHT TO RELIGIOUS FREEDOM AND ENVIRONMENTAL ETHICS

Environmental law is facing a new direction with the increasing recognition of some kind of legal personality to non-human entities, both individually and collectively considered (animals, species, ecosystems,[52] and also sacred natural sites).[53] This new kind of law that is being developed in different parts of the world is actually the result of a reflection on the aspirations of the deep ecologists of the sixties.[54] The concerns about more respectful ethics are now coming to the legal sphere.

Since the ILO Convention of 1989 (No. 169), where the issue of the special relationship with land was addressed, passing through the UN Declaration on the Rights of Indigenous Peoples of 2007, and culminating in the American Declaration on the Rights of Indigenous People of 2016, the importance of land for indigenous peoples, in its full complexity, has been recognized, directly or indirectly. There has been an evolution in addressing the issue, what was the 'special relationship with the lands'. Article 13 of ILO Convention No. 169 now pervades the whole text of the last of the declarations referred to, and Article XVI, dedicated to the indigenous spirituality, deals with this issue specifically.[55]

The sacredness of natural elements is being contemporarily addressed from another perspective: through the attribution of legal personality to non-human entities. The not so recent cases of the Ecuadorian[56] and Bolivian[57] constitutions have been followed by the Whanganui Case in New Zealand,[58] the Atrato river case in Colombia, and by the case of the Ganges River in India.[59] Furthermore, in the last Advisory Opinion of the Inter-American Court of Human Rights on Environment and Human Rights, the court notes that recognizing legal personality of non-human entities is a new tendency in environmental law.[60]

52 Gordon, G.J. (2017) Environmental Personhood, Columbia Journal of Enviromental Law, Vol. 43, No. 1.
53 Studley, J. and W.V. Bleisch (2018) Juristic personhood for sacred natural sites: a potential means for protecting nature, PARKS Journal, Vol. 23, No. 1.
54 Naess, A. (1993) The Deep Ecological Movement in M.E. Zimmerman (ed.), Enviromental philosophy: from animal rights to radical ecology, Prentice-Hall, p. 196.
55 Article XVI.
56 Ecuador (2008), Constitution of The Republic of Ecuador.
57 Bolivia (2009), Plurinational State of Bolivia Constitution.
58 Charpleix, L. (2018) The Whanganui River as Te Awa Tupua: Place-based law in a legally pluralistic society, The Geographical Journal, Vol. 184, No. 1.
59 A summary of all these different cases can be found in: Gordon, G. J. (2017), Environmental Personhood, Columbia Journal of Enviromental Law, Vol. 43, No. 1.
60 Inter American Court of Human Rights (2018), The Environment and Human Rights: State obligations in relation to the environment in the context of the protection and guarantee of the

What we are seeing in environmental legislation, both at international and national levels, is a progressive extension of those entities that deserve a person-like treatment, instead of an object-like one. In some sense, the fact that this movement is being recognized in the legal sphere could be a sign of a bigger change, like the one predicted by Thomas Berry, consisting in considering the world as a community of subjects instead of the actual perception where this feature is only present for humanity.[61]

All norms and court cases related with some form of recognition of personality to non-human entities are yet related with chthonic traditions: given their traditions, indigenous populations and Hinduism are akin to this idea. A broader adherence to this form of environmental regulation could spread in the western world without any direct religious association. Intimacy with the planet could be promoted through emotions of wonder, or beauty, or through the sense of mystery that pervades the whole human existence, and the Universe, with its dimensions and scales.[62]

In the case treated in this paper, the recognition of personality to non-human beings could be considered an interpretative tool to reinforce the subjective right to religion freedom, because they both are framed over the same paradigm shift in human-nature relationships and they both consider that in some cases, for instance the SNS cases, the relationship established is one of a subject-subject kind.

5. CONCLUSIONS

Religion matters. That is an indisputable assertion in environmental issues. It matters on different levels and scales: at policy and management level; and at litigation level. Besides that, it matters on an international scale, and on a national one. It matters because of a number of quantitative reasons, but also because of its qualitative aspects, like the values it enhances.

To fully understand all the aspects of the interaction between religious practices and environmental issues it is necessary to be aware of the importance of religions for believers. It implies not only different visions of the same nature, but, in some cases, completely different cosmologies and ways of existence, that is to say different kinds of relationships between humans-humans and humans-non-humans.

---

rights to life and to personal integrity – interpretation and scope of Articles 4(1) and 5(1) of the American Conventi.

61 Berry, T. (1999) The great work: our way into the future, Bell Tower, p. 11.

62 Ibid., p. 163.

Worship, as one of the central parts of any religion, is protected by subjective rights, recognized since the first's human rights declaration. In the case of SNS, the interactions between nature conservation and religious rights can be mutually reinforced, especially in litigation cases. In addition to these two aspects, the new recognition of personality to non-human entities is another direction in international environmental law that could become an important interpretative device for the application of the right to religious freedom in relation to SNS.

www.ingramcontent.com/pod-product-compliance
Ingram Content Group UK Ltd.
Pitfield, Milton Keynes, MK11 3LW, UK
UKHW051922100926
8556IPUK00021B/1313

9 781780 6875